# Speaking to the
# Heart
## Volume 1

Bruce McDonald

ISBN: 1500240826
ISBN-13: 978-1500240820

# DEDICATION

First of all to my Lord and Savior Jesus Christ I dedicate this book, and may He receive much glory from these words and thoughts. Secondly, I dedicate this book to my two sons and daughter. To Jessica who has worked so hard on this project, and who has been my special "Scooter" all her life. She has been a delight to me. To Joshua who has brought me such joy, and has always sought to honor me and encourage me. He has brought godly Ehrin into our family, and has blessed us with 3 wonderful grandchildren - Talia, Toby and Tyler. To Jeremy, our oldest, who has amazed us at his adventuresome spirit and risk-taking. I have never stopped being grateful for him since the day the doctor told us "It's a boy!". He has brought godly Wendy into our lives, along with our sweet granddaughter Presley. I am grateful to God for each of you.

# CONTENTS

Bruce McDonald

Bruce McDonald

# INTRODUCTION

This book is a compilation of weekly devotionals that
were written over a eight year period. The devotionals
were designed to be intimate talks with people who, like
all of us, need strength for the journey. There are 300 of
these devotionals, and they are contained in three books.
You are holding Volume One. Each volume has 100
devotionals. Initially written to those in ministry, they
grew to become devotionals for all believers. The
response and testimonies from those who have read these
Speaking to the Hearts have been warm and encouraging.
They are put in this collected form to encourage a greater
readership. May God speak to your heart in a way that is
both helpful and Christ-honoring.

# 1

# THE SCAR

I was driving back from climbing a mountain in the Colorado Rockies. In the car with me was our daughter, Jessica. She had talked me into hiking/climbing Colorado's highest mountain, Mount Elbert. Mount Elbert soars to a height of 14,400 feet. Jess, who is an unbelievable hiker/climber, was excited to climb another fourteener (what Coloradoans call mountains higher than 14,000 feet). She set a quick pace, and eventually reached the top about a half hour before me – certainly had to be some sort of land speed record for climbing Elbert! With great difficulty and challenge, I arrived at the summit, and we both enjoyed some PB&J sandwiches at the top of the world. The views were stunning.

So, after the harrowing descent back down the mountain, we were riding in the car and both retelling the joys of the journey up and back. A good day...and then the cell phone rang. It was my wife, Bev, telling us there was a fire in Waldo Canyon. Waldo Canyon is just outside of Colorado Springs where Jess lives, and not far from our town of Woodland Park. There had already been several fires in our area (many of them started by an arsonist), so although we were concerned when hearing about this fire, we hoped and prayed it would soon be either contained or put out. Jess kept checking her smart phone to see how the fire was doing. By the time we reached our house outside of Woodland Park, the fire had grown tremendously. So much so that Jess needed to run down to her house and pack some things as she was under pre-evacuation. The next day, she and Bev went back down to her place to get some final documents and pictures. On the way down, the police closed the main road going into Colorado Springs. They had to come home via Denver, adding about 2 hours on to their drive.

Jess stayed at our house while we watched the news of the fire. It quickly went out of control and homes and developments were evacuated. And then the unthinkable happened, the fire leaped the mountain ridge and consumed 346 homes. A horrific catastrophe. The homes literally were right next to my daughter's development.

We left the next day after hearing this news, and with a "pre-evacuation notice" for our own home and development (Jess had already been under mandatory evacuation at this time), we headed north, and were gone for 10 days. While away, we kept checking live feeds on the Internet to see how the fire was doing. It was heartbreaking to watch the reports.

After 10 days we drove back to Colorado and to Jess' home. We had received news that her development was now safe to go back into, and that the mandatory evacuation had been lifted. Her power, water, and gas had been shut off for part of that time. When we crested the hill overlooking her development we saw the devastation of the fires firsthand. It was almost too much to take in. Where homes and developments had been, there were now just charred ruins. The fire had also burned up much of the beautiful forest covering the surrounding mountains - mountains and forest where Jess normally hikes.

But something else was noticeable from that hill's vantage point, something that almost took my breath away. Jess' entire development was standing, with trees and yards fresh and green. Not one home was destroyed, and not one piece of property was touched. On both sides of her development, homes and property were burned. There was literally a horseshoe of green in the midst of charred ash.

Why had that happened? Why devastation and destruction so close by, but not in her development? The answer was the scar. Behind Jess' development, and the surrounding neighborhoods, are mountains. They come down right to the borders of the houses. Beautiful tree lined mountains. That is, all except at Jess'. Behind Jess' development and home is a mountain that has been scraped for rock and gravel. It's huge and noticeable. It's like a large slice of "red rock" covering most of the mountain. Locals call it the "scar", and have often complained about its unsightliness (compared with the other sides of the mountain).

As I sat in my car on top of the hill, I realized that the reason the fire didn't come into her house and development was because the scar protected it. When the raging inferno (1500 degrees) reached her development from behind, there was nothing to burn - the "scar" kept any inflammable material from being present. As I looked, I saw black surrounding her house and development. But hers had the previously thought "ugly scar", that now flowed down with green. The scar was its protection.

Tears came to my eyes, first of all because of all the great loss to homes (especially) and to the forest. But, then, tears of a different sort came to my eyes as I saw the reason her house and development were spared. For so many years people complained about the scar – me too, but now, the scar shone as a beautiful barrier to destruction and ruin.

I thought immediately of the cross and the wounds of Christ. It was His Scar that saved us. When sin with its destruction and spiritual death came racing towards us, it found nothing to kindle. It couldn't touch us because of the scar of Christ. II Peter 2:24 says, "he himself bore our sins in his body on the tree, so that we might die to sins and live for righteousness; by his wounds you have been healed." Isaiah 53 reminds us, "Surely he took up our infirmities and carried our sorrows, yet we considered him stricken by God, smitten by him, and afflicted. He was pierced for our transgressions, he was crushed for our iniquities; the punishment that brought us peace was upon him, and by his wounds we were healed." Those scars He bore for us, those nails driven into His hands and feet, were for us, and by them we were healed and shielded. The Apostle Paul reminds us, "When you were dead in your sins...God made you alive with Christ. He forgave all our sins...he took them away, nailing them to the cross."

What a reminder that day was for me. Had there been no scar on that mountain, Jess' home would be gone. Had there been no scar on my Savior, my life would become consumed by the eternal fires. That scar, once thought so ugly, now is viewed differently. Christ, who was once viewed as unattractive – "He had no beauty or majesty to attract us to him, nothing in his appearance that we should desire...Just as there were many who were appalled at him-his appearance was so disfigured beyond that of any man and his form beyond human likeness." (Isaiah 53:2 & 52:14) now is viewed in all His beauty – "I shall see the King in all his beauty." (Isaiah 33:17). The scar now actually enhances the beauty of our Savior.

Did you know that the only reminder and evidence of sin in heaven – is on our Savior? He retains the scars of our atonement and redemption. The Apostle John writes, "I saw a lamb looking as if it had been slain" (Revelation 5:6). In the

Greek, the language is actually, "looking as if freshly slain". Oh beautiful scars of Christ! He has saved and rescued more than a house or development; He has rescued us from the fires of perdition.

## 2
## WHAT'S IN A NAME

Names are very special. Think how strange it would be not to have a name, but instead a number. Can you imagine being addressed by a number? Have you ever wondered how many names there are in the world? Think just of the variety of names here in the states, and now add that to the different names that are in other cultures and countries. The number, so I'm told, is incalculable.

My name is an "old name", not too many people name their child Bruce anymore. If someone is named Bruce, you can be relatively sure they are older. There are actually 4 Bruces in our church, and you guessed it, we're all older. Now I must rush on and say, my middle son, Joshua, and his wife Ehrin, named their middle child Tobias Bruce! That's pretty amazing! I could give you a list of current popular names for boys or girls, but that would only be for our culture. Other countries and ethnic groups would all have their own "favorite and most used names". In fact, if you go outside our country, the variety of names is astronomical.

When I was ministering in Hungary, I had one gentleman tell me that parents in his country must choose from an "Official List" of names that have been approved by the government. Rather shocking, to say the least. In recent years, the list has expanded, but years ago (when this man was born), the list was smaller. So, as you can imagine, there were a lot of "repeats", that is, people with the same first name. I'm sure many of you have had the challenge that I have had, when hearing a new name (one you're not familiar with) for the first time. You either have trouble saying it, or spelling it. This is, of course, especially true when you're in another country.

Since names are so important – especially to each of us, it really becomes challenging to address a person by their name if it is a difficult name (to you) to hear or pronounce. Perhaps there is another thing you can identify with me, it is when you've forgotten a person's name, or you weren't really paying attention when they said their name – and suddenly, you're in the awkward moment of not addressing them by their first name. Each of us probably knows someone who has a "good knack for names", and if you do know them, you probably have wished you had their gift.

Have you ever wondered how God is with names? Have you wondered about that great day when we are all before God, and as He scans the immense crowd, will He recognize you and call you by your name? Can you imagine God calling you by your first name? Hi Marcia, Hi Chris, Hi Cathy, or Hi Frank, Hi Dave and Hi Keith. Won't that be amazing? Think of someone you know, who perhaps to some people is rather famous. When you're in the presence of that person, especially if others are around you, and that person singles you out by your name, that's pretty cool!

For some reason, as I typed that line, I thought of one of my favorite movies. The movie is now quite old, but I still like to watch *The Man from Snowy River*. In the movie, there is a young man named "Jim" (the eventual hero of the film). Jim has recently lost his dad, and has come down from the "Snowy Mountains" in Australia to get a job. He has a rough time of it, and particularly takes ridicule for being "from the mountains". During one interaction with people at the ranch where he has just been hired on, one of the ranch hands excitedly says to some other workers, "Clancy" is coming to the ranch tomorrow. Now Clancy was a famous horseman, and was already a legend in his day. When Jim hears this, he says, "I know him, he and my dad were mates." At which, all of the ranch hands break out in laughter, and tell Jim there is no way anyone like Clancy would know Jim. Jim is totally embarrassed and humiliated, and he walks away. As you might guess, the next day Clancy comes riding into the large ranch. Everyone is gathered around staring at him (like a present day Rock Star). Clancy scans the crowd and sees young Jim. He looks at Jim and says, "How are you doing Jim? Sorry about your dad, he was a 'good mate'". Classic moment! Something about being recognized by someone, and your name called out.

Back to the question about God and names. So, how is He with names? Have you ever noticed the times when God called people by name? I know, there are too many to recall, but you might want to take a moment to think of a few of these; "Moses, Moses", "Abraham, Abraham", "What are you doing here Elijah?", "Joseph, son of David, do not be afraid", and of course, the numerous times Jesus addressed His disciples. "Simon Peter do you truly love me?" But I think one of my all-time favorites, is when Jesus had first rose from the dead. Mary went to the tomb, and then she heard His voice. Jesus simply said "Mary" (John 20:16). Can you imagine that moment! How wonderful, to just have Him utter your name. In her most troubling, perplexing and anxious moment, He said simply "Mary", and everything changed.

I do believe one day you too will hear Him say your name - what a wonderful moment that will be. It is not only that He has a good memory, but that it was His idea for your name in the first place. "Before I was born the Lord called me; from my birth. He has made mention of my name." (Isaiah 49:1) Hey, if God has named each of the stars (Psalm 147:4), then you're important enough to Him to have a name! God loves names, especially personal names, and think how often Jesus was giving His followers new names; "You are Simon son of John. You will be called Peter." (John 1:42)

Yes, one day, the King of kings will call you by your first name. He will know it, not because there are just a certain number of names to go around, but because He knows you. And guess what? He likes personal names so much, that He has a new one for you! It will be just between the two of you. In Revelation 2:17, Jesus says He will give us a new name. How cool is that!

But it gets better. He will also whisper to you a new name you can call Him (Revelation 3:12). Names are special; names are ways of sharing closeness and familiarity. You are not just another "number" in God's great host of children. You are known, and you are special. And your moment will be greater than young Jim's when Clancy signaled him out in the crowd. No, you'll have the King of glory address you – affectionately and personally by your name. Like Mary that early Easter morning, just for Him to say your name, will be priceless.

3

# EXPUNGED

Do you remember "Pardongate"? Pardongate was the derogative term critics gave President Bill Clinton's actions on his final days in office. President Clinton pardoned so many criminals just before leaving office that news outlets and critics gave that very unflattering term to his actions. Presidents are of course known for their "pardonings", especially as they are leaving office. Though President Clinton was singled out for his actions, he takes a back seat to President Richard Nixon, who pardoned 190 criminals while he was in office. As you can imagine, many of the people who have been pardoned by each of our presidents have come under close scrutiny, and usually criticism. There have been murderers, drug dealers, sex offenders, crime lords and a host of other so-called nefarious criminals that have been pardoned. Probably depending on your personal convictions, understanding of the criminal charges and even political persuasion, you would pick certain ones that should have or should not have been pardoned.

In the last 50 years, perhaps no presidential pardon has sparked so much outrage and controversy as that of President

Gerald Ford's pardoning – President Richard Nixon! And undoubtedly, the most unusual and universal pardoning of someone was President Andrew Jackson's pardoning of the entire Confederate Army. Pardoning is oftentimes questioned, but it is most welcomed by the one charged with a crime. To receive a pardon, means that you have received forgiveness for your crime and the penalty that was associated with it.

To be pardoned, for the convicted, is undoubtedly beyond belief and wonderful. There is, of course, an analogy that can be made for the believer – duly convicted of sin, to be wonderfully pardoned by God because of the satisfactory, atoning work of Christ on the cross on our behalf. Praise God our sins are forgiven and the penalty associated with it. But the believer is more than pardoned; the believer has also had his record expunged. The word expunged is perhaps not an unusual word for us, thanks to all the crime and detective shows on TV, but it is worth looking at this word more closely. To have your record expunged means to have it completely removed, but even more than that, to have your records permanently sealed. To be truthful, some of our states vary in regards to what being expunged looks like. For some, like Texas, the records of a criminal being expunged is totally wiped out and forever concealed. For California, there can be variance in its criminals being expunged. Sometimes the charge is "dismissed", but the details are left there. But generally speaking, to have your record expunged, means to have it completely removed and the details sealed forever. This is especially true for the believer.

I believe that sometimes when we approach God, we have a fairly firm grasp on the fact our sins are pardoned, that is, the crime is forgiven and the penalty removed. But I wonder if oftentimes we really don't grasp that our sins have been expunged. We thank God that He has forgiven us, and we're grateful Christ paid the penalty for our sins, but God still knows all about our sins, they are kind of still in the  back of

His mind. So, if we are experiencing difficult times and God seems distant, or we have prayed long and hard about something, but found no answers, we begin to entertain thoughts in our mind. For instance, "Well, this makes sense, because, after all, God knows my sins, and is it any wonder that He has never answered me?" Or perhaps it's something like this, "I hope God sees how serious I am about living better for Him, and doesn't hold me too responsible for some of my present sins and struggles." Does this sound familiar? I believe that for many of us, the Devil gains victory, not by accusing us of our sins and that God hasn't forgiven them, but that God hasn't forgotten them.

The teaching of sins being expunged is wonderful in the Word of God, and understanding and believing it can change everything. You probably know, and for some of you, can quote many verses on the assurance of forgiveness of sin, but you may have either forgotten or never grasped the wonder of our sins being expunged. The doctrine of sins being removed from God's mind is mind-boggling. It doesn't mean that God is senile and forgets things; it means He chooses not to remember them in association with us, but with Christ. Our unforgettable sins have all been attached to Christ. When we approach Christ, whether now in prayer or one day before His throne, God has no reference point for us as far as our sins being ours. This is an unimaginable truth. God doesn't now think, "Okay, I'm listening to your request, but your record has been rather shaky lately." Oh no, never in a million years! Nor will we stand before God one day and He will say, "Okay, you lived a pretty good life, but I have a few things I want to bring to your attention." Once again, no way!

Let these promises wash over you today; "I will remember your sins no more"; "I have put your sins behind my back"; "Your sins are buried in the deepest sea"; and perhaps here's a new one for you; "In those days and at that time – this is the Lord's declaration – one will search for your guilt, and there will be none, and for your sins, but they will not be found, for I will forgive." (Jeremiah 50:20) This verse was first given to Israel and Judah, but certainly applies even more to us today who are in Christ.

Listen dear friend, I sin and you sin, and forgiveness and pardon are certainly not a license to sin more. But the truth of the matter is, that believers don't "sin as much as they want to", we "sin more than we want to". God is not keeping track of your sins, or how many sins you've committed. He has forgiven us all our sins (Colossians 2:14), and He no longer calls them into account when dealing with us – He held Christ responsible for all our sins. Learn the wonderful, liberating truth of our sins, not only being forgiven – praise God, but expunged, never to be remembered. Sins pardoned is wonderful, sins expunged is freeing. You and I approach God with no record of wrong doing, the sins have been sealed, and even God (by His sovereign design) can't open the record. Don't listen to the evil one, approach God with the assurance that your sins are both forgiven and forgotten. Sometimes, as it relates to sin, you have a better memory than God! Your sins are expunged!

# 4
# CONSCIENTIOUS OBJECTORS

Justin Colby, Dan Felushko, Patrick Hart, Brandon Hughey, Peter Jemley, Ryan Johnson, Christian Kjar, Dale Landry, Kevin Lee, Brad McCall and Phil McDowell. Sound familiar? Most likely not. These are the names of a partial list of conscientious objectors during the Iraq War. All of them fled to Canada, and are still living there. I remember the first time I heard the term "conscientious objector"; it was during the Vietnam War. I was a High School student (painful to admit my age!), and there was a fighter that many of us followed in the Olympics by the name of Cassius Clay. He was an Olympic hero, and then went into the Professional Boxing ranks and won three Heavyweight Boxing Championships. Clay decided in 1964 to embrace the Islamic faith, and, as a result, he changed his name to Muhammad Ali. When he was called upon for the draft, he "Conscientiously Objected". He wasn't the first, but the first I had heard of.

Seems like since the Civil War there have been conscientious objectors. And in a broader sense, there have always been those, who for various reasons – including religious ones, have "objected" to war. Some because they were simply pacifist. The technical term for conscientious objector is "an individual who has claimed the right to refuse to perform military service". So the men listed at the top of this chapter chose to do this, and, as a result, they had to flee the country. It's one thing to "object" to war as a civilian, but quite another as an enlisted soldier or one that is being drafted. The latter means you're breaking the law.

I thought of that phrase the other day when I was reading an account of Moses. He had been leading the Israelites through the Wilderness for 40 years, and now they're finally ready to enter the Promised Land (Canaan). But before doing that, leaders of two of the Tribes (families) of Israel come up to him and ask if their families can instead stay on "this side of the Jordan River", and settle there. In other words, not go into Canaan. Moses is furious, and sees this as cowardice and backtracking into disobedience and not going forward into the land God has promised.

Here is how his words are recorded that day to these leaders of the two tribes; "Should your brothers go to war while you stay here!" (Numbers 32:6) He actually had more to say to them than that, he actually "railed" on them for 9 more verses, including calling them "a brood of sinners". To say the least, he was not happy. Now, truthfully, you need to read the full account found in Numbers 32 to see what was really going on there, but for the sake of this chapter, I want to examine Moses' words of "should your brothers go to war while you stay here", and muse on that for a few moments. I'm not the first person to see these words as a powerful question for each of us in our Christian walk.

In some ways, one of the aspects of our Christian life that is often neglected, or at least not talked about, is our spiritual warfare. There are many descriptive names and associational words for Christians in God's Word. Among those are: Bride,

Body, Sheep, Building, Athlete, Fishermen, Ambassador, Pilgrim, Priest, Farmer, Branch – and a Soldier. Most of us are uncomfortable with the term "Soldier", because it speaks of war and warfare. Perhaps one reason we don't like it is it can speak of having a "militant attitude" towards others. That is understandable, and in some ways it's good to shy away from that approach to "Christian Soldiering". The "enemy" is not other "people", but our enemy is Satan and his hordes that use other people, our flesh, and this world system.

The Bible leaves no room for Christian Pacifism in regard to spiritual warfare. Eight times in the New Testament we are told to "fight the good fight of faith" or "that our fight is not against flesh and blood". Even at the end of his life, the Apostle Paul said "he had fought the good fight of faith". (See I cor. 9:6; II Cor. 10:4; I Tim. 1:18; 6:12; II Tim. 4:7) Whatever "fighting" in the Christian life may mean, it certainly includes the following: Constant Vigilance, Potential Setbacks and Defeats, Added Conflicts (when you enter into spiritual warfare intentionally), and Rearranging of Priorities. Absenteeism, avoidance, and conscientious objection are the norm, but unfortunately, not the call in Scripture. There will always be a temptation to not want to be involved in spiritual warfare; "Let others do it" would be our mantra, but we must not be guilty of "staying at home while others are fighting". There are no "armistice" days in our Christian life, no big extended "furloughs from conflict". Our weapons must never rust and our armor must never be discarded. (Ephesians 6:10-18)

Warfare for the believer is both "outward" and "inward". Spiritual warfare means fighting against all that would come against us in this world-uncompromisingly so. The attacks that the Devil would do on us through this world's delights and priorities, and through the Devil using others to carry out his nefarious plans, must be fought with resistance and confidence in the power of Christ. Again, we don't "hate and fight unbelievers", but we do fight that which assaults Christ and His message. On a recent trip of mine overseas I was introduced to a fellow believer and minister of the cross of Christ who had been beaten for his faith. Understandably, I had to ask myself this question; "would I be so willing to identify with Christ in this culture?" Many of our brothers and sisters throughout this world are uncompromisingly standing strong for Christ with dire consequences. But it is not just in life-threatening situations that we are called on to be valiant soldiers for Christ, I know students who have been brave in the face of losing friends and popularity, athletes who were valiant and it cost them endorsements and playing time, and businessmen who unflinchingly stood strong for Christ and it cost them a promotion or even loss of a job. Valiancy can take place in many arenas – and it must!

But outward attacks are only a part of the battle, sometimes the greatest battles are waged "within". The good fight of faith is to resist all the "natural temptations" to give into the flesh. Battles in the area of pride, fear, lust, anger and a host of others are a constant battle grounds for the believer. The Devil never takes a holiday, and neither does our flesh. If you or I do not remain vigilant, if we set aside our armor, we will have the Devil to pay.

Personally speaking, I find myself more vigilant and more prepared to fight the good fight of faith when I'm in the midst of "doing" something for Christ. However, in the times when I'm restful, things are peaceful, and there is actually a "lull" in my frenetic (exaggeration) activity, those are times I'm most likely to experience defeat and setbacks. I call this the battlement of ease.

The bottom line is this: "I can't stay at home while others are in the battle". Look again at the list I began with. Lord willing, there will never be a list posted in heaven of those who were "conscientious objectors" to the fight of faith. Pray that our names are not found there.

"*Must I be carried to the skies on flowery beds of ease, while others fought to win the prize and sail through bloody seas? Sure I must fight if I would reign – increase my courage Lord! I'll bear the toil, endure the pain, supported by Thy Word.*"

Isaac Watts

# 5
## COSTLY LOVE

The story made the headlines for several days in the fall of 2010. Not only did the major news outlets report the story, but the Today Show actually did a piece on one of the people involved in the story. On September 13, 2010 Brian Wood and his pregnant wife Erin were traveling across Washington State to visit family. The Woods were from Vancouver, British Columbia, and were looking forward to spending time with friends and loved ones. As they were traveling down the highway a Chevy Blazer was heading in their direction in the opposite lane. As it approached the Woods, the Blazer suddenly  swerved into their lane heading directly at them. Brian saw the impact would be immediate with no alternative, so he slammed on his brakes, pulling to the right so that the Blazer would hit his driver's door full on and miss his pregnant wife. They collided and Brian died instantly, saving his wife and his unborn child. It was found out later that the driver and passenger in the Blazer had drugs in their possession.

Brian's act of love and courage inflamed the nation – "What sacrificial love!" Erin later told the today show that her husband made that decision to save her and the baby's life. What costly love!

As I write this chapter, it is Valentine's Day. A day our country has set aside for us to show love to the special people in their lives. Some will scramble at the last minute and get a card and perhaps flowers. Others will have been more premeditated, and thought through plans for dinner, gifts, etc. Valentine's Day is a great day, and just gives us another opportunity to say "I love you". I realize cost is relative, some may give some extravagant gift – because they can, others may give something of less price, but more sacrificial for them. It is safe to say that no one plans on laying down their life for a loved one as Brian Wood did. Brian's decision was reactive and immediate, he loved his wife and it was "natural" to sacrifice his life when the car sped towards him. Brian did not start out the day, or for that matter, the year, thinking "I'll show my wife how much I love her by dying for her." There have been others down through the years, who, when it came a time to make a decision to give your life for a loved one, did it.

Hearing Brian and Erin's story cannot help but make you think of the One who gave His life for His Bride. Each Valentine's Day we have the opportunity to think about the costly love our Savior displayed for us. Christ's love was not reactive, it was not something that was suddenly thrust upon Him, and He made an immediate decision to die for us. Christ's love was premeditated and planned in advance. The Bible makes it clear that "Christ was the Lamb slain before the creation of the world." (Revelation 13:8) In eternity past, long before Christ created everything that was made (John 1:3-4); He knew He would give His life for His Bride. But please don't think that because He knew what He would do, that it didn't fill Him with dread when He came to earth. Listen to just a few of His words: "I have a Baptism to undergo and how distressed I am until it's completed." (Luke 12:50) "Now my heart is troubled, and what shall I say? 'Father save me from this hour?' No, it was for this very reason that I came to this hour." (John 12:27-28) You remember when Christ was approaching Calvary, His agony in the Garden of Gethsemane; "And being in great anguish, he prayed more earnestly, and his sweat was like drops of blood falling to the ground." (Luke 22:44)

Just how costly was this love for us that caused Him distress, trouble and anguish? Sometimes we sanitize the death that Christ died, but we should not. Isaiah 53:7 tells us He was led as a lamb to the slaughter. Sometimes in the old King James they choose not to use the word "slaughter", but instead "kill". However, I personally believe the newer translations have it right in referring to it as "slaughter". In Leviticus and Numbers you have the word slaughter used in describing the sacrifice of lambs over 40 times. The Hebrew word, which should always be translated slaughter – not killed, actually can also be translated "massacre"! You would not have wanted to watch a lamb, bull or goat "slaughtered" during sacrifice. Neither would you have wanted to watch our dear Lord and Savior slaughtered on Calvary. When the Apostle John saw Christ in heaven (Revelation 5:6), he described Him as "a lamb that had been slain". The CSB (Christian Standard Bible) Translation rightly translates it as "a lamb who had been slaughtered". The Greek word there literally means "savagely slaughtered".

The next time we celebrate Valentine's Day (and every day) let's show love to those we love, but let's also think much of the One who loved us when we didn't love Him – "Christ died for the ungodly" (Romans 5:6). Does that sound too harsh, that Christ died for the ungodly? Then perhaps this verse makes it clearer; "This is love; not that we loved God, but that he loved us and sent his Son as an atoning sacrifice [slaughtered for us] for our sins." (I John 4:10) Christ's love for us was both costly and premeditated, and we say today; "I love you Lord, and I thank you for your love for me."

# 6
# DONATION VERSUS DURATION

$P$at Tillman, Lou Gehrig, Karen Carpenter, Keith Green, Glenn Miller, Wolfgang Mozart, Frederick Chopin, Heath Ledger, River Phoenix, Joan of Arc, Amelia Earhart, Ann Frank, David Brainerd, Robert Murray McCheyne, Martin Luther King, and Jim Elliot. What did all these people have in common? They all died at a very young age, whether athlete, musician, actor, historical figure or minister and missionary, they were connected by dying at a seemingly "too-young" age.

Death is never welcomed, but when it strikes the young, it seems especially confusing and heartbreaking. The year I write this has seen many "notable" people die, their names trumpeted across the Internet pages, and many of these seemed to have died "too- young". But it's not just the notable or newsworthy people who died unexpectedly this year--many who this world knew nothing of died tragically and unexpectedly. Several natural disasters took the lives of the young as well as the old. Our hearts broke when we heard of deaths through fires, floods and tornados. Others died through human violence, many of these children, and others passed from this world through sickness and disease. There are always many questions asked when death comes knocking, but none so many as when death strikes the young. Earlier this year I was asked to speak to a gathering of High School Students after a friend and fellow student was killed in a tragic accident – the 5th student to die from that High School in an automobile accident in the past year.

Truthfully, death at an early age is something that breaks all our hearts, and it is something that brings troubling questions to all our minds. Certainly questions such as "why", but deeper down, perhaps questions about our own mortality. For most of us, and for most of our lives, we push the thought of death to some far distant recess in our mind. Reserving those thoughts for a "distant day" when we get "old". That distant day keeps getting pushed back because "old" seems to always be "getting older". Death, especially death in the young, shocks us because we feel "so much was ahead". Cut off too short, with way too much life still ahead.

I remember the first time it really hit me about someone dying early. I was in my early 20s working as a Youth Pastor at Northfield Baptist Church in Northfield, Ohio. The first year I served there our senior pastor Lynn Rogers was gone on Sabbatical. The church had brought in an interim pastor by the name of Earl Willets to do the regular preaching. Pastor Willets was 72 years old at the time, and had served for thirty years in another church, and also had been Pastor Rogers' pastor. One day Pastor Willets told me about the story of John and Betty Stam. Pastor Willets had been a student at Moody Bible Institute in the 1930's when word reached the college that former students John and Betty Stam had been martyred in China. The Stams were 27 years old, and had a three month old daughter at the time of their beheading by the Chinese Communist Army. As Pastor Willets told me the story of this young couple's martyrdom, my heart and mind raced to grasp the "why" of this. Why would God allow this? Later I purchased their biography, *John and Betty Stam: A Story of Triumph,* and was totally engrossed in their story and testimony. Sometime later, Pastor Willets picked up on the "rest of their story"; he said when their death and martyrdom was announced at Moody there was such a revival that broke out on campus that hundreds of students volunteered to take their place. At the time he was telling me the story, this was the greatest outpouring of missionary volunteers that the school had ever experienced.

I thought about the Stams recently when I was reading my Bible. The passage that triggered my thoughts was II Kings 2. The beginning of the chapter says, "The time had come for the Lord to take Elijah up to heaven." Elijah, as you probably remember, was "caught up to heaven" in a fiery chariot and he went without dying. Evidently, one of only two people who left this world without dying (the other being Enoch). But as I thought about Elijah, I also thought about "Elisha". Elisha was Elijah's protégé, but when Elisha left this world, he wasn't caught up in a fiery chariot; rather he died from an illness, "When Elisha became sick with the illness he died from…" (II Kings 13:14). Two men of God who held similar positions, yet very un-similar departures. That got me thinking further about people's "departures".

A few days later in my reading of scripture I read this verse about a godly priest named Jehoida, "Jehoida died when he was old and full of days; he was 130 years old at his death." (II Chronicles 24:15) One hundred and thirty years! Wow, that's a long time! But then I thought of another godly man, this man was not a priest or prophet, but instead a king. His name was Josiah, and he was wonderfully used of God and brought revival to Judah. But Josiah didn't live 130 years, he lived 39 years! "Josiah was 8 years old when he became king and he reigned 31 years in Jerusalem. (II Kings 22:1) Josiah was not carried to heaven in a chariot, or left this world via illness or old age, but he died in battle.

So reading of these men's departures and it happening in different seasons of life got me thinking way back to when I heard and read of John and Betty Stam. Though they had been dead for 40 years when I heard the story, it impacted me. It still does to this day, but I think of the influence and impact their lives had, albeit, short lives.

So what can we take away from all this today? Well, for one thing, only God knows the day of our birth, and only He knows the day of our death and departure. Every day of our life is written in His book, before one day happens (Psalm 139:16). Even the death by beheading the Stams suffered at the hands of the communist Chinese had to pass through a sovereign God's hands. No tyrant, terrorist, doctor or natural **X** disaster holds the keys to life and death – only God (Revelation 1:18). But there is something else that is very important to think about when we consider life's brevity and unexpectedness, and that is the importance of living in the moment with eternity in view. We do want to plan for the future and set goals, but always in the context of the "immanency of life's departure".

Perhaps a better way to put it, is the way that former Senate Chaplain, Peter Marshall said; "*Life does not consist in the duration of life, but the donation of life.*" It's interesting that Peter Marshall said those words, because God's day for his departure would come early. Peter Marshall died at the age of 46. When you think of life, truthfully, in the final analysis, it's not how long we live, but what we have done with that life that God has given us. The fact is, our lives will all end "short", because in light of living for eternity, this mortal life will be short even if we live for 130 years.

We need not live fearful lives, and certainly not morbid lives, but we must live prepared lives, purposeful lives. Plan for tomorrow, but live for today. None of us should die "too short", but ready and invested. I think we all know a person who died early, in fact, He was only 33 years old. But when He died, the world could say, "His life was not about duration but donation." Jesus Christ set the pattern for us, so be all that you can until "that day", whenever the Lord determines it will be.

# 7
# EASILY AWED

I'll never forget our private guide who was of "Inca bloodlines". We had just finished our meetings in the large coastal city of Lima, Peru. So, we decided to take an extra few days to fly "up," as in elevation, to "Cusco" (12,000 feet elevation), and then take a train ride to the fabled city of Machu Picchu. We took a bus up the steep mountain to see and explore the site that is called "one of the seven wonders of the world". We had our own private tour guide, who just happened to be of Inca descent. After the early (very early) morning mist and clouds disappeared before our eyes, we saw it – Machu Picchu! Unbelievable! The most stunning natural wonder we have ever seen. And what I most want to share here with you, is what our guide did after he showed us the amazing, and very high, panoramic view of Machu Picchu. He simply turned around and walked away. Our brief, very brief tour was over. We were now on our own (which was great).

We scrambled about for hours. I would occasionally look for our guide, and would see him, normally sitting talking to friends – looking off the other way! Eventually, he left the ancient massive city, and walked outside the complex into the shops. I bring him up because he is a great reminder that we can live next to greatness, or with greatness, and totally lose awe in what we see and experience. It can happen to all of us.

How does a person maintain their awe? How does one not lose the art of wonder? I can speak somewhat to that, since we live in one of the most stunningly beautiful places in the world – the Rocky Mountains. But I am not so much thinking about losing wonder or awe in natural environments, but how does one lose wonder and awe in our relationship with God.

Before I share some thoughts on this, which truthfully, is rather convicting to me, let me share a Bible Story that is both delightful and convicting. The story is found in John's Gospel, the first chapter. It concerns Jesus' calling of some of his disciples to "follow me". In verse 43 Jesus calls Philip, and right away Philip goes and gets Nathanael. Nathanael comes to Jesus, whereby Jesus says; "Here is a true Israelite, in whom there is nothing false." Nathanael is shocked by these words, and replies, "How do you know me?" Jesus responds, "I saw you while you were under the fig tree before Philip called you." Now, listen to this, you gotta love this, Nathanael is "blown away", and he exclaims, "Rabbi, you are the Son of God, you are the King of Israel!" Wow, don't you love that! I mean that is so cool! Nathanael gave one of the most astounding praises to Christ on who He was, and he did it with just Jesus saying "I saw you under the fig tree". Don't miss this! Disciples would see Jesus heal the blind and sick, they would see Him cast out demons and multiply food, they would even see Him raise two different people from the dead, but none made a statement like this. It wasn't until a couple years later that Peter and the others began to put the pieces together, and they too made statements like this. But Nathanael made this when Jesus simply said, "I saw you under the fig tree".

Wouldn't you like to have wonder like this? Just what does

God have to do to get your awe up? Something major, something new, not the same old, same old, of what you've grown accustom to? Nathanael's faith may not rate up there with Mary's, who believed she would have the Messiah, even though she had never known a man, or with Daniel's, who trusted God to keep the mouths of lions shut. But you have to believe that Jesus loves those who trust and worship Him over the smallest things. We talk about childlike faith, and perhaps there is some of that here, but I think it goes deeper than that. Being awed easily doesn't have to be childlike. Being awed easily, I believe, is a sign you haven't developed a system of expectations.

We all have to watch out for a walk with Christ that is characterized by "what have you done for me lately?" Or, "I need you to do this really big thing, and then, watch my awe go up!" Must Jesus only do great things for us to be in awe of Him? Can so-called "smaller things" still elicit awe from us? Author Erica Goros says, "*I thank God I have seen an orange sky with purple clouds. How easy it is to forget that we have the privilege of living in God's art gallery.*" I wonder what "fig tree" experiences you are currently seeing? Have you become not easily awed? There is so much around us, and not just God's handiwork in creation. The air your lungs take in, the carpet you feel underneath your toes, the giggle from a child, the note from a friend, and a dog laying his head on your lap. But more wonderful still, is pausing to reflect on being made right with God, having a God who loves you and joyously laughs over you. When you think of the wonders of the cross and all that it means for you, have you "grown accustom to it", because you can recite all the benefits of the cross – redemption, forgiveness of sins, reconciliation, adoption, propitiation (you get the idea). When you look at the stars, or even our moon and sun, does it not register as a potential moment of awe, because you've pretty much learned "how things work" in our Solar System. Mark Twain once remarked, "*We have not the reverent feeling for the rainbow that the savage has, because we know how it's made. We have lost as much as we have gained by prying into the matter."*

Oh for a faith like Nathanael's! Maybe that faith doesn't move mountains, but it is awed that there are mountains. What does it take for you to say; "Jesus, you are the Son of God! You are the King of Kings!" Have we journeyed so far in our "understanding of things", that it takes much to awe us? Perhaps those of us who "professionally dispense the Word of God" are in the most danger of losing "the easy aweness". I know that's not a word, but maybe your knowing it's not a word is an indication you know too much! Not really, but let's have more "Nathanael Moments", where the slightest thing, whether it's in the creative world, the relational world, or the spiritual world, sets us off to saying, "Jesus, you are the Son of God, you are the king of Israel". And here is an "insider secret", if you practice awe of the small things, Jesus will really wow you with bigger things. But probably not until then!

Here's the rest of the John 1 passage, Jesus so loves Nathanael's response that He tells him, "You believe because I told you I saw you under the fig tree before Philip called you? You shall see greater things than that! You'll see heaven open, and the angels of God ascending and descending on the Son of Man." It's a win, win situation. Scale back; learn to appreciate the small, everyday things. Learn to be in awe of what you already know, and you'll be much happier – and you'll make our Lord smile too. And then, on top of that, he will show you greater things, not that you're looking for them, but because He loves how you loved to be awed. Let's be easily awed people.

# 8
## EXPECTATIONS

I still laugh out loud when I hear my friend Ryan tell this story. He and his wife Julie had been married just about a year when they were presented with a "Time Share" opportunity. They had enough wisdom and resistance to not buy into the property that was being offered, but they had agreed to the "presentation", because if they just sat through it, they could receive a "luxury cruise". Yes, you read that right, for just listening to the presentation they could have a cruise of a lifetime. So they made it through the presentation, and sure enough, were awarded the cruise trip. Ryan and Julie flew to a city near the port they would be leaving on the cruise. They rented a car at the airport and traveled to the port. As they neared the port, both Ryan and Julie could see in the distance the beautiful, very large white Cruise Ship. You know the one, the one you see in the advertisements of Carnival and Princess Cruise lines. They both were excited, having been only married a year, and now this! It made listening to the presentation more than worth it. After parking the car, they headed towards the ship, but when they inquired about boarding – they were told that "this was not their ship, but theirs was 'over there'". When they looked at "over there", they saw a small (one quarter the size of the large white Cruise Ship) blue ship, which, in Ryan's words, "looked more like a tug boat". That was their "Cruise Ship"! Not quite what they "expected"! Ryan recalled the first night at dinner; the little ship tossed so much in the waves that the dishes were sliding on the dinner table! That night, as a result of the "rock and rolling", they both got seasick. So much for expectations!

Expectations are normal, who of us have not had expectations? They range from expectations about jobs, marriage, parenting, vacations, investments and degrees. Expectations come with humanity, and they can be a bane or a blessing. Some, in order to avoid disappointment, seek to eliminate all expectations. Bill Watterson of (comic strip) Calvin and Hobbs fame, says; "*I find my life is a lot easier if I lower my expectations.*" Alexander Pope, 18th Century English poet said; "*Blessed is he who expects nothing, for he shall never be disappointed.*" But truthfully, can determining not to have expectations really keep us from expectations?

Christians are not exempt from expectations. Some expectations are healthy and good, and others can lead to disappointment, and in worse case scenarios, even frustration with God. A casual glance at scripture reveals many incidences of disappointment over expectations. Here are just a few: Naaman – Expecting Elisha to do some magical gesture for his healing (II Kings 5:11- 12); Two Disciples on the Road to Emmaus – Expecting Jesus to not be killed and crucified (Luke 24:18- 24); Jewish Religious leaders – Expecting John the Baptist and the Messiah to look and appear different (Luke 7:31-35); John the Baptist – Expecting Jesus to have acted differently (Matthew 11:3); Hiram – Expecting better cities from Solomon (I Kings 9:12). I think you get the picture, God doesn't "sugar coat" expectations ending in disappointment.

But, of course, the greatest disappointment portrayed in

scripture is over God's seeming delays or denials over promises or our personal desires. Failed expectations in scripture, as well as our own lives, can "stagger our faith" unlike almost any other thing we face in our walk with Christ.

So, what do we do about expectations? As already mentioned, they're kind of built into our lives. When expectations merge with hope, they can be good. We can't really live our lives without hope, and as scripture says, "Now faith is being sure of what we hope for and certain of what we do not see." (Hebrews 11:1) So, expectant hope can be good, but most of us struggle with expectations because we seek to imagine or request God to answer and provide in a specific way – one we have chosen or determined, or at least imagined. You might want to reread that line. Let's face it; truthfully, we've all been disappointed with God not meeting certain expectations, especially when we believe these are good, Christ-honoring expectations. I know, we would not share that in a testimony meeting, but it's true nonetheless. So, how do expectations fit in with our Christian walk?

If you have not bought and read this wonderful "Table Book", I'd encourage you to buy and read it. The book is *The Art of Abundance,* and its author is Candy Paull. The book is not about "Wealth and Prosperity", but about identifying what God has already blessed us with. Anyway, here's a line from her book; "*Letting go of expectations is a big part of the art of abundance. Expectations dictate the way we think God's goodness should come to us – what kind of box life is supposed to come in. But that limits what God can do in our lives, because He is a God of surprise and diversity and wonder. The only boxes God likes are surprise packages! Our box of expectations labeled "what should be" can become a trap. True abundance welcomes the surprises of life.*" If it can be said this way, "God is a God of 'beyond expectations'". Isaiah 64:3 revels in the wonder of this God of "beyond expectations" – "You did awesome things we did not expect." Of course He did! He is that type of God; "God can do anything, you know

33

– far more than you could ever imagine or guess or request in your wildest dreams!" (Ephesians 3:20)

It's hard to let go of expectations, especially ones we have already defined and shaped. Most of the time our expectations of how and when God will respond and do something meet with disappointment. But if we leave with God His timing, method and what the answer will look like, we can set ourselves up to be "surprised by God". Samuel Johnson once wrote; *"Our brightest blazes of gladness are commonly kindled by unexpected sparks."* It's not that we should abandon all expectations – or even lower them, but instead, we should entrust our expectations to the God who is wise, all-powerful, loving and infinitely creative. God is still able to do "jaw-dropping, eye-popping, and ear-ringing things", it's just that it may not be what we thought or imagined.

Ryan and Julie saw the "big white cruise ship," but then saw the "little blue tug boat". Jarring disappointment. Much of life hits us this way. But let's lay at Jesus' feet our expectations, we won't know always what He will do, or when or how, but He can be trusted to supply and provide in a way that's commiserate with His infinite Being. God's plan for us is not life in a "Happy Meal box with a toy in it", but a "Surprise Package delivered at an unexpected time containing unexpected blessings". Our expectations, no matter how lofty, are low and meager, compared to God's infinite wisdom and creativity. Trust Him for this – and you won't even have to sit through a "presentation" to receive His wonderful gifts!

# 9
# BMI OR SMI?

$O$kay, that was embarrassing. I had a physical check-up on the day I write this. Truthfully, though I know better, I try to avoid these. I know, I know, that's not wise, but it's the truth! Anyway, after experiencing the joy (cough, cough) of a complete physical, including perfunctory blood test, etc., I left to run some errands.

While waiting on a certain item at the store, I went over to Starbucks and got a Chai tea. As I was sitting there at a table, I felt the paper in my pocket that the Doctor's office had given me when I left from my appointment. I hadn't thought to look at it, since I figured it was simply an itemize list of the charges I just had incurred. But when I pulled it out, it wasn't, instead it was a report of the temporary findings (minus the blood test results) of the exam. I was looking down through it, and I saw these letters "BMI", and a little asterisk next to it. I thought "what's that?" So I called the Doctor's office and asked the receptionist. She told me it was Body Mass Index. Hmm...I didn't like the sound of that, it sounded kind of like Body Fat Potential that I heard often when working with the professional athletes. The Body Fat Potential was how much of their body was made up of harmful fat (not all fat is harmful, our body needs fat). With the athletes this was oftentimes ridiculously low. I remember the basketball player, Herschel Walker, had something like 5 or 10 percent.

But BMI is different; basically BMI tells you if you're overweight. And I had an asterisk next to mind! It's not fool proof, the BMI, because a muscular person – weightlifter, bodybuilder, athlete or Speaking to the Heart writer (wink, wink), may "seem" to be overweight, but their muscles weigh more than their fat. So, here it was on my chart, recommending that I "lower" mine. BMI is determined (got a pen) by multiplying your weight by 703, then multiplying your height in inches by your height in inches (still with me?), and then dividing your new body weight number by your height number. Doing this, they (whoever "they" are) can determine your BMI. Theoretically, they would like your number 24 or below. According to whoever keeps these types of statics, more than 2/3rd of all Americans are overweight. I was figuring mine out, and realized I was "undertall", that was the reason for their "mistakenness" on my chart!

But as I sat in that Starbucks, I began to think what if believers had a SMI, that is, Spiritual Mass Index. What would mine read? What "percentage" of my body (life) is spiritual? As far as BMI, maybe I struggle with too much "fat", but with SMI, I wonder if I struggle with too little "Spiritual". How can I, or anyone, know their SMI? Are there indicators or factors that show up – or don't show up, that would let me know my SMI? And are there people who can help me identify my SMI?

Taking the latter first, there are people who can help me know my progress of growth in Christ. They are not medical practitioners, but spiritual practitioners. And, unlike in the medical world, these observers and helpers are not necessarily "professionals" or "experts". They are just people close to us, who can see our lives, and truthfully, can see things we sometimes can't. These would be our family, our close friends – and sometimes, not so close friends, our pastor or mission's director, they can even be people we have ministered to ourselves. One of the things the "Evil One" desires is for us to remove ourselves from those who would have access to our lives, so that they can see things "up close and personal". We'll never be able to get a control on our SMI, if we avoid people or put ourselves "above" others. Proverbs hits the nail on the head when it says, "Iron sharpens Iron, and one man sharpens another." (Proverbs 27:17) Centuries later the writer of Hebrews said, "And let us be concerned about one another in order to promote love and good works, not staying away from our meetings, as some habitually do, but encouraging each other…" (Hebrews 10:24-25). So God has placed all around me people who can help me know my SMI.

But what about the first point, "How can I know my SMI?" Well, unlike the complex and complicated "formula" to determine my BMI, my SMI is much easier to spot. Basically, and primarily, the first way to tell, the first indicator of what my SMI is, is to ask the question – or ask others this question about myself, "Do you see change in my life? Do I seem more Christ-like right now, are there evidences that things that should not have been a part of my life, are diminishing?" It's important to realize we're not talking about "perfection" but "direction". In my meetings I've often told missionaries and pastors that it's easy to try and "stay one step ahead of those we minister to", but all the time, we ourselves are not really growing. I say this to them because I know my own heart, and see that temptation is an easy pathway to take. I can speak from experience!

There are no exceptions to the repeated admonitions in scripture to "bulk up spiritually": "Grow in grace and knowledge"; "Grow up in your salvation"; "In an ever-increasing way be transformed into his image"; "Perfecting holiness out of reverence to God." (II Peter 3:18; I Peter 2:2; II Corinthians 3:18; II Corinthians 7:1) We don't grow to a more loved position by God, and we cannot become more holy and righteous in His sight, but we can become more like Him in our walk and conduct.

But in addition to asking ourselves the question "Am I growing", we can know our SMI by asking ourselves "Do I love Him more now, then I have in the past?' If not, then I have a problem with my SMI. Is He the joy of my life? Do I find myself regularly worshipping Him? There is a reason that Revelation 2:4 is in our Bibles, it reminds us that we can lose our first love. A third question helps us determine our SMI, we first ask "Am I growing", then "Do I love Him more" and third, "Is my trust in Him and His ways stronger now than before?" Do I trust Him to do abundantly and beyond what I can imagine? Do I trust Him in the dark, when I can't see His face or hand? Have I given up on Him answering certain prayers, have I begin to doubt His goodness and power – His wisdom? If so, my SMI – Spiritual Mass Index is in trouble.

I really didn't like seeing that statement on my sheet from the doctor's office. First of all, I didn't even know what BMI was, and secondly, when I found out what it meant, I was frustrated – but not with my need and failure, but with them! How dare they! There must be some mistake, there has to be exceptions! But, there is a reason that they have a medical certificate, and I do not! Sometimes shocking evaluations are necessary. The Apostle Paul said, "Let a man examine himself" (I Corinthians 11:28). I think at this point, it is so very important to understand examination and evaluation – by ourselves and others, examination is always with the motive of growth and maturity. It is not meant to discourage or even cause embitterment, but to remind us "that there's more out there" in our Christian growth and Christ-likeness. Any evaluation and examination must be first of all centered in the love of God for us, and our forever standing in grace. It must be that way. But growth is not an enemy of God's love and grace.

So, how about it, are you willing and ready to find out your SMI? The BMI may mean consternation and a lot of self effort, but improving our SMI has the added benefit of coupling our effort with the glorious inner power of the Holy Spirit. And as it has often been said, "We work from Righteousness, not to righteousness." "Work out your salvation with fear and trembling, for it is God who is working in you, enabling you both to will and to act for his good purpose." (Philippians 2:12) Hey, I can't say "2/3rd of believers struggle with SMI", all I know is – it's definitely something I should address in my life! Would you care to join me?

Bruce McDonald

# 10
# FACE TIME

To say we live in the day of Social Media is a great understatement. As recently as 15 years ago no one could have imagined the explosion in this phenomenon. The most known and recognized Social Media, is of course, Facebook. The statistics on Facebook are rather staggering. Here are some statistics I read recently, and the rate they have changed yearly will probably make these obsolete when you read this. The current number of Facebook users is 700 million worldwide (you may want to look at that number again!), with more than 70% of the users coming from outside the USA. Approximately 175 million people log on each day and over 200 million visit it monthly. More than one half of all people who visit the internet visit Facebook, and Facebook is used over 700 billion (not million) minutes per month. And two and one half million websites now have integrated with Facebook. And some of you thought Social Media was just a current fad with certain members of our society!

Facebook, of course, is not the only Social Media, just the best known. There's Twitter, Google Plus, Instagram,

LinkedIn, and some other lesser known and used ones. LinkedIn is a Social Media site for professionals, and boast a world-wide number of users at over 225 million. Twitter has actually passed Facebook in the amount of teen users in the United States. And Instagram will most likely soon overtake Twitter for teen users.

So what does all this mean? I'm sure you have your own thoughts on Social Media, whether pro or con, but whatever it is, we probably all need to come to the realization that "it's not going away". Facebook was, and continues to be an interesting phenomenon. Just the name "Facebook" speaks of a current trend to move relationships from physical to viral. Now just using "viral" makes me realize that I'm becoming a product of my society. When I use viral, I'm of course, not speaking of infection or disease, but of "fast-moving electronically". People, or so it would seem, are moving from "face to face" interactions to electronic images and words. In recent surveys teens have reported that they now have "many more friends than they have ever had". It's not uncommon for people to report of scores or hundreds of "friends" on Facebook. One sight claimed that the average regular user of Facebook here in the states has 130 friends. Many users have less, but some seemed to determine to break some sort of record for number of friends on Facebook. In my research, it seems like Facebook has put a limit of 5,000 "friends" for any particular user!

I find the name "Facebook" rather intriguing, I mean, isn't Facebook anything but face time? I think we'd all agree that a major part of genuine communicating is looking directly at someone's face. How often have we said to a child, "Please look at me when I'm talking to you"? But it's not only true for a child, but for adults as well. So, at this point you may be thinking, "Well, we certainly know what you think of Social Media. And yeah, we get it, it's not the best form of communicating". But that's not the point of this chapter. The thought I'd like to pass along is one that God would seek to remind me about, and that is this; "the best communicating times with God involve face-time." Perhaps our current trend in social relationships is also reflective of current trends in our relationship with God. Let me ask you a question, "Is face-time with God important?" Or perhaps another question would be this; "Is face-time with God actually possible?" In Social Media we can actually read things about friends, loved ones or acquaintances, and maybe even see pictures or videos, but we're truly not spending "face-time" with that person. The same can be true for the child of God with His Heavenly father. We can read things about Him, or about Christ, we can even see videos of the things of God (or for that matter, movies portraying Jesus), but are we actually spending time with God in an intimate way. Are we drawing close to Him, seeking His face?

Please don't think this is just using some clever semantics to make a point, the believer must cultivate face-time with God. This was a serious pursuit of the followers of God in the Bible. Could they, can we, actually see the face of God? Of course not, not yet anyway, but when I speak of face-time with God, I mean intimate, personal and revelatory time with Christ-time that is life-transforming. It is reported that Moses spoke with God face to face (Exodus 33:11), and in fact God Himself made that statement (Numbers 12:8). But at the same time, God told Moses that "no one could see His face and live" (Exodus 33:16-20). So what does that mean? It means that we can have face to face time with God, intimate and revealing time, looking longingly into God's face without seeing Him. The Psalmist repeated on several occasions that he desired to "seek God's face above all things and at all times". "My heart says of you, Seek His face!' Your face, Lord, I will seek." "Look to the Lord and His strength; seek His face always." (Psalm 27:8; 105:4) "Face", is the anthropological term God uses for intimacy and acquaintance. We must seek His face always.

Much happens when we spend face-time with God; first of all we get to know Him better. We recognize God for who He really is. We are intimately acquainted with Him, because we know "what He looks like" (spiritually speaking). But, secondly, when we spend face-time with God, we change. Something happens to us, we become transformed; "But we all, with open face beholding as in a glass the glory of the Lord, are changed into that same image from glory to glory, even as by the Spirit of the Lord." (II Corinthians 3:18) Somehow, when we spend face-time with Jesus, when we gaze at His face, we are changed, and the change is that we begin to look like Him. Again, not an actual likeness to His literal face, but our demeanor, our attitude and actions, the graces of the Spirit of God are molded into our very being. One day we will actually bear His image. I don't know exactly what that means, but I do know it means what it says! "We know that when He appears we shall be like Him, for we shall see Him as He is." (I John 3:2) That day is not here yet, but we can begin to "resemble" Him now.

I have said that face-time with God will result in knowing Him better and ourselves being changed. But there is a third result of having face-time with Jesus, and that is that it makes us better qualified to minister to others. Shortcuts to friendship with God (remember Social Media?) will result in powerless lives in regard to impact and influence of others. More than a century ago James H. McConkey wrote; "*No man is fitted to look into the face of men in service until he has looked into the face of God in communion.*" We may have some legitimate concerns over the potential shallowness of Facebook, or any other Social Media in regard to genuine friendships and relationships, but our greater concern – and self-examination, should be with our potential shallowness with time with God. Am I spending face-time with Christ? Do I seek His face? Do I know His face? One day I will see His face (Revelation 22:4), will I be shocked or will I say, "That's the God I have known and pursued. That is the God that I have diligently spent time face to face with."

# 11
# FROM CRADLE TO GRAVE

We all to like moving forward in life, it's generally not good to stop or go "backwards" – career wise, relationship wise, and health wise. As I'm writing this I'm currently traveling a long distance. Actually I'm traveling more than half way around the world. I'm ready to get home, but we have these breaks in our travel – called airports! On this one there's 5 of them, and one "stop" is 6 hours and another is 9 ½ hours. Just get me home! Let's keep moving, what is it with all these stops?

But stops are a part of life, whether in music, refueling cars or waiting on a roast in the oven. Still, we chafe most of the time at stops. This is especially true in our Christian walk. We want to grow in grace and knowledge. We want to, in an ever-increasing way reflect God's Glory, and we want to grow up in our salvation (I Peter 3:18; II Corinthians 3:18). All these are Biblical admonitions and most of us do want to grow in our faith and walk with Christ. Unfortunately, we tend to think that our Christian life is a life of constantly moving forward, or at least we feel we should be moving forward. Along with that comes another desire (assumption?), and that is that the more we go and grow in our walk, the less we'll have "stops". Somewhere along the line we were told that, as we grow, we reach new stages in our Christian life, never to "revisit" the old ones. Along with that, is the belief or assumption that eventually, we'll have grown to the point where the old stops are not necessary. In other words, when we've experienced something along the way i.e., a trial or difficulty, we'll learn and grow from that, and that will be the last we see of it – we've moved on.

The feelings of being over stops in our lives, either comes from reaching a certain age (whatever that may be), or else having finally passed through some pretty significant trial or sorrow in our life. But, sadly (at least from our personal viewpoint), we find that unexpected stops still suddenly come into our lives. Okay, here is a good time to "stop" and explain what a stop is; "A stop is a time or event in our lives where God seeks to bring some new (to us) transforming truths into our lives. It is a moment where He intercedes – intersects, our lives, to continue the Christ-forming process." Trials bring with themselves all sorts of challenges, but trials that continue to show up later in life, or at least later in our experience with Christ, have double the potential challenges. We usually don't verbalize this, but our thoughts are, "Why now, why after all these years?"

This is not a light or trivial subject; trials strengthen in nature when they come at a time when we feel we are "over" the trial and growth stage. I have seen older Christians, and strong vibrant Christians, reel when new trials and difficulties hit them. But truthfully, I only need to look in the mirror to see examples of that. Why would God allow – or send, a trial into our lives that "stops us in our tracks"? It doesn't make sense, we've had trials of all sorts already, and we're in the midst of seeking to love and serve Him – "what's this all about!" The truth of the matter is, we'll never outgrow the growth stage-never! Trials are from cradle to grave (or rapture). Think of the trials brought into the Patriarchs' lives; Abraham is in his 90s, Isaac is in his 100s, and Jacob is in his 100s. Daniel's in his 90s and thrown into the lion's den. John's in his 90s and exiled to Patmos. The point is, age or experience – or even usefulness, makes no exceptions for "stops" in the Christian life.

God tips His hand for His desire to continue the growth process throughout our earthly existence by a story that's found in the book of Exodus. Most of us are familiar with the story of Moses and the Ten Commandments, and you probably also remember the ten plagues visited on Egypt. Over and over again (ten times), God tells Pharaoh (through Moses) to "let my people go". God wanted His children out of Egypt, and He went to great lengths to get them out. Finally, the day comes when, through the last plague (death of the firstborn), the Israelites are set free. God tells Moses to have the people ready to go—right now! And go they do, heading out of Egypt, finally, after all these years (430 to be exact). So, as they're leaving, well, let's let scripture pick it up; "Then the Lord spoke to Moses! Tell the Israelites to turn back and camp in front of Pi-lahiroth, between Migdol and the sea; you must camp in front of Baal- zephron, facing it by the sea." (Exodus 14:1-2) Okay, so despite the strange sounding names, you just need to know that the Lord said "stop" when He told them to go.

Finally, after all the trials and difficulty of Egypt, they were leaving. Ah, a breath of fresh air, a release from all the heartache and suffering. The Promise Land was in sight (at least symbolically)! But, no, not now, God is once again putting a hold on their plans. And the Israelites are thinking, "Not again!" And you probably remember that throughout their wilderness wanderings they were taken back by new trials (stops), and they constantly showed their unpreparedness for God's trials by complaining and wishing they could go back to

Egypt.

So, God has them stop, just before leaving Egypt. Now, just because you know the "rest of the story" don't lose the powerful importance of this stop in their lives. You may recall that by stopping, the Israelites faced two major fears and obstacles; one, the Egyptian army would catch up to them, and two, the Red Sea blocked their path. God had them right where He wanted them – at one of His stops. Though common sense, and human expectation, all seemed to say that they had had enough trials already and that God was telling them to move ahead to "better times", their common sense was not God's perfect plan. They still had much to learn about trusting God in impossible situations, and they had much to experience about God desiring events – when we're at our weakest, that's when we will display His glory. Not much has changed today.

As you read this, and as I pray over this for myself, are we frustrated at a 'stop' by God? Does it not make sense? Do you feel like you've already had enough trials and heartache? Does it seem like you've grown enough or aged enough to now be on the backside of stops? I appreciate your thoughts and – they're very real. But the truth of the matter is that the stops will never stop! Not if we want to continue growing and not if we desire God to continue to receive glory. It's not just the "steps" of a good man that are ordered by the Lord, it's also the "stops" of a good man that are ordered by the Lord. Our forward progress will always be characterized by "stops", from cradle to grave.

# 12
# GLORY STEALING

Since 1999 there has been a rumor going around that Al Gore "said" he invented the internet. The reason for this rumor is because of an interview that Gore had with Wolf Blitzer on CNN's Late Edition on March 9, 1999. This chapter is not to address the validity of the claims that people have made on either side of this accusation. A part of his interview included these words; "*I took the initiative in creating the internet*". If you read the rest of the transcript, you can see how either side of this controversy can use some validity in either accusing or denying the report. The point of using Al Gore at the beginning here, is there are people out there – whether Gore is one or not, you'll need to choose – who take credit for other's success, accomplishments or words. A much older accusation of "taking credit for someone else's accomplishments" centers around William Shakespeare. For centuries now, there have been critics who believe that Shakespeare really didn't write his plays, that it was actually someone else. In fact, some critics believe that Shakespeare copied from as many as 70 other writers, most notably, Francis Bacon and Christopher

Marlowe. Since Shakespeare wrote during the late 1500s to early 1600s, there's no way to really know for certain.

Currently there is a debate raging about the authenticity of British climber Edmund Hillary actually being the first one to climb the summit of Mount Everest. In some circles it's almost blasphemous to doubt his "first climb" achievement. On May 29, 1953 Hillary and Tensing Norgay made it to the top of Mount Everest, and the accomplishment was greeted with the hurrahs of other first time explorer's accomplishments – crossing to America, going to the South Pole and finding the source of the Nile River. But recent information on Mount Everest may reveal that the summit was climbed almost 30 years prior to Hillary's success. Two men, "Sandy" Irvine and George Mallory, climbed Everest in 1924. It was thought that they made it to within a few hundred yards of the top. But now, new evidence may reveal they made it to the top and were on their way back down when they died. Previously it was assumed they died on the way up. Found in the pocket of Mallory (famous for climbing Everest in a three piece suit!) was his pair of sunglasses. The theory is that they were descending and he took off his glasses in the fading light. The search is on now for the camera that young (23 years old) Irving had on him. The thought is, that if they reached the top, he'd have pictures of the summit – still intact because of the deep freeze weather – so it could be verified if he indeed did reach the top before Hillary. What a find that would be, and change the face of the first climber(s) to the top of Everest!

Whatever is discovered about Irving and Mallory, there certainly are no accusations that Hillary and Norgay deliberately sought to deceive anyone into thinking they were the first to do this monumental achievement. Mistakenly identifying someone for someone else's accomplishments is understandable. Perhaps the mistake can't be corrected, but there are times when it is. What is more heinous, and sometimes despicable, is when there is deliberate intention to take credit for someone else's accomplishment. This can happen in Christian circles – and truthfully it is happening more frequently now, when it shows up in the area of Plagiarism. There seems to be an almost epidemic of plagiarism happening among clergy and writers today. Copying someone else's work (deliberately) and taking credit for it yourself. Bad stuff and grieving to the Holy Spirit.

But Christians can be guilty of another form of taking credit for something, and that is taking credit for the work in which God is doing. I think of this as "Glory Stealing". Surprisingly, and sometimes unknowingly, it can show up in many forms. What can sometimes prompt this dangerous and sinful action is, believe it or not, success. Here are some possible scenarios: God chooses to bless a church with significant church growth, we then rush to write books and hold seminars on "how to grow a church". God chooses to start a church from scratch, and have it also grow, and we write books and speak at conferences on "how to plant a church". We have, by God's grace, a good or great marriage, we then feel prompted to tell people publicly and in print, "how to have a great marriage". God in His infinite grace blesses our children, and they turn out well, so we get busy writing books and holding conferences on "how to parent well". God blesses our business, and we now are "experts" on business growth, and speak or write on "how to run a business". God in His kindness blesses our finances, and we now can tell others – even scold them, on "how to handle your finances wisely". We are becoming pretty adept and creative in writing about and speaking about, our "secrets to success" in all these areas. Please don't take lightly what I am writing about. It's something all of us – beginning with myself, should remember. God doesn't like "Glory Stealing". The Apostle Paul warns us about this; "For who makes you different from anyone else? What do you have that you did not receive? And if you did receive it, why do you boast as though you did not?" (I Corinthians 4:7) It seems like we live in an age that has a great propensity for taking credit for what God does. Really, think about it. Where do you read of this in any other church age (at least to this degree)?

In case we think this is a "light matter", keep in mind God's Word – "I will not give my glory to another!" (Isaiah 42:8) Both a warning, and sobering words to us, God had already gone on record saying He is a jealous God, and does not share His glory (Exodus 20:5). Want to see a picture of how serious God is about this? Think of God's dealings with King Herod, and see what action by Herod caused God to "react" violently. Here's a snippet from Herod's life: Herod arrests John the Baptist and has him beheaded (Matthew 14:3-10); Herod is given Jesus, and then he promptly has Him beaten and mocked (Luke 23:8-11); Herod arrests James, the brother of John, and has him beheaded (Acts 12:1); Herod arrests Peter and puts him in prison with the intent to kill him (Acts 12:3). And in all this, Herod seems "to get away" with these acts of atrocities. But one day he brings a speech before a group of people. Well, here, let me have you read what took place: "Herod wearing his royal clothes sat on his throne and began making a speech to them. The people started shouting, 'The voice of a god and not of a man!' Immediately an angel from the Lord killed Herod for not giving glory to God. Herod was eaten by maggots and died." (Acts 12:21-23) Wow, enough said! God didn't seem to react to all his heinous crimes, but when he stepped over the line and took credit for what God had gifted (in this case, ability to speak well), God struck Him down. I think the word for myself and each of us, is "let's make sure we don't glory steal" - we can in subtle ways. And though we don't wrongly fear he "will strike us down", we desire to not grieve His Spirit, and always give Him glory. "Not to us, O Lord, not to us but to your name be the glory, because of your love and faithfulness." (Psalm 115:1)

# 13
# GOD IN THE DETAIL

I write this somewhat hesitantly and embarrassingly. But, for whatever reason, God in His sovereign grace and determined purposes has allowed us to experience the benefits of world-wide travel. There is no explanation for it, except that it is His predetermined will to use us – for however long He may choose – to minister to people here in the states and many countries overseas. Truthfully, we are unlikely ones to be used of God, and certainly many others would be more deserving and fit for this ministry. Be that as it may, He does have us in this ministry of travel, and as a result, in the midst of our ministry we have had the unexpected, and sometimes, unparalleled joy, of seeing many amazing wonders of this world - both man-made and Creator made. I won't bore you with a litany of these things-you have your own you can share. But, for the sake of this chapter, I will mention a particular blessing Bev and I have experienced during travel. And that blessing is seeing many of the finest art museums in the world. I won't list all of the ones we have seen, but just to mention a few: The Louvre in Paris; The British Museum in London; The Vatican Museum in Rome; The Hermitage in Saint Petersburg,

Russia; The Smithsonian in Washington DC; The Ufizzi in Florence, Italy; and The D'Orsay in Paris. There are others, but these particularly stand out in my mind. My personal best is the Hermitage in Saint Petersburg.

It would be doubly hard to list what things in these museums really were special to us. Michelangelo's statue of *David*? Da Vinci's *Mona Lisa*? Rembrandt's *Return of the Prodigal Son*? Rodin's *Thinker*? Or the *Venus de Milo* statue? For me, the fascination has always been in the detail of the work of art, and, surprisingly, not the fame or history of the art. Now granted, I'm no art critic and I have literally no "artistic side." But I do enjoy craftsmanship of any type, and these museums obviously put craftsmanship on display! What really draws me are the incredible intricacies and details of great works of art. When we were in the Hermitage in Saint Petersburg, I was captivated by a small carved scene in a cabinet from several centuries ago. I stood there totally fascinated by the detail that went into making this piece of art. I can't remember how long it took to carve this cabinet, but it was quite a long time. The artist took great measure to go into every detail of his work.

That reminds of me of something that is repetitive in scripture, but one I don't always appreciate. Each year for the past 30 or so years, I read through the Bible – cover to cover. It's been very profitable and helpful to me, but I must share a "secret" with you. The secret is this, having read through the Bible so many times, in addition to my normal studies and devotions, there are parts of scripture I kind of do a "drive-by", or just skim at best. You can probably imagine which ones these are; the genealogies, the rules and regulations for purity and cleansing (you know, the ones about mildew and sores!), the ones about dividing the land and the dimensions of it, and especially, all the details about the design and building of the Tabernacle and then the Temple. There, I confessed it! I feel much better now! But, in all seriousness, think about it, exactly how many verses and chapters do you need to describe the dimensions of the Tabernacle and Temple, and how many verses and chapters do you need to describe each item in the Tabernacle or Temple? Here's an example of what I mean; just in I Kings you have 4 chapters and over a hundred verses describing the building of the Temple, and, are you ready for this? Even such a small thing as building and designing the "water carts" takes up 12 verses! Amazing! So what's going on here? I mean – "Who cares about the water carts?" Okay, tough words, but I ask the question, "Why?" What is God doing? Doesn't He know that so many of us who will have read the Bible, will have done it centuries and millennia's after all this had been destroyed and become irrelevant (at least in this age of grace)?

I think I finally figured out the "why." God is in the detail – He loves it. All the intricacy of the minutia is His delight. He wants you to see His craftsmanship; He wants you to see His architectural abilities. As I was meditating on this, it's as if God is saying; "I don't want you to miss a thing, look at all the detail I put in this!" Who knows, maybe in heaven, as we see all the glories of the New Jerusalem (remember all the detail listed in the design and dimension of it in Revelation 21 & 22?), Christ will walk around pointing out the "Gates of one pearl" or the "Streets of gold". Like a great artist and craftsman, God is infinitely involved in the detail – and nothing is rushed or overlooked.

Which (finally) brings me to this point – God is in to the detail of your life! Every aspect of it, from the design of your body, the parents or lack of them you had, the gifts and abilities you have, the experiences He has allowed you to have, and the way in which you will bring Him glory. It's true, He is even more into design and detail as it relates to your life than He was with the Tabernacle and Temple. The most clarifying and powerful verses in our Bible on this truth is Psalm 139:13-16. In these verses God says; I was intricately wrought in my mother's womb. Every aspect of my being and every detail of my life were hand-crafted." Verse 15 says I was "woven together" (NIV), the old KJV says "Curiously wrought", but the ESV says "Intricately woven". That's the closest idea. The word each of these translations seeks to translate is a word that literally means "embroidered". It could also mean "needlework". I encourage you to go back and read Psalm 139:13-16 in your Bibles. God, the Master Craftsman and Artist, was working every detail of your life while you were still in your mother's womb. In fact, verse 16 says "every day of my life was written in a book before one of them came to be." But truthfully, though God's work on you started in the womb – and continues every day of your life – His design of you and your life, started in eternity past. Think what that means, who knows how long Da Vinci or Michelangelo had a work "in their mind" before creating it? Perhaps days, weeks, months, or maybe even years. But God's design of you went way back – way back before space, time and eternity. The Apostle Paul reminds us that this all took place "before time began" (II Timothy 1:9).

Hey, the Louvre and the Hermitage are great, and I hope you can go there one day. But it only takes a look at you to see a "masterpiece". And one that reveals that great design and detail went into that work. You know why I know you are special, and you're not the "scrapheap" that the Evil One accuses you of being? Because I know your designer – and God doesn't make any junk! Only great works of art and ones that much detail went into. You too can say to God; "I will praise you, because I have been remarkably and wonderfully made." (Psalm 139:14)

14
# HAVING TROUBLE FINDING A GIFT?

Christmas is wonderful, for all the right reasons. First, and most obvious, is because we stop and take time to celebrate Christ and His entrance into this world. But it is also a time to show good will towards others, and most enjoyably, those we love and cherish. Receiving gifts is a big part of it – "who of us doesn't like to receive gifts!" But truthfully, giving gifts and seeing the response of those who we give gifts to, has its own special joy. Of course, if it's a gift that the person really didn't want (ties, footie pajamas and fruitcake), their response may not be so precious to us! But, with the gift giving, there can also be some significant challenges - like, "what do you get a certain person?" That's not always an easy thing to do, and you probably know of someone whom it's really hard to find something for them. It may be that they already seem to have everything, or simply that they are people for whom you find it complicated to get something.

Then, there is another scenario, where you unexpectedly receive a gift from a person, and now you have to scramble and find one for them. It probably has happened to you. Or, how about this one? You buy something for someone, and they for you, but when you open their gift, you realize theirs was a much more expensive gift than yours! Yep, gift-giving can present its own unique set of challenges.

I mentioned above the challenge that may arise if you desire to give a gift to someone who has everything, or at least seems to have no needs. How about Royalty? What would you give to a King or a Queen, or a Prince or Princess, or any other type of dignitary? There are people who face that challenge. If it's one Royalty to another, the choice may be a little easier – but not necessarily. Did you hear this one about the gift exchange between President Obama and Queen Elizabeth? There's a story that back in April of 2009, President Obama and his wife Michelle had a private audience with the Queen. When the President arrived, the Queen presented him with some wonderful gifts. These gifts were rather amazing and spoke volumes of her thought process in this gift-giving. She presented President Obama with one of the earliest known copies of William Shakespeare's Henry V. She also presented him with a framed original sheet music of John Newton's "Amazing Grace". To President Obama's daughters, the Queen gave a dollhouse-sized replica of Windsor Castle with a functioning train station. They also received a prized Shetland pony. Mrs. Obama was given a ruby ring commissioned and worn by Queen Victoria. The Obama's gifts seemed to reflect that they had not really been prepared or thought through the gift-exchange. President Obama (rather unceremoniously) handed the Queen a shopping bag from the Duty Free shop at Heathrow Airport. It contained a copy of *Dreams of My Father*, purchased at the WH Smith shop at the Heathrow airport. Also in the bag was a bottle of Johnny Walker Scotch, a CD of the Swedish band ABBA's Greatest Hits and 10 bags of M&Ms with the Presidential Seal on them.

Okay, I think I got your attention! The story, of course, never really happened, though several of the tabloids reported this story to be true. The President (now this is the truth) gave the Queen an iPod with songs and pictures of her visit to America, and she in turn gave him a valuable silver tray with her picture and Prince Philip's on it. Like I said, it's hard to give Royalty a gift! This Christmas, you and I have an opportunity to give a gift to Royalty. No, it's neither our president nor the Queen of England, but it's the King of kings. Some people are in the habit of baking a "birthday cake" for Jesus on Christmas day. Others will have a gift wrapped present under the tree for Jesus, usually one containing some words of thanks to our Savior, or some promises for the coming year.

But, truthfully, what do you get someone who has everything? What do you get someone who has already given you a gift that can never be matched? Many of us become weighed down with all the commercialism of Christmas, and the amount of money that is spent during this time of year. We know Christmas is not about focusing on trees, gifts and travel. And we desire to somehow bring Christ back into the picture – more than a child figurine in a small Nativity set. I think there is a way to give a gift to the One who is "The Indescribable gift". (II Corinthians 9:15) It is by going back in time, going all the way back to when Christ was a small child. It is seeing what the first gifts given to Christ were. We are all aware of what the Wise Men brought to the young child Jesus in the home where Joseph and Mary were living. The Magi brought gifts of gold, incense and myrrh.

If you and I stop and think about it, these three gifts represent the greatest gifts that one can give to Christ. The gifts in themselves seem rather extravagant for a child; I mean, what can a child do with these gifts? But as you know, these gifts "represented" something, something that was well thought out – and not purchased at a "Camel Roadside Shop" just before arriving. Those three gifts are gifts which please our Savior and bring a genuine response of appreciation. The gifts, as you recall, were to represent the following things; Gold – His Kingly presence, Incense – His Deity, and Myrrh – His sacrificial death.

This Christmas, as you present your gift to Him, give Him worship and gratitude for the fact that He is the King of kings, that He is sovereign over your life and all the governments of the world are rightfully His (Isaiah 9:6). Second, give Him worship and gratitude that He is God over all (Romans 9:5). He left all of heaven's glory and His rightful worship to come here. He is God Almighty and the Everlasting Father (Isaiah 9:6). Third, give Him worship and gratitude for suffering the ultimate death, dying for our sins. He is the Lamb of God that took away the sins of the world. Jesus loves nothing better than worship (John 4:23). It is the gift He never grows tired of, it is the gift He never has too much of. Though these are gifts that should be given to Him all year long – and daily, why not this Christmas stop and take time, as a family or individually, and present Him His gift, a gift of praising Him for His kingship, His deity and His suffering. Hey, it's pretty amazing to receive an original copy of William Shakespeare's Henry V, or original sheet music of "Amazing Grace"! But, to open up gifts for Christ of Gold, Incense and Myrrh, is priceless.

# 15
# HIGHER

Do you know any tall people, I mean, really tall people? You probably do, or at least have seen someone who is tall. I know tall is a relative term, and depending how "height challenged" you are, tall may be very relative. But there are tall people, and then there are really tall people. The other day we had neighbors over for a cookout. I was outside grilling some burgers and my wife, Bev, needed something put back on the top shelf, but she couldn't reach that high. So our neighbor, who is around 6 feet tall, put it back for her. That was really convenient, but 6 feet is not that tall. We have had a few friends that were over 7 feet tall, and compared to them, a six-footer seems rather small. Seven foot tall friends come in especially handy when seeking to reach something, but there is a downside to having 7 foot friends. There was a time one of our 7 foot friends remarked to Bev that she needed to clean the top of our fridge! During my time as a basketball chaplain for the 76ers, I hung with friends who were 7 foot 6 inches - okay, that's tall! You ever try talking to someone that tall? After a while it gives you a sore neck!

So, here's a question; "just how tall is God?" I mean, will even 7 footer's look up to Him? Okay, quick answer – I don't have a clue! But here's something to think about, and it's the reason for this chapter; "When thinking about God, we should always look up!" In fact realizing and remembering that God is "up" is crucial in our Christian lives. Did you know that when the Bible speaks of God, and primarily when God speaks of Himself, He usually uses the term "up". That is, that God is normally up or above. This is pretty fascinating, especially when you think of all the promises and proclamations about being "near or present". Sometimes the promises are in the same passage of scripture; "The Lord God is in heaven above and on earth below." (Deuteronomy 4:39). I believe this is a passage that is more than just explaining the omnipresence of God. It is more than just revealing that God is transcendent. God is indeed a very present help in time of need and One who has promised that He will never leave or forsake us. (Hebrews 4:16 & 13:5) But the nearness of God is not comforting unless we understand the far-ness of God. That may sound confusing, but let me try to explain. Scripture reminds us that "God is up", so that when our present circumstances tend to overwhelm us, we want one who is near us that is above us. Confused? The "Up-ness" of God is essential in us having the right perspective on current challenges and problems. We want someone who is higher than us; we want someone who is above us, to come to our rescue, to be our deliverer – to be our hope.

Do you remember the story of Jacob's ladder? Modern translations call it "Jacob's staircase". More accurate than "ladder", but to be even more accurate, we should call it "God's stairway or the Angel's stairway". Anyway, the story is found in Genesis 28, and in that story Jacob falls asleep (on a rock) and has a dream/vision of a stairway reaching to heaven. On that stairway, angels are coming up and down from heaven to earth. Pretty amazing vision! But notice something powerfully important to our topic in this chapter. Let me cut into Jacob's dream/vision: "He saw a stairway resting on the earth, with its top reaching to heaven, and the angels of God were ascending and descending on it. There above it stood the Lord…And He said; 'I am with you and will watch over you wherever you go…'" Did you notice something? Did you notice God was first "above" and then He was "with" Jacob.

Strange as it sounds, even though we love the thought of a God who is there, and there for us, we need a God who is first "above". We preeminently find comfort in a God who; "sets His glory above the heavens" and "Who sits enthroned above the circle of the earth." (Psalm 8:1 & Isaiah 40:22) We love our Lord Jesus Christ, and we take courage in His words, "I am with you always, to the very end of the age." (Matthew 28:20) But the reason we take such comfort and courage from that is because Jesus is the one, "Who is seated far above all rule and authority, power and dominion, and every title that can be given." (Ephesians 1:21) When we pray, we can be encouraged that God is near, even in us, in the presence of the Holy Spirit. But when we pray, we should first and ultimately pray to a God who is above. "I lift my eyes to you, to you whose throne is in heaven." (Psalm 123:1) We need to have Isaiah's vision and awe; "I saw the Lord, seated on a throne, high and exalted." (Isaiah 6:1) We need to be confident that the one we come to us is higher than us. "Lead me to the rock that is higher than I." (Psalm 61:2)

There is a reason that the Apostle Paul says to "set our thoughts and affections on things above" (Colossians 3:1). It's because we need someone higher than ourselves. There are perhaps several advantages for a basketball player who is 7 feet or taller. But the advantages for a God who is higher than all, is incalculable. His "high-ness" speaks of the fact that He has authority over all. This is huge! All are under Him, even the evil one and the evil people on this earth. His "high-ness" speaks of the advantage of perspective - He sees what we cannot see, and He sees the whole picture. A flight in a plane gives us a perspective of the earth we don't have when we walk about here. Even much more, God's view from heaven gives a perspective that we could never have – plus He knows the future! His "high-ness" reminds us that He is not bound by our circumstances and dilemmas. He is "above" them, not entangled by them, not confused by them, and not at a quandary at what to do. And, perhaps, the greatest advantage of His "high-ness" is that He is above us so that when we look up at Him, we give Him our full attention. When we look around for Him, we get distracted, we lose focus. But when we lift our gaze up to Him, we see only Him. He is high and lifted up, and He has our full attention.

There is a phrase from a verse in the book of Daniel that I love, and it speaks to the topic of this chapter. It's found in Daniel 4:34, and here's what King Nebuchadnezzar says; "When I lifted my eyes to heaven, my sanity was restored!" That's it isn't it? Lifting our eyes to God restores everything. You probably noticed how often I used the word "high-ness", and that was intentional. You undoubtedly thought of the word "highness", and now you know there is only one person in the universe that deserves the title "Your Highness"! Praise God that He is near-by, and praise the Lord that He will never leave us or forsake us. But the comfort of those promises is the fact that God is over and above all. He is high and lifted up. Abraham was a unique follower of God – he is called the Father of our faith (Romans 4), and God gave Abraham a special title. God called Abraham His friend! Wouldn't you love that! But in turn, Abraham had a special name for God, and that name was God Most High or "El Elyon". (Genesis 14) Some of you use the names of God in your prayer life. Here's one we all should use and proclaim – El Elyon, God Most High. Do you know somebody tall? Well, you can certainly say you know someone "high", in fact higher than anyone else. Lift up that head!

# 16
# I CANNOT NOT

Okay, how's that for a title! Hopefully it will make sense in a few moments – hopefully. First of all, let me tell you about a pair of dogs, Shelby and Cooper. They're inseparable friends, and they're also are my daughter's dog and my dog. They are great dogs, both are Yellow Lab/Golden Retriever mixes, and both are large dogs. They have many wonderful qualities, smart, obedient, loving and loyal. They also like to role in dead things or the nasty stuff that comes out of live things! Now, again, as I mentioned, they're great dogs. I mean they come when they're called, they're loving and gentle with others, they do lots of tricks – but, then again, they role in dead things. No matter what we (our daughter or Bev and I) try to do – speak kindly to them, speak authoritatively to them, or give them treats, the temptation when walking with them to role in something dead or nasty is too much for them. I've even tried sharing Bible verses with them, and have resorted to crying out to God about this, but our dogs still want to role in dead things (hard to imagine, I know!).

Alright, now would be a good time to introduce a word

here into our chapter, it's the word Inherent. You're probably familiar with that word, though we don't use it often in a sentence. The word inherent means: Part of the very nature of something; Inseparable element; Permanent characteristic. So, here's the sad truth, our dogs inherently love to role in dead things – and that other nasty thing. I can't change it, even though I've tried several different approaches. People have inherent issues as well, although hopefully not rolling in dead things, or things that come out of live things! But we do have inherent issues. I'm not talking here about generational sins or physical or psychological traits that are sometimes passed down - that is for someone else to write on. But, for now, just by way of illustration, we do have inherent traits and idiosyncrasies that are, well, inherent! Have you heard someone say to you; "You know, your father/mother used to do the same thing." Perhaps it's clearing your throat, running your hands through your hair, jingling coins in your pocket, hitching your pants up, or any number of other mannerisms. When someone has pointed these out to you, you may at first deny it, then you may try to correct it, but you find it comes too "natural" for you to easily change. Okay, good news here, you're not a dog, so you can change; it just will seem "unnatural" for a while.

It seems like when we talk about inherent things, that, for the most part, they're not good, or at least, not the best things. But I want to share with you an inherent trait that all believers have, and that is faith. Notice I said "believers", because only believers have Biblical faith in God. When Christ saved us, His Holy Spirit came into our hearts; this was a wonderful, life changing moment. The Bible addresses this several ways; "God sent the Spirit of His Son into our hearts, the Spirit who calls out, 'Abba Father'"; "Having believed, you were marked in Him with a seal, the promised Holy Spirit"; "He anointed us, set His seal of ownership on us, and put His Spirit in our hearts." (Galatians 4:6; Ephesians 1:13; II Corinthians 1:22) And because He saved us and sent His Holy Spirit into our lives, everything has changed. We now have a new nature (II Corinthians 5:17), our spirit has come alive (Ephesians 2:4; John 3:3-7), and we are now forever (Jude 1) the glorious possession of the God of the universe – bought by an unimaginable price, His Son's blood (I Peter 1:18). Everything has changed.

So here's the comforting and glorious news, I cannot not believe! Oh, I can doubt, even quite a bit sometimes, but I cannot not believe. I may go through days, or even seasons, when my faith is stretched and tested, but God's children will still believe – it's inherent! Hey, you'd probably be encouraged to hear just two Biblical examples of this. In this case, they come from the same individual; he is the Old Testament Prophet Jeremiah. Here's the first verse and illustration: "If I say, 'I won't mention Him or speak any longer His name', His message becomes a fire burning in my heart, shut up in my bones. I become tired of holding it in, and I cannot prevail." (Jeremiah 20:9) What Jeremiah was experiencing was frustration and confusion. He felt God had become unfair, and that God wasn't answering his questions. But, what Jeremiah found out, was that he could not not believe. In another passage, and at a different time, Jeremiah again expresses his frustrations and confusions; "He pierced my heart with arrows from His quiver…He has broken my teeth with gravel; He has trampled me in the dust…I remember my affliction and my wandering, the bitterness and the gall…My soul is downcast within me. Yet this I call to mind and therefore I have hope: Because of the Lord's great love we are not consumed, for His compassions never fail. They are new every morning, great is your faithfulness." There it is again, that inherent burning in his soul, that irresistible Spirit of God. God won't let him go! He cannot not believe.

I have been using an Old Testament believer as an illustration, but how much more for the believer today, who is indwelt by the Holy Spirit. At times you and I have doubts, you may be there right now, and I don't make light of these. They can be the dark night of the soul, but you're not alone in this - you will come through. Christ has not lost one believer yet! "No one can snatch them out of my hand." (John 10:28). That no one includes you! Hey, you may have tried to suppress some of your inherent traits, but this is one, thankfully, you can't suppress or change. You've tried to stop praying – you can't, you've tried to stop believing – you can't. For a time, yes, but the inherent new nature coupled with the Holy Spirit makes spiritual death an impossibility. This inherent trait didn't come from our parents, nor did it come from my natural self. This came from the new birth and the entrance into God's family. Okay, so jingling change in your pocket may be annoying, but irresistible faith in Christ is glorious!

# 17
# ICY HOT

There are many things in this world that do not make sense to me, and one of those is Fried Ice Cream. I mean "fried" "ice cream"? Think about that! Now I love Mexican food, but when I see fried ice cream on the menu, I stay away from it. I mean, does it come out melted or frozen? (Don't worry, I actually know the answer.) Another thing I've struggled with is seeking to figure the concept behind Bengay®, Icy Hot. When you rub it on your aching joints, are you supposed to feel cold or hot? For that matter, while I'm thinking about it, how can you get chills from a fever? Okay, I admit it; I actually know that one too. There seems to be a lot of contrasting or opposite words that describe the same thing. It seems like I remember somewhere that these are either contranyms or autantonyms? At this point I'm probably going to hear from an English teacher or some linguist!

But I don't know if anyone has tried to name the experience that believers have when they feel both abandoned by God and kept by His presence. It is a pretty common phenomenon, even if we don't like to admit the first part of it.

It certainly is prevalent throughout the characters in scripture. And the Psalmist, David, seems to have it reoccur in his psalms at different times. "Why have you forgotten me...By day the Lord directs his love, at night his song is with me." (Psalm 42:8-9) And again in Psalm 10:1, 17 "Why, O Lord, do you stand far off? Why do you hide yourself in times of trouble...You hear, O Lord, the desire of the afflicted; you encourage them, and you listen to their cry." There are other Psalms where David expresses these same conflicting thoughts. You may even have noticed a number of them where David starts out complaining – crying out to God, and concludes by words of confidence and worship to God.

But it is not just the psalms, over and over again in scripture men and women felt both abandoned by God and kept by Him. Again, the incidences are too numerous for this chapter, but let me remind you of just a couple. Naomi, the mother-in-law of Ruth, felt so abandoned by God, that she said to her two daughter-in-laws, "The Lord's hand has gone against me!" Later, when folks from her home town saw her, she said to them, "Don't call me Naomi, but call me Mara, because the Almighty has made my life very bitter." (Ruth 1:13, 20) Yet, sometime later, she rejoiced in God's faithfulness as she held in her lap the child of Ruth and Boaz, named Obed. Think of Jacob, who said on three occasions that "He would go down to the grave mourning and filled with grief." (Genesis 37:35; 42:38; 44:29) But later he gave this testimony, "God has been my shepherd all my life to this day." (Genesis 48:15) Both with Naomi and Jacob, they seem to believe both things are true – and they are! Believers who walk with God will feel abandoned and they will feel forgotten. At times this is a very real thing, but like "Icy Hot", they will also feel kept by God. They will express God's faithfulness in a way that someone who has not experienced feelings of abandonment could ever express.

There is a line from the life of Old Testament Joseph that

really speaks to this. As you recall, much of Joseph's early life was spent in prison. At one point, it looks like God is finally going to deliver him by providentially arranging for the King's Cup Holder and Baker to be in prison with Joseph. When Joseph accurately interprets the Cup Holders dreams, and the Cup Holder is released, Joseph asks him to tell Pharaoh he's innocent. This is surely – finally, his way out! But then there are simply these words; "The chief cupbearer, however, did not remember Joseph; he forgot him." These words are followed by, "When two full years had passed." (Genesis 40:23; 41:1)

Don't think lightly of Joseph's plight, he had many a "God-forgotten" moment. From being mistreated by his brothers, sold into slavery, betrayed by Potiphar's wife, and forgotten by the cupbearer – all over a 13 year period. But, as you know, on two occasions, Joseph reassured his brothers that God had been faithful all that time. "Do not be distressed, and do not be angry with yourselves...because it was to save lives that God sent me ahead of you...Do not be afraid, you intended to harm me, but God intended it for good." (Genesis 45:5; 50:19-20) This is going to sound strange, but somehow (remember fried ice cream) those – each of us, who have felt abandoned and forgotten by God, believe Him most to be faithful. It's the icy/hot principle of scripture. The two don't seem to go together, but they do. I know that right now there are many of you who are reading this, who are examples of this. You know what I'm talking about. You have felt alone and confused, and God was nowhere to be found. Perhaps for 13 years. But, somehow, in the midst of that, as well as the conclusion of it, you are more than ever convinced of His faithfulness.

Perhaps you've never voiced Job's words; "Though He slay me, yet will I praise Him." (Job 13:15) But, in some way, your life and lips have reflected that. Unanswered prayer, loss of a job or home, a rebellious child or failed marriage, illness or unsettling health news, or loneliness - all these seem to point to being forgotten by God. But, you know something of God's faithfulness that no one else knows. There are many things I don't understand in this world; fried ice cream, icy hot rubbing gel, and chills from a fever. But what really mystifies me is how you can feel forgotten, and yet, feel God is faithful. Thank you for this. It is the icy/hot principle of a life yielded to God.

"Though you've not seen him [at times in your life], you love him; and even though you do not see him now [in this particular situation], you believe in him and are filled with an inexpressible and glorious joy." I Peter 1:8

Bruce McDonald

18
INGREDIENTS

We all have our favorite foods and dishes. If this was a blog, I could have many of you give testimonies of your favorite culinary dish. I'm married to a great cook, and my daughter is also a fantastic cook. For that matter, so are my two daughter-in-laws, so I pretty much am blessed with women who can cook! My wife and daughter like to watch the food channel. Personally, I'm not into that, but, on occasion, I'll walk in when they're watching something, and it is pretty fascinating to see the chefs bring all the ingredients together into a fantastic dish. Dishes (meals) are only as good as the ingredients that go into them – and obviously, the skill to bring it all together. I came across something recently that was rather fascinating; it was a list of the most expensive ingredients in meals. Here they are: Most expensive fruit: Yubari King Melons (a pair of these auctioned off in Japan for $26,000!). Most expensive fungus: White Truffles ($3,000-$5,000 per pound). Most expensive poultry product: Swiftlet Nests ($1,000 per pound, $20 per nests). Most expensive pantry staple: Acsto Balsamico Tradizionale ($200 for 100 milliliter bottle, or $60 per ounce). Most expensive coffee: Kopi Luwak

($500 per pound). By the way, if you're wondering what that is made from, it is coffee beans that have passed through the digestive system of a civet (cat)! Most expensive meat: Jamon Iberico de bellota ($87 per pound). It is the cured leg of a pata negra pig from Spain. Most expensive spice: Saffron ($30 per gram). And one last one; Most expensive seafood: Sturgeon Caviar ($500 per serving).

Ingredients are important to make up the final product. That is of course true in just about everything. I came across a passage of scripture recently that helped me find the necessary ingredients for something very important to God, and that is worship. It is one thing to say that God loves worship (John 4:23-24), and that worship should be our primary focus (Ephesians 1:12 & I Corinthians 10:31). But what goes into genuine worship? The best way to see what goes into making worship great is to look to heaven and see how it's done there. Everyone in heaven is worshiping – angels and humans. But probably no class of beings worship like the Living Creatures, or as the older translations say, the Cherubim. We don't know who these mysterious creatures are. There has been much speculation, and we don't know their relationship to the Seraphim. But, whatever they are (whoever they are), they were definitely built for worship. Perhaps gazing at them (can you imagine that we'll do that in heaven!) right now can help us understand about our present worship and what goes into making it great. Here are some ingredients that you would readily pick up from them in Revelation chapters 4 & 5:

Ingredient # 1: They were close to the throne (4:6). Genuine worship, even now, comes from when we stay close to the throne, when we are regularly looking at God. Distance from God will result in cold, sterile worship, but gazing at God regularly, seeking to stay near Him, will result in a fire that ignites worship.

Ingredient # 2: They gazed at Him in every imaginable way

(4:6). They were covered with eyes! They saw everything they could about God. Close proximity is good, and looking towards God is good, but "being covered with eyes" is the best ways to see the manifold greatness of our God. We're not covered with eyes, obviously, but we should look to God in every way possible. We should constantly be searching for His perfections – gazing through worshipful meditation, but also immersing ourselves in the worshipful study of God in scripture.

Ingredient # 3: They sang worshipful songs (4:8; 5:9): I don't believe they were "chanting" "Holy, Holy, Holy"; I believe they were singing it. Beautifully! I often write about this. God loves music, and music that is sung close up and personal. In chapters 4 & 5 there is lots of singing. In fact, they seem like they cannot not sing! Worship definitely is a premium in singing.

Ingredient # 4: Their actions prompt worship in others (4:9-10): Whenever they sing and proclaim worship to God, the 24 elders (representatives of all of us), fall down and worship – and proclaim! Cherubim, or Living Creatures, definitely lead and motivate others in worship. Our worship should also be contagious and prompt others to worship our God.

Ingredient # 5: They incorporated prayer in their worship (5:8): They poured out (literally) prayer before God. A great reminder that a big part – the biggest part, of our prayers, should be worship. We all know that this can be a challenge, working in as a priority praise and adoration, in the midst of our petitions and requests.

Ingredient # 6: They incorporated both praise for who God was and what He has done (throughout 4 & 5): When praising God for His works (things He has done), we often express thanksgiving, and when praising Him for Who He is, we often are filled with awe. Genuine worship is attributing "worth" to His Being and Character.

I don't know how expensive each of those ingredients is, but I do know this, "They make up the most costly thing we can offer up to God." I enjoy a great meal, and especially one that has been served with tender loving care. But I know that meal just "didn't happen", it just didn't "come together." There were intentional ingredients that were brought together to make the dish. The same is true with worship to God. It must be intentional (does not negate spontaneous at times); it must include what the Master Chefs of Worship have shown us. Hey there's no worship channel to watch that shows you how to bring the right ingredients together, but you do have your own Master Chef/Worship Book. Crack open those pages and mix those ingredients together. You never know, you might just bring together worshipful culinary delight to our God.

Bruce McDonald

# 19
# ISOLATION

It is said to be the highest form of torture – Solitary
Confinement. Recent studies have revealed the horrors of
being in solitary confinement. For most of us, the word or
term solitary confinement is familiar, and whether we have
seen it depicted in movies or read about it, we feel we have a
comfortable familiarity with this form of punishment. But the
actuality of the punishment is far beyond what we can begin to
grasp or imagine. Doctors and psychiatrist tell us that sustained
time in isolation can produce all sorts of physical and mental
ailments. The typical "cell" for solitary confinement can be a 6
foot by 9 foot cell, no windows, gray walls, steel doors and no
pictures allowed on the walls. The prisoner can be held in the
cell for 23 hours a day, and let out for an hour to exercise, but
at no time seeing any other prisoners. Fifteen days in such
conditions can cause irreversible health issues. In an almost
unfathomable act of cruelty, Herman Wallace was kept in
solitary confinement for 41 years! He was incarcerated at the
Louisiana State Prison in Angola, and was released October 1
this year. He died two days later at the age of 71.

Solitary Confinement is horrible enough in our prison systems, but it is unfathomable in other countries. Particularly during times of war. Many a soldier has been confined to this form of punishment at the hands of despicable human beings.

The most notable and shocking story of isolation and solitary confinement took place during the Korean War, and it involved 36 American Soldiers. The 36 American airmen were shot down from the sky during the Korean War and were falsely accused of plotting to bomb civilian targets. The world and, our country in particular, were shocked when all 36 confessed to this crime. The North Koreans were known for their cruel and inhuman punishment of prisoners, and their acts of torture and other atrocities were legendary. But Americans were shocked to find out that none of the prisoners were tortured and none had suffered severe physical punishment.

The highest ranking officer among those 36 airmen was Marine Colonel Frank Schwable, who went on record to state emphatically that he did not undergo any physical torture. In fact, none of the 36 men experienced physical torture. Col. Schwable later said he wished he had, if he had, he felt he would have survived better. Instead he and his men were subjected to something new: touchless torture. Each soldier was kept in solitary confinement, the least for 10 months, the most for 13 months. They never saw or talked to each other, they were interrogated by their captors, but always in isolation. During their time of isolation they were made to sit or stand in awkward positions, sometimes sitting on the edge of a chair for 33 days at a time, the entire time in a position of "saluting". Others had to stand saluting for 30 straight hours. After months of isolation, confusion set in, and fact and fantasy blended together until each one of the 36 in isolation confessed to the crime they did not commit. They all lied.

The public was incredulous. How could they have

confessed to a lie, especially after it was learned that none were physically tortured? In the approximate 60 years since that event, the military has learned the powerful damage of isolation in solitary confinement.

If you want to read of an individual's solitary confinement during World War II, read the powerful book, *Unbroken*, by Laura Hillenbrand. It is the incredible story of the imprisonment of Louie Zamperini. I can guarantee that you will not be able to put it down. And if you'd like to know more about the 36 airmen who falsely confessed to plan civilian bombings, read Joseph Margulies excellent article "The More Subtle Kind of Torment." (October 2, 2006)

But why bring up isolation and solitary confinement? What are the chances that we might experience that, or that we have experienced that? Well, perhaps slim, but no one knows for sure the future. And there is an isolation that we can experience, and in fact, most have. That is the feeling of being isolated from God. Make no mistake about it; it is a very real "feeling". And, truthfully, the feeling of being isolated from God can have far greater results than confessing to a crime you didn't commit. Of all the struggles that Christians face, surely, the greatest is the feeling of being cut off from God. There are many reasons for this feeling: severe trials, unanswered prayer, prolonged experiences of the seeming silence of God, and disappointments over godly expectations. These are but a few of the causes of feeling abandoned by God. No one is exempt from this. Age does not matter, occupations do not matter (even for those in ministry), gender, health, race or culture, wealth or poverty - none grant exemptions.

The feelings of being isolated from God have been paraded before our eyes on the pages of scripture. Many Bible characters struggled with feeling isolated from God, and, on occasion, even the feelings of being alone in solitary confinement. Here are a few of these words: "Do not hide your face from me when I am in distress." "Why O lord, do you stand far off? Why do you hide yourself in times of trouble?" (The Psalmist) "He has made me dwell in darkness…He has walled me in so that I cannot escape." (Jeremiah) "He has shrouded my paths with darkness…If I only knew where to find him." (Job) These are but a few of the heart cries in scripture, and, just at face value, they sure seem like people who felt isolated and even in solitary confinement. But we don't need to look at scripture to see feelings of isolation from God – we need only look in the mirror. You know in your heart of hearts there have been times, and perhaps now is one of them, that you have felt cut off from God. You have felt He is nowhere to be found. You have felt isolated and far from God. It is a horrible feeling.

I would like you to take something with you into those times of feeling isolated and removed from God. I want you to take with you a powerful truth, quite staggering in its implications, and that truth is your inseparatableness from God. There are certainly many passages that reassure us about "God never leaving or forsaking us" and "That His presence will go with us," and even the fact "That the Holy Spirit is in us and our bodies are His holy temple". But sometimes our circumstances cause us to struggle with these promises. So, let me remind each of us of an amazing and comforting truth about how we can never be separated from God. Let me start by having us listen to Jesus' words in John 14; "In that day you will know that I am in the Father, you are in me and I am in you." Now, here's the astounding truth as it relates to God never abandoning you, and you never being in isolation. You can't be alone, because you are in Jesus and He is in you! If you could be separated from Christ, then Christ can be separated from the Father. Christ can never be separated (isolated) from the Father, and vice versa. Jesus says, "If you can separate me from the Father, than you can separate Me from you." It's an impossibility! Tonight, rest your head on John 14:20-23. You'll never be isolated from Christ – He can't leave Himself, and

He's in you and you are in Him. And, oh yes, the Father will never leave you either. "My Father will love him, and we will come to him and make our home with him." (John 14:23) No solitary confinement for you!

20

# KNOWING THE DIFFERENCE

There are things that are natural, and there are things that are reasonable. Understanding the difference between these in our Christian life is crucial. In Scripture there are many occasions when the children of God were put in frightening or overwhelming situations. It was natural to feel fear and a sense of impossibility. But in each of those incidents, it was also reasonable to trust God for the provision or victory. In the Bible, you constantly had events or situations that caused a natural response of fear or uncertainty. No food or water in the desert for the Israelites, no weapons for the armies of Saul to fight the Philistines, no rain in the land of Israel to provide crops and water for livestock and people during Elijah's life, no land bridge to cross the Jordan during flood stage, no money to pay taxes during Jesus' earthly ministry, no way to escape a violent storm in the midst of the Sea of Galilee, and no way to get a dead self-proclaimed Messiah back from the grave.

You and I face things that are naturally unsettling, confusing, and at times, downright frightening. For instance, a call from the doctor after a series of medical test, losing your job, not being able to pay the mortgage – or even losing your home, the end of a relationship, orders to ship overseas, and uncertainty about our children. These all are causes to create natural anxieties and fears. But the question is, "are they reasonable fears and anxieties?"

That is the question of this chapter. Perhaps the best place to start is with a definition for "natural" and for "reasonable". Any definition you would find for natural would contain the following: "normal, lifelike, innate, not acquired, and 'true to nature'". The word that is most often translated natural in our New Testament is a Greek word that means "lower nature, bestial". Quite descriptive, wouldn't you say? To respond naturally may be understandable and normal, but it's not the way that God would have the believer respond. The word reasonable includes definitions such as "sensible, the ability to think and draw conclusions, to think logically". Reason, in a Biblical context, is to "think logically and sensibly about a situation or event, and then make logical conclusions." In Scripture, reasonableness is drawn from knowing who God is and what He is capable of - added to that, the remembrance of how He has worked in the past. You might be surprised – I know I was, how often people in the Bible responded "naturally" to a major challenge or crisis, rather than "reasonably". In fact, when we read these events, we may find ourselves saying things like, "why didn't they trust Him?" or "where was their faith?" But, as the Bible reminds us, "For everything that was written in the past was written to teach us, so that through endurance and the encouragement of the Scriptures we might have hope." (Romans 15:4)

We could pick many illustrations of people responding "naturally" as opposed to "reasonably", but I'd like to isolate one event that speaks into my own heart. The story takes place in Numbers Chapter 11, and it involves the Israelites complaining that they had no "meat", and they had already (less than a year) grown tired of "Manna" (wafer like cakes).

Moses was frightened at their outburst and felt totally helpless, this was not the first time they had talked of rebelling and killing him. In verses 11-15 Moses bitterly complains to the Lord about the people, and the Lord, in response, says: "I'll give them plenty of meat for a whole month" (11:20). At this, Moses replies incredulously. "Here I am among 600,000 men on foot [not including women and children], and you say, 'I will give them meat to eat for a whole month!' Would they have enough if flocks and herds were slaughtered for them? Would they have enough if all the fish in the sea were caught for them?" (Numbers 11:21-22) Now, before I comment on Moses' words, let me remind each of us that this was "Moses," God's friend, who He spoke to face to face. See chapter 12 to find out how much God loved Moses and how – in human terms – close they were to each other. But, here in this passage in chapter 11, Moses reacts "naturally". He did the numbers, calculated the resources, and determined it was impossible. It was a "natural" response. But hear God's words to Moses upon hearing Moses' evaluation of the problem, "Is the Lord's arm too short?" (11:23). Other translations have, "Is the Lord's power limited? " "Do you think I'm weak?" "So, do you think I can't take care of you?" You may recall the rest of the story, God causes a strong wind to bring in millions of quail – three feet deep for a "day's walk" in every direction! No Israelite gathered less than 60 bushels! Wow, are you kidding me?

So here's the lesson for all of us. Moses responded naturally rather than reasonably. The reasonable thought (remember, reasonable is weighing logically the facts about who God is, what He can do, and what He has done in the past) would have been, "Well, I've seen God do greater things than this, and He certainly has told us time and time again that he will take care of us." That was the reasonable decision, but Moses chose the natural one. Think about it, Moses had seen the 10 plagues, seen his own hand turn leprous and then whole again, and his rod turn to a snake and back again to his rod. He had seen the Red Sea part, Pharaoh's army drown, water come from a rock, manna appear in the desert – he had been with God at the burning bush and the rumbling mountain! Yet he still reacted naturally. Sounds like the disciples, who ran out of food and questioned Jesus where they would get food – after He had already miraculously fed 5,000 men with a few fish and loaves of bread (Mark 8:4)! Moses saw the hand of God powerfully provide time and time again, but he acted – reacted, "naturally". In my Bible I have a quote from Ian Thomas that I wrote down almost 30 years ago. Here is what he said, *"Do not allow the poverty of self-sufficiency to rob you of the miraculous! It is a particularly subtle form of conceit which denies to God the possibility of doing what you consider to be beyond the bounds of your own carnal self-esteem."*

You and I will always find ourselves facing things that are beyond our ability, and many times, beyond anyone else's ability to help us. "Only God" can be Jehovah Jireh, the Lord who provides. Think "reasonably", remind yourself of who God is, what he has done, and what He has promised. Assimilate and calculate those facts, and then act in faith to what you know to be true about God. The temptation to react "naturally" to the impossible will always be there, even in the best of us (remember Moses). But choose to know and exercise the difference between natural and reasonable.

"Then Job replied to the Lord: 'I know you can do all things; no plan of yours can be thwarted." Job 42:1-2

# 21
# TO KNOW WHEN TO RETREAT

Late in the summer of 1812, La Grande Army of Napoleon marched into Russia with the goal of conquering and subduing this vast nation. Napoleon had systematically been conquering one nation after another, and now set his sights on Russia. Napoleon expected to face the Russian army and win a decisive battle. His army was the largest Europe had ever seen, more than 500,000 soldiers accompanied Napoleon. Napoleon's intent was to force Russian Emperor Alexander I to surrender to him. Alexander I appointed a new General for his army by the name of Prince Mikhail Kutuzov. Kutuzov employed a new tactic for military conflict – he retreated! As Napoleon's massive army continued their march across Russia, Kutuzov ordered his army to set fires as they retreated. Basically scorching the countryside, so that the French army would have no food or provisions to gather. Periodically, Russian Cossack soldiers would ride in and pick off French soldiers who were on the fringes of the advancing army.

Eventually, Kutuzov engaged in a battle with Napoleon's forces on September 7, a battle that was held at Borodino

Field. 108,000 men died that day. Kutuzov realized that he could not defeat Napoleon's massive army that way, so he continued to retreat farther away. When he got to Moscow, he ordered the city to evacuate. But, before leaving, he released all the prisoners who were in jail. Shortly after that, Napoleon arrived in Moscow on September 14, shocked to find the city abandoned. Napoleon set up headquarters there, but some of the prisoners and former inhabitants began setting fire to the French Headquarters. Days turned into weeks, and the French Army was running out of supplies. With cold weather soon approaching, Napoleon made a decision to leave the city and head back to Russia.

As they began the long march back, a brutal early winter set in. With little food, frigid temperatures, and occasional Cossack attacks, Napoleon's great army found itself in great disarray. By the time Napoleon made it back to France he had an army of less than 27,000 soldiers! 380,000 had died in battle or weather, and 100,000 had been captured. Napoleon's great reputation as an undefeated military hero was forever crushed. Soon other, countries rebelled against him, and two years later he met his Waterloo.

General Kutuzov displayed a great lesson for peoples of all time, "sometimes running away is the best strategy for victory you can employ". Up until that time, no one had been able to defeat the mighty Napoleon. Even believers can learn much from Kutuzov. Not for military battles, but for spiritual battles. The Bible talks much about "fighting the good fight of faith" (I Timothy 6:12) and "being more than conquerors through Christ who loved us" (Romans 8:37). We can be confident that "greater is he who is in you, than he who is in the world" (I John 4:4), and that "with God we will gain the victory" (Psalm 60:12). But there are times when God's plan for victory for us is to run or flee. Listen to these words of Jesus in Matthew 6:7-13; "When you pray…This is how you should pray…'Don't allow us to be tempted. Instead rescue us from the evil one.'"

Christ is making it clear here that there are times we are not to face our enemy – the Napoleon of the spirit word, Satan himself. Instead, flee, run away as fast as you can. In fact, this passage tells us to even pray, "God don't let me be tempted, keep me from his temptations". I believe that what Christ is saying is that there are certain sins you know are more potentially disastrous for you. They are ones we are more susceptible to, ones that are besetting sins, or even potentially stronghold sins. Those we don't want to have an attitude of "come on, bring them on, I'm strong in Christ". Instead, we honestly say, "God, I don't want to be a hero here in this struggle – just keep it from me!" It's not that we doubt God's power, it's that we're heeding what He is saying. Some sins we fight valiantly, others we flee, and we retreat. Lust would be one of those. Paul writes to Timothy, "Flee youthful lust" (I Timothy 2:22). By the way, any lust is youthful lust – it's that strong. But Paul exhorts fleeing other sins as well. "Flee all these things." (I Timothy 6:11) Some sins are best dealt with our heels and not shields.

What are those sins you and I have a greater propensity towards? Lust, greed, anxiety, gluttony or pride? Or perhaps some others I haven't listed. Whatever it is, don't play with it, don't challenge it, and certainly don't take it for granted. I'm tempted to give illustrations of the above sins, and how we dabble in them, thinking that at the right moment we "can stop" and get victory. But I think you get the picture. Run away from that temptation. Flee engaging it in battle (when possible). Have a "scorched earth policy." "Make no provision for the flesh." Burn away all that would fuel that temptation. Who knows, perhaps if you and I flee enough, and farther enough away, then, like Napoleon, our enemy's dominance will be broken. We know that Satan's Waterloo is coming. Let's keep his wins in our life at minimum right now. Sometimes the bugle sound for retreat can lead us to great victories.

Bruce McDonald

22
LOVE SINCE FOREVER

So, do you know what happens when the ventral tegmental area in the brain floods the caudate nucleus with dopamine, which in turn causes the caudate to signal for more dopamine? Not sure? Well, you've most likely experienced it; it's what happens when you "fall in love". Well, at least that is what scientist say happens. Not sure too many of us would agree that's what causes love. I guess if you did agree with that, then perhaps something could be bottled for us to take to create that sensation and feeling, no matter who the other person was. No, I'm afraid love is much more mysterious and complicated than that.

There has probably been no subject written on more than that of love. More songs, poems, plays, books and movies have been centered on the theme of love than anything else. We've read about it, sung about it, seen movies about it, and, for many of us, experienced it. Yet, it still is beyond description and understanding. It certainly cannot be boiled down to simply a "chemical reaction in the brain". And, truthfully, nothing we can do on our own intentions can "make it

88

happen". We can seek to somehow control surrounding events and use props to create the potential mood for love to happen. But these do not make love appear. Most of us have heard of Montezuma, although normally not in the context of something we'd care to experience (if you're baffled by that line, talk to someone who travels much). Montezuma was a 15th century Aztec Emperor. Montezuma believed he knew the secret to love, and, truthfully, I like his attempt on this. He believed that love was generated and produced by consuming chocolate (see I told you I liked his idea!). So much so, that he drank 50 cups of chocolate a day! Alright, the illustration breaks down a little here, because he had a harem of 600 women.

But what causes love? How do we know when it's going to hit us? Jim and Daisy certainly didn't see that coming. Jim and Daisy were childhood friends from as far back as they could remember. They can't recall a time when they didn't know each other. But then one day, just a few years after WWII, Jim and Daisy's friendship turned to love. They were married in 1951, and have been married for over 60 years now. Jim and Daisy Bashan cannot remember a time they didn't know each other, nor can they remember just when it was that their friendship sprouted into full blown love. But it did and it has. In their minds, they loved each other, like since, forever.

Have you ever wondered just when it was that God started loving you? Pretty interesting thought isn't it? Did you do something to prompt His love? Were circumstances just right for that love to happen? Knowing when God first "began" loving you is one of the most important things you and I could ever know. God hasn't left us in the dark about this. Listen to these staggering words; "I have loved you with an everlasting love; therefore, I have continued to extend faithful love to you." (Jeremiah 31:3) When we think of God's love for us, sometimes we try to grasp how He can love us forever. I mean forever and ever! Though it's hard to comprehend, it is so assuring and comforting – "Nothing will separate us from the love of God." (Romans 8:35) But have you ever thought about this everlasting love? God's love for us is not only eternal, in the sense that it goes on and on and it will never end, but His love is also eternal, in that it never had a starting point! You read that right, God, who has always existed, and in whom are no new thoughts, loved you eternally. This is unfathomable!

God, who is Father, Son and Holy Spirit, always existed – and always loved you. When He created the world, He now could show this unfathomable love to creatures He was ready to create. Even the fall of man did not deter God from showing this amazing love. The staggering truth of the provision in the Garden of Eden would one day come to fruition in the sending of His one and only Son; "For God so loved the world that He gave His one and only Son…" (John 3:16) You and I did nothing to warrant, deserve or prompt this love – it was eternal; "This is love; not that we loved God, but that He loved us and sent His Son as an atoning sacrifice for our sins." (I John 4:10) Don't misunderstand me, we did need to put our faith and trust in God's Son for our forgiveness, but when we did, we then found out that God's love "was from old", as one translation puts it. Many of us can quote, or at least we know in part the verse, "God demonstrated His own love for us in this: While we were sinners, Christ died for us." (Romans 5:8) But God's love for us is even more amazing than that – He loved us before we were born! You may love God, but God's love for you predated that love; "We love because He first loved us." (I John 4:19)

Knowing God's love is since forever has the potential to change everything. No more working and striving to get God to love us or to love us more. No more fretting that God will remove His love or decrease it. It is an eternal love – beginning to end, or better yet, beginningless and endless. The writers in the New Testament understood this freeing empowerment. Take the time at some point to see how often they remind us of this amazing love. Here are just a few samples: "Be imitators of God, therefore, as dearly loved children." "God's chosen people, holy and dearly loved." "For we know, brothers, loved by God." "Who are loved by God the Father and kept by Jesus Christ." (Ephesians 5:1; Colossians 3:12; I Thessalonians 1:4; Jude 1:1)

Jim and Daisy cannot remember a time when they began loving each other, it seemed like it's been forever. In the same way, only in a much greater way, God can never remember a time when He didn't love you. He is eternal and His love for you has existed since then! A practice that has always been associated with love is the wedding ring. The wedding ring placed on the left hand has been a symbol of marriage and undying love – that's why it's a ring, because it is circular and has no end. Even if we've marred that picture, it still is a wonderful picture. But what about the left hand and the fourth finger on our left hand? The ancient Greeks believed that the fourth finger on the left hand contained "vena amoris", the vein of love. They believed this vein ran directly from the fourth finger on the left hand into the heart. A beautiful and noble picture, but, truthfully, the love of God goes farther. There is a rich vein running from God's heart to our heart, and this vein runs back into a distant past, one without beginning or end. Put your head on the pillow tonight, thinking of this immeasurable love, this unfathomable love, this enduring and eternal love. A love that would risk all for us, even the life of God's one and only Son; "Because of God's great love for us, God, who is rich in mercy, made us alive with Christ." (Ephesians 2:4)

Bruce McDonald

23
MIP

Paul George was named Most Improved Player in the National Basketball Association (NBA) for the 2013 season. Quite an honor for the young, 22 year old, player for the Indiana Pacers. Even at his age, he has already played 3 seasons in the NBA. When you stop and think about it, the Most Improved Player Award triggers some interesting thoughts. First of all, to be named this, you have to have improved (rather obvious). But also to have been named this, you have to have displayed ability the previous season that needed improvement. That's not a bad thing. Hopefully, everyone who enters the NBA knows that they haven't already arrived at their "peak". But very few players have as a goal, "I want to earn Most Improved Player". They want to earn MVP (Most Valuable Player), or First team All NBA, or Defensive Player of the Year – or even an assist or rebounding title. But if you asked an NBA player if he'd like to get the MIP, he'd look rather shocked.

Perhaps that's why Paul George's comments upon receiving the reward were rather surprising. George said he worked hard all last summer (the NBA's off-season) to improve his game. And, after accepting this award, his goal was to work even harder to improve for next season. That's refreshing to hear, because, you see, NBA ball players have something in their lives that sometimes makes "improvement" challenging, or at least not as desirous as it may appear. The "thing" in their lives is called guaranteed contracts. The NBA leads all other sports in this area, and all of the NBA players, excluding second round picks (only two rounds of picks in the NBA), have guaranteed contracts. In other words, you ink a contract for three or more years, and the amount you signed for is what you are "guaranteed" to get – regardless of how you perform. It is true that some players "step it up" in the last year of their guaranteed contract, hoping to get a new, longer and more expensive contract. But to seek to improve when you know everything is guaranteed is a big challenge. Paul George took that challenge!

I have often thought about the parallels to NBA Player's contracts and our "guaranteed contract" as Christians (I know, you may have "winced" at that descriptive title). When a person puts their faith and trust in Jesus Christ and His finished work on the cross, we are saved for all time and eternity. We've passed from death unto life, and the Holy Spirit has come into our lives to seal us for the day of redemption (John 5:24; Ephesians 4:30). By God's grace, and the saving life and work of Christ alone, we are "guaranteed" salvation and eternal life. So, for the believer, is there ever a desire to achieve the most improved award? For that matter, is there a Most Improved Award given in heaven? Is it part of the rewards and crowns that will be handed out on that great day in glory? Okay, I think I got your attention now! Let's muse on this for a moment. I mean, what if there really was such an award? The Bible certainly makes it clear – abundantly so, that God desires "improvement" in our Christian life. You could look up Hebrews 10:14; I Peter 3:18; Ephesians 4:15 and II Corinthians 3:18 to see this clear admonition in scripture to improve our "walk" with Christ. But let me share two other verses that particularly speak to the necessity of improvement. II Peter 1:5 – "For this very reason make every effort to add to your faith goodness knowledge, self-control, perseverance, godliness, brotherly kindness and love." The word "add" in the Greek incorporates the idea of "bring alongside of". There's something "we do" and that is we make "every effort" to bring these Christ-like characteristics into our life.

But perhaps a stronger verse is II Corinthians 7:1 – "Let us purify ourselves from everything that contaminates body and spirit, perfecting holiness out of reverence for God." Probably the word "perfecting" causes you some concern. Don't let it. Our salvation is secure in Christ; we can neither add to nor take away from what Christ has accomplished. I can't make it better, and anything I do will not cause God to love me more or love me less.

It's important that you and I understand this, so you may want to read that line again. But "effort" in our Christian life is not an enemy to grace. I love the words of Philippians 2:12: "Work out your salvation with fear and trembling, for it is God who works in you…" In other words, what God has worked "in you", you work to "bring it out and into the open" so people can see you are Christ's. The word translated "work out" comes from a Greek word that means "bring to summation"; it actually is a mathematical term. The word "perfecting" in the above II Corinthians 7:1 verse means to "bring to completion" also. The Greek word epiteleo (perfecting) is made up of two other Greek words, one means to "seek or desire intensely" and the other word means to "complete or finish". So, in other words, work (effort) to join in the process of practical sanctification (not positional). Some translations translate II Corinthians 7:1; "Bring holiness [practical] to completion." "Bring our consecration to completion." "Making our sanctification [again, practical] complete."

Well, how about it? Should we be seeking to win "The Most Improved Award" (MIP)? Really, when you think about it, we have no say over rewards or awards that will be given out in heaven. But one we can work at is "improvement". Sometimes it's easy to criticize athletes that never seem to improve, or worse yet, are content to live off their guaranteed contracts. But am I, as a blood-bought believer in Christ, one who has been guaranteed heaven, living off my contract? I like Paul George. I like his attitude. I would like to see improvement in my walk with Christ – I'd like others to see that in me! Maybe athletes should enter the professional sports world with the goal of winning the most improved trophy – each year! Maybe, those coveted words we long to hear from Christ, "Well done good and faithful servant", are really about the improvement He saw in our lives. After all, we all start off our Christian life the same – fully saved, fully forgiven, fully loved and fully sanctified (positionally). And we all start off our Christian life fully in need of growth and transformation.. Maybe, to the degree that happens, will be the words "Well done good and faithful servant". Here's hoping we'll see you get that MIP Award in heaven.

24

MIRRORS

Well, I learned something new recently. I found out the criteria for determining the best and most first- class airlines. I was on a flight heading from the west coast to Des Moines, Iowa, and seated next to me was a businessman (rather successful, I found out). He was flying in from Taipei, Taiwan, where he had a series of meetings. We engaged in conversation, and he mentioned to me that in all his travels he had discovered that the best airlines were the ones that had the youngest and prettiest flight attendants. At first I thought he was kidding. But as he continued to talk, I realized he was serious. He named the airlines that fit these criteria and those that didn't. Now knowing this, I needed to share this with my travel agent – my wife, who could then begin to narrow down the search for our flights to the "best airlines"!

The man who spoke to me was not a "bad man", or even a lecherous old man (he was in his 40s). In fact, he spent much of the time telling me about his wonderful wife and family. This businessman, sadly, represents what our culture has come to embrace, and that is outward beauty. Which brings me to the subject of this chapter, "are mirrors a good thing?" Before we move too farther along in this reading, ponder the answer to that question. What would our world be like if we had no mirrors? Perhaps a better question is, "what would your world be like if there were no mirrors"? Has there ever been a time when there were no mirrors? And, if so, how long was it before there were mirrors to gaze into? Most certainly the first "looking glass type mirror", was simply water. Looking into still or standing water would reveal one's reflection - their image. As you can imagine, there certainly were challenges associated with using water to see your image. As far as archeologist and scientist can tell, "mirrors" were invented around 6,000 BC. They have found "polished stone" (obsidian) in many sites around that time. Around 4,000 BC polished copper appears as mirrors. The earliest mirrors were hand mirrors, and it wasn't until 1 AD that full length mirrors appear.

I recall on a trip to Corinth (Greece) seeing an early mirror, which was from New Testament times. It was somewhat hard to see a reflection in the polished bronze, and made sense that the Apostle Paul used this imagery when he said "Now we see but a poor reflection as in a mirror" (I Corinthians 13:12). The mirrors of Paul's day revealed only poor reflections. It wasn't until the Middle Ages that mirrors began to reflect more clearly and accurately one's image. And by the mid-1800s, mirrors were being coated by Metallic Silver to give a clearer image. Today the images are even better, since most mirrors are either molten aluminum or silver.

So, there you have it, mirrors took a little while to appear, at least ones that gave a clear image. But, still, they've been around a long time. It's probably hard to imagine going through life not being able to see what you look like. And there are certainly times when we'd want to check out a mirror before we go in public – you know, a piece of spinach in your teeth or your hair sticking straight up. So, mirrors definitely have value as it relates to making sure we look proper in public.

And mirrors have certainly helped in other areas. Mirrors are used in telescopes, lasers, cameras, and a host of other inventions. The largest manmade mirror is in the telescope located on Mount Graham. It's 8.4 meters in diameter, and weighs 20 tons! However, it has to take a back seat to the largest mirror on earth; this mirror is 4,086 miles in length! It's actually a large flat area in Bolivia, covered with a thin layer of water. In the winter the water forms into a thin sheet of ice, and literally becomes a mirror. So big, and so reflective, it can be seen from outer space. You should go online and check out pictures of this phenomenon. It's quite amazing.

So, mirrors have value, but mirrors can often create some real problems, especially as it relates to identity. If I shape my understanding of who I am by what I see, I'm in trouble. This can work both ways. If I like what I see, I can take my self-esteem on current appearance. If I don't like what I see, I can forget who I really am. Recently I spent the night at our daughter's house, and the normal guest room I stay in has a wall-length mirror leaning against the wall. I love this mirror! You see it has an ever-so slight curve to it. And when I look at my image in this mirror, I've actually slimmed down and gained a few inches in height. I mean, it amazes me what good shape I'm in when I look at her mirror. It saddens me to walk away from that mirror, especially if I have to walk away and see myself in another mirror - one that's not bent! For some reason, the other mirrors show me much shorter and wider!

Yes, mirrors can be a bane and a blessing. I mean, who am I really? Unfortunately I'm not the man I see in my daughter's leaning mirror, but, thankfully, I'm not the man I see in a regular mirror. In God's eyes, I am loved, cherished and beautiful. This is not a small thing to understand. Identity is huge for the believer. Since we live in a society that puts a premium on outward appearance (not to mention styles), the mirror becomes the barometer to how I perceive myself. How wonderful to know that God operates on a totally different dimension. In one of the most important passages in regard to this, the Lord reminds the prophet Samuel, "Do not consider his appearance or his height…The Lord does not look at the things that man looks at. Man looks at outward appearance, but the Lord looks at the heart." (I Samuel 16:7)

What is the perfect look? We have no clue, and truthfully, each culture and century has its own idea of what that is. What will we look like in heaven? After we have had a complete makeover, we'll have glorified, resurrected, immortal bodies. But we still don't know what we'll look like. God hasn't revealed that. I John 1 says we'll "be like Him", but what does that mean? I find it interesting that when the infinite Son of God chose a body for this earth (Hebrews 10:5; I Timothy 3:16), He chose one that was rather normal at best. Certainly nothing notable or attractive. The prophet Isaiah says this prophetically about Jesus Christ; "He had no beauty or majesty to attract us to him, nothing in his appearance that we should admire him." (Isaiah 53:2)

Who are you? Are you the person in the mirror? Or are you the person who has been bought with the precious blood of Christ (I Peter 1:18) and is loved and cherished (Zephaniah 3:17)? Appearances wax and wane. Current trends come and go. God does not value outward appearance as something to be pursued or highly esteemed. And here's a thought, what if our future – and eternal appearance, will be determined by how we developed the "inner person". What if those who spent all their time on the "outer person" will not have the beauty as the person who has worked on the "inner person"? The only "mirror" we should put great value on, is the "mirror of God's Word" (James 1:23-25).

Hey, I'd like to carry Jess' mirror around with me; I like the guy in that mirror. But how much better for me to carry God's mirror with me at all times? And, oh yeah, in all my flights, I've not noticed a correlation between so-called beautiful flight attendants and great flights and service. So, don't throw your mirror away (remember the spinach in your teeth), but spend more time gazing at yourself in the mirror of God's Word.

25
NOT YET

Not sure if you are one of the people who put presents under their tree in the days leading up to Christmas. If you are, and if you have children, you know how desirous the kids are to look at, touch, shake, and feel those presents. It's oh-so hard for them to have to wait for Christmas day! Some families, knowing how hard it is for the children, allow them to open one gift on Christmas Eve. Of course, I've been speaking of children, but some of us (cough, cough) live in a household where certain adults have been known to snoop around looking for their gifts – and even pick them up and feel them!

Anticipation is difficult, especially when you can see the gifts right in front of you. The holidays not only present challenges with waiting for gifts to be opened, but waiting in general; "Don't touch the pies, they're for Christmas Day", "Get your hands off the turkey, wait until it's on the table", and "Wait to pop that Christmas video in until the relatives get here". Wait, wait, wait - it's no fun waiting! Most of us have had the experience of children finally breaking their "wait" by getting up unbelievably early on Christmas Day.

Bruce McDonald

What we see played out right here and now with our families during the holidays is similar to what is being played out with God's family. Our Heavenly Father – who loves to give gifts (Matthew 7:11) – has purchased for us many wonderful gifts. But, like our own children, He has told us to "wait, the time to open them is not yet here". Our gifts from our Heavenly Father are not under a tree, but they are our gifts because of a tree – Calvary's tree, where our Savior died. And the gifts, though not under a tree, are still visible. They are visible on the pages of the New Testament. When we see many of those gifts, we long for them, but also feel somewhat frustrated, because they are for a time "not yet".

As we think about the Holiday Season, and the celebration of Christmas, think with me for a moment of our gifts that "are not yet". Perhaps no other scripture captures this truth for us more than Ephesians 2:7. Here is this wonderful verse and promise: "God raised us up with Christ and seated us with him in the heavenly realms in Christ Jesus, in order that in the coming ages he might show the incomparable riches of his grace expressed in his kindness to us in Christ Jesus." (NIV) Here are two other translations and one paraphrase: "And [God] raised us up together, and made us sit together in the heavenly places in Christ Jesus, that in the ages to come He might show the exceeding riches of his grace in his kindness towards us in Christ Jesus." (NKJV) "God has brought us back to life together with Christ Jesus and has given us a position in heaven with him. He did this through Christ Jesus out of his generosity to us in order to show his extremely rich kindness in the world to come." (GW) "He took our sin-dead lives, and made us alive in Christ. He did all this on his own, with no help from us! Then he picked us up and set us down in highest heaven in company with Jesus, our Messiah. Now God has us where he wants us, with all the time in this world and the next to shower grace and kindness upon us in Christ Jesus." (Message)

102

The "gifts still not opened yet" are a tantalizing present. Like a brightly wrapped gift under the tree, we stare at it in wonder, wanting to hold it, shake it, and unwrap it. What indeed, are the incomparable riches of His grace? Whatever they are, they're still to come. The above verse says that they will be ours in the ages to come. We are blessed with many things in the here and now, but, evidently, there are more blessings (gifts) to come – a whole lot more! These "presents unopened" both excite me and frustrate me. Why? Because truthfully, like a small child, "I want them now"! As much as I might know "heaven will be worth it all", I still struggle with difficulties and disappointments here.

So often it does not seem like we're rewarded and honored for our efforts and sacrifices. Sometimes, it seems like we even live under "The law of diminishing returns". Oh there are blessings – undeserved and generous ones, right here and now. But it seems like there are more times of difficulties and hardships, even disappointments. God, in His infinite wisdom and sovereign purpose, has designed a program (called the Christian life) that has benefits and rewards – in the future! He doesn't abandon us here, but neither does He always bless us here. Ephesians 2:7 (and many other passages) remind us that there is coming a day when rewards will not only be commensurate with our sacrifices and service, but will be exceedingly above and beyond what we could ever imagine in the way of "deserving".

Bible scholars have found much gold to mine out of Ephesians 2:7. They tell us that the phrase "the coming ages" means "the ages that are coming one upon another". That is, the eternal ages that roll in, one after another. We live "in this age". It seems an eternity, but it is only a brief passing moment on the line of eternity. We are in the Age of Grace, an age that will soon pass. Then will be the thousand year earthly reign of Christ – and then eternity. One age after another, forever and ever. Each age, each year, each day – each moment, will find God "unwrapping a new exceedingly rich treasure of His grace". For the child of God, it will be Christmas morning – each day! Can you grasp that! God loves to give gifts. And though this world can be very hard, wearying, and confusing, God will reward His children. Why? Because, as Ephesians 2:7 reminds us, He is kind!"

I don't think children believe their parents to be cruel and mean because they are not allowed to open their presents yet. But, as believers, we may question God as to "why we have to wait". We may have to wait, but then again, when we open our new gifts (God's exceeding treasures"), it will not be "a one day event", but a forever and ever event. Oh dear friend, I know that seeing Jesus will be enough for us in eternity. But, for God, it is not enough! He wants to continue to show you His love and grace, that began at Calvary's Tree, and will last throughout eternity. Oh how He can't wait to see your eyes as He opens up one treasure after another. May the "not yet" not discourage you, but fill you with hope and anticipation.

# 26
# PRODUCT REQUIRES PROCESS

I think it's pretty obvious that in order for someone to accomplish something, they have to put the time and effort into that particular desire or achievement. If we see an Olympic athlete standing on the dais to receive a medal, we know that person has put much time, effort and practice into accomplishing that feat. Whether it's in swimming, wrestling, gymnastics or any other event, we've all heard stories of the hours of practice and discipline that the particular athlete put in to accomplish this feat. The same would be true for an accomplished musician or singer. The hours of practicing the violin or piano, or the disciplines of voice training, would also be necessary for outstanding achievement.

In reality, this could be said about any skill, vocation or pursuit. Without putting in the time and effort, there will not be much of an accomplishment. At this point in this chapter, you may think I might go the direction of talking about "personal discipline and training" in our Christian life to accomplish the desired Christian growth mentioned in scripture. But, actually, I'm thinking about a different aspect of the Christian life that necessitates a process before there can be a product. As much as "spiritual disciplines" can be challenging, and truthfully, sometimes avoided, this "product" is often times shunned more than spiritual disciplines. Yet, at the same time, it is a "product" that is desirable for all of us.

The desired product I speak of is to be an encourager and helper to other believers. Who doesn't want to be this type of person? Who of us has not benefited from this in others or been blessed by a person with this attitude? Any casual reading of the New Testament reveals the call and challenge to be an encourager, come-along-sider, and a helper to others. But truthfully, just the admonition to do this, to be this, doesn't produce it in us. And neither is it something that just "naturally" happens in certain people because of temperament or upbringing. No, the product of being an encourager and supporter requires a process that often causes us to avoid the journey to being an encourager and comforter. The best way to describe this process of becoming an encourager is found in the New Testament book of II Corinthians. Let me have you read these verses, and then I'd like to make some comments about this passage.

"Praise be to the God and Father of our Lord Jesus Christ, the Father of compassion and the God of all comfort, who comforts us in all our troubles, so that we can comfort those in any trouble with the comfort we ourselves have received from God...If we are distressed, it is for your comfort and salvation; if we are comforted, it is for your comfort..." (II Corinthians 1:3-4, 6) Here is how God's Word Translation translates these verses; "Praise the God and Father of our Lord Jesus Christ! He is the Father who is compassionate and the God who gives comfort. He comforts us whenever we suffer. That is why whenever other people suffer, we are able to comfort them by using the same comfort we have received from God...If we are comforted, we can effectively comfort you when you endure the same sufferings that we endure."

I have often spoken on this important topic, and God spoke these truths afresh into my life on the morning I write this. If I may, let me share with you what I wrote in my journal. I want you to see that this is something that God is seeking to teach me, and not just something I am "speaking to you about". Here are the exact words from my journal:

*"I've thought on this before – and have spoken on it, even wrote about it, but it is such an important truth. I think we all love the fact that God is a 'God of all comfort'. And we love the fact that we should encourage and comfort others when they are suffering or going through difficult times. What we don't particularly embrace, or at least think about, is that for God to comfort others, He usually uses people. And for God to use people, He first of all has had to comfort them. If that is true, then before we can comfort, we must experience His comfort, and before we can experience His comfort, we must suffer. Like the rest of us, I'd just as soon show God's comfort, without having to have experienced His comfort in suffering. But sadly – speaking from my own heart – God's comfort normally comes from our having experienced suffering, so that we would have experienced God's comfort. Different translations translate the Greek word 'thlipsei' either suffer, trouble, tribulation, or affliction. Thlipsei in its most basic translation can mean any of the words used in the various translations. But the root meaning carries a couple ideas; 'restricted without options' and 'a narrow place, to be hemmed in'. So this word can in some ways mean trials of various sorts. So, practically speaking, it can mean health issues, financial pressures, relationship problems, loss of something, and a host of other things that are 'thlipsei' to us. We need God's comfort in these areas, and we are surrounded by people who are experiencing these things. God wants to comfort them through us, so He allows – brings difficulties and disappointments into our lives, so He can show us His comfort. Then, in return, we can show His comfort to others. We know God comforts, and we do want to be a help and comfort to others, we just don't often think that the process and development of this, is our own suffering and comfort."*

Well, that's what God has been reminding me lately. You

can't have product without process. Granted troubles, trials, affliction and disappointments will take various shapes and forms, but none of them are wasted. In them, God will comfort us, so that His comfort will flow out of our lives into others who are experiencing these similar conflicts. Perhaps it would be good to close with this powerful quote from Ugo Bassi; "*Measure thy life by loss and not gain; not by wine drunk but by the wine poured forth, for love's strength standeth in love's sacrifice, and he that suffereth most, hath most to give.*"

# 27
# REFUSING TO SURRENDER

In 1972 two American hunters stumbled across a cave on the island of Guam. Inside that cave a man was living. When the Americans entered the cave they found Shoichi Yokoi, a former Sergeant in the Japanese Army. Yokoi had been hiding from the U.S. Forces ever since the end of World War II, some 27 years earlier. He had refused to surrender to the American Military, and instead, like many of his fellow soldiers, was trained to fight to the death, and never give up, to never surrender. He had been living in the jungles of Guam and survived by eating fish and rats. The two Americans turned him into the local police, who then shipped him back home to Japan. He had been declared dead back in 1944, so you can imagine the surprise and shock to his relatives upon his arrival home. You can also imagine his shock to find a Japan 27 years into the future.

Down through history there have been many tales and accounts of people, cities and countries that have refused to surrender, some against amazing odds. Not all stories of refusing to surrender are noble and inspiring. Let me share with you another story of refusing to surrender that is both historical and temporary. This refusal, rather than being noble and inspiring, is chilling and crippling.

The greatest Warrior General in the Old Testament was undoubtedly Joshua. An entire Old Testament book is named after him, and the pages are filled with his unbelievable exploits and victories. Taking untrained soldiers and armies into the Promised Land, defeating kingdoms, walled cities, and battling tested warriors and giants is a thrilling read. The victories were obviously of Jehovah God, but the man he chose to use was Joshua. When reading the book of Joshua you come to chapter 12, and there is a recap of what has been accomplished so far. You have 31 kings listed who had been defeated in Canaan (The Promised Land). North, South, East, and West, no matter what the size of the army, no matter what alliance the enemy formed, they all fell to Joshua and the Israelites. Well, almost all of them. Chapters 16-20 reveal that eventually there were pockets of resistance for the twelve tribes of Israel. They (the resistance groups) were defeated and dethroned, but some still, like Yokoi, refused to surrender. Years later these small groups would come back into force to harass, and even dominate the Israelites. But these small groups were nothing compared to one city that stubbornly refused to surrender or be defeated.

When Joshua first entered Canaan, there were many strong and powerful fortified cities; one of those was the Jebusite city of Jerusalem. Joshua and his Israelite army moved west from crossing the Jordan River, and began a series of campaigns that included walls of cities falling down, hail being hurled from the sky at the enemy and the sun standing still. No one could stand before Joshua and his army...that is, except the Jebusite City of Jerusalem. There it stood, impregnable, unscalable, and imposing. Several times in the Old Testament, it is mentioned that this Jebusite city could not be taken. The first time is in Joshua 15:63; "But the descendants of Judah could not drive out the Jebusites who lived in Jerusalem. So the Jebusites live in Jerusalem among the descendants of Judah to this day." The "this day" was at the conclusion of the book of Joshua, some 21 years after the Israelites conquered the land. But the Jebusites stayed entrenched in Jerusalem well beyond 21 years. They stayed there – undefeated, unconquered, for another 400 years (There was a brief victory at Jerusalem's outpost, but it was short- lived. Judges 1:8, 21)!

I have always been amazed at this story. Why couldn't they get the Jebusites out of Jerusalem? Think about it, what was different about Jerusalem with the Jebusites, than any of the other walled cities? I mean, Joshua and Israel had a God who parted water, threw hail stones down – caused walls to tumble! Joshua was right there. Caleb and the first judge Othniel all would defeat the surrounding cities (and giants!). Down through the centuries, in the times of the judges, people like Gideon, Barak, Samson – and even the Prophet Samuel, could not budge the Jebusites out of Jerusalem. No, it was not until the year 1048 BC that a young man, fresh off of being a shepherd boy and a young giant slayer, was crowned king of Israel, and fastened his eyes on the walled city of Jerusalem. It was still inhabited by the Jebusites, and he said "I want that city". Here are the exact words; "The king and his men marched to Jerusalem to attack the Jebusites, who lived there...David captured the fortress of Zion, the City of David...David then took up residence in the fortress and called it the 'City of David.'" (II Samuel 5:6-9)

Perhaps the Jebusite city of Jerusalem stood for hundreds of years in defiance of occupied Israel to teach us a lesson today. All throughout Israel, for centuries, God's advancements could be seen everywhere. But sticking out conspicuously was this stubborn city and people who would not surrender. Does that picture sound familiar? Our lives as believers have seen so much growth and advancements, so many victories, so much to be grateful for...but there is, in most of us, that "walled city" that "defiant Jebusite" who refuses to surrender. Why is it? Why, when so many other victories have been wrought? That one stronghold, that one "pocket of resistance", that one…bondage, it haunts us, mocks us, and stubbornly refuses to leave. Like the Jebusite city of Jerusalem of old, standing in the midst of subdued and surrendered Canaan, with heroes all around, it still mockingly stands. We've prayed, we've planned, we've fought, we've sought help, we've cried out to God, but the Jebusite City stands unwavering and unconquerable. And in our worst moments it "taunts us". Yes, we're defeated in our attempts – no matter how valiant, to bring down this stronghold. That is, until He comes!

Go back with me again to II Samuel 5 and the account of David's winning Jerusalem from the Jebusites. Listen to the Jebusites mocking words to David the Giant Slayer; "You might as well go home! Even the blind and the lame could keep you out. You can't get in here!" (II Samuel 5:6 Mess.) You've heard that before, right? The mocking and taunting of the Jebusites. But this time, they said it to the wrong man! There was one there greater than Joshua, Caleb, Othniel, Gideon, Samson, Barak and Samuel - there was David the giant slayer. But for us – there's one greater than David! And hear me on this, He, the Lord Jesus Christ, has set His eyes on that stronghold in your life and has said "I want that for my residence". It will no longer be an enemy stronghold! Why has it taken so long? Perhaps for a couple of reasons.

First, in our victories and growth, this area humbles us, makes us aware that we have not arrived. It keeps us gracious towards others and flat out dependent on God. And second, It has been waiting all this time for the "one greater than David" to show up. Those days, weeks, months, and years that have seen this resistant stronghold are about to come to a glorious end and victory will finally be experienced. Like David of old, Christ wants the very area that has been a stronghold in our life to now become His residence - now known as His Stronghold.

Think of the glory He will now receive, the very area that you were your weakest, where you experienced your greatest defeats, becomes His glorious throne. Perhaps the time has come for that "walled Jebusite city" in your life to fall, and become the new home for our King. It would be just like Him to do that – and at this time.

## 28
## THE RING OF POWER

No, not that one! You were probably thinking of the Ring
of Power that Gollum had and sought, and that Bilbo Baggins,
and then Frodo, carried. That's of course, from *The Hobbit* and
*The Lord of the Rings* trilogy. Great story, but a different ring
than what we want to consider. The ring I'd like us to consider
is much more powerful than Tolkien's ring. The ring I'd like us
to consider is God's Signet Ring. You may or may not be
familiar with signet rings. A signet ring can be simply an ornate
ring designed with numbers, letters or symbols. It can be a ring
that's passed down through families. A ring that is associated
with some club, achievement or society, or it can be the sign
and signature of Royalty. I'd like us to consider the latter, a
sign and signature of Royalty.

In by-gone days, signet rings were quite common for
Royalty. Kings, Queens and Emperors wore Signet Rings, and,
as you can imagine, they could be quite decorative and
intricately designed. But the purpose was not just for
ornamentation sake, the ring served a purpose. The signet ring
was a means to verify and authenticate any message that had

the approval of the ruling power. History has many illustrations of this, and even in our Bible we have on two separate occasions where a person in power uses his signet ring in a key Bible account.

You have undoubtedly thought of those two already: one was when Pharaoh took off his signet ring and gave it to Joseph (Genesis 41:42), and the other was when Xerxes gave Mordecai his ring (Esther 8:2). The reason for both of these ring transfers were identical, the King was showing that the person receiving the signet ring (Joseph and Mordecai) had the King's authority in matters delegated to these men. Most often the ring was given so that any edict or decree, as well as decision made, could then be written down, and sealed with wax with the imprint of the signet ring on the document or decree. The sealed document with the king's signet ring pressed in the wax was official, and was to be obeyed – and anyone who broke that seal before its' intended delivery would be subject to death.

There's a fascinating passage of scripture in the Old Testament book of Haggai. In Haggai 2:23 a person is called God's Signet Ring. That person is Zerubbabel, and God was going to use him to be shepherd/governor of his people in Jerusalem upon their return from the Babylonian Captivity. In a broader way, it was also a picture of the Lord Jesus Christ and His future role. But in the immediate context and time of Haggai, it referred to Zerubbabel. Evidently, God has a Signet Ring. I don't know if it actually is one "on His finger", but He definitely has one "symbolically". And God is in the habit, much like Pharaoh and Xerxes, of taking that ring off and giving it to someone – and guess what? You're that someone!

Understanding our favored position in receiving God's signet ring is of powerful importance to each of us. For Joseph and Mordecai to receive the king's ring, they had to hold the highest position of esteem and honor in the kingdom. They had to be loved, trusted and commissioned to receive the ring. As followers of the Lamb and subjects of the King of kings, you have been given God's Signet Ring.

Let's consider what this vaunted position means to you. The ring means for you at least four things; Approval, Access, Assignment, and Authority. Please don't just buzz by those four words, they're not just some fanciful alliteration, they are powerfully pointed in showing how you and I have God's Signet Ring.

Approval: Signet Rings were not just given to anyone; they had to be trusted and loved subjects. There was only one Signet Ring, and the King would only give it to someone highly esteemed – and trusted. We are "approved" by God; "We speak as men approved by God..." (I Thessalonians 2:4, see also II Timothy 2:15; II Corinthians 10:18) God loves us and has made us joint-heirs with Christ (Roman 8:17) and our approval is at the highest level.

Access: Those with the approval of the king had constant, immediate  and welcome access to the king. They could walk into his presence at any time. When the king heard they were outside approaching him, he would say "let them in". We have access always to our King; "Through him we have access to the Father..." (Ephesians 2:18, see also Romans 5:2; Hebrews 4:16). Having the Signet Ring – the Ring of His approval, gains us immediate access into His presence.

Assignment: The "Ring Bearer" was not just a "courtier", someone who had access to the King's court, but they had work to do, they had an assignment. They represented the king; they bore his signet ring, and carried out matters for him. We too have assignments by our King, we are commissioned by Him; "You did not choose me, but I chose you and appointed you to go and bear fruit..." (John 15:16; see also  II Timothy 1:9; II Corinthians 5:18) Our King has given us each assignments, like Joseph and Mordecai of old. They are important, urgent and designed by the King.

Authority: having the signet ring not only meant approval by the king, access to the king, and specific assignment from the king, but the ring meant real power. All the authority of the king was behind that ring. We go out on our marching orders from our King, knowing that the King of Glory has given us His authority. "All authority in heaven and earth has been given to me. Therefore go…" (Matthew 28:18; see also Mark 1:27; I Peter 3:22) As Abraham Kuyper once said; "*In the total expanse of human life there is not a single square inch of which the Christ, who alone is sovereign, does not declare, 'That is mine!'*" Our King's supreme power and authority goes with us, as if we had His signet ring on. We don't go out in our own might and authority, but the mighty Christ's.

Gollum, Bilbo and Frodo all sought the power of the "ring". Forces of good and evil lined up to fight for its power. But the sovereign Lord of the universe has granted us His signet ring, and with it comes approval, access, assignment and authority. Oh, how special that day was when Pharaoh slipped his signet ring off and gave it to Joseph. What a scene we would have wanted to take in. And the day when Xerxes slipped his signet ring off and gave it to Mordecai, how that changed everything. But dear friends, unbeknownst to you, without great pomp and ceremony, the King of kings has given you His signet ring. Go forth with confidence, assurance and gratitude. You represent the King!

29
# ROAD TRIP

One of the questions that are frequently asked of Bev and I is, "Do you enjoy traveling?" Because God, in His grace and sovereign purpose, has us in a ministry that requires – and has the benefit and blessings, of travel, it is a question often directed towards us. As I write this, it has been a rather typical year; we have had some years with more travel, and a few with less travel. Counting trips up in my mind as I sit here at my computer, I figure we have taken close to 40 flights this year. Now, that's not a lot compared to some of you who are reading this, and especially my close friend Dave, who probably puts that many flights in every couple months. But still, it's a lot of travel. In just over a year, we have been in 11 countries and 17 states. So, again, it's not "off the charts", but neither is it "staying put". But back to the question, "Do you enjoy traveling?" The answer, in brief, is that we enjoy "being places, especially overseas, but the getting there is not always fun, and grows tiresome very quickly."

Getting to and from airports becomes a hassle, checking in and going through security is bothersome and can slow things down considerably. And making connections, especially when there is little time or a great distance in terminals, can be a real "travel breaker". Missed flights, bad flights, and cramped seating conditions all add to making the travel part not as fun and exciting. Okay, right now I'm in danger of losing you. To some it has become "blah, blah, blah", or worse yet, "whining". But hold on if you will, there is a reason I took some time to express the non-fun part of flying. So, yes, we enjoy travel, in the sense that we love to be different places (most obviously, because of ministry opportunity), and we love seeing and experiencing other cultures and customs. But, no, the travel part can put a real damper on traveling, or at least take the fun and excitement out.

Now here's the purpose for this chapter. Unfortunately, you and I spend most of our time, wait, let me correct that - we spend all of our time traveling. In the truest sense, we're never really home. Paul tells us in Philippians 3:20 that our home (citizenship) is in heaven. And the writer of Hebrews tells us that, for all practical purposes, we spend our entire lives as sojourners, pilgrims and wanderers (Hebrews 11- 13). Hebrews sums it up by saying, "We don't have a permanent city here on earth, but we are looking for the city that we will have in the future." (Hebrews 13:14) As much as we seek to dig in here and make this our home, we all have a sense that "this isn't home" and we're still traveling. We're to have a mindset that constantly sets our thoughts and affections on things above (Colossians 3"1-2) and to store up treasures above (Matthew 6:19-21).

But it is not just that this isn't our home. In one real sense, this is the home of the enemy. This is (temporarily) Satan's turf, and he has, in the words of scripture, "the whole world under his control." (I John 5:19) Switching metaphors here briefly, we are not only constantly on a "road trip," but we're constantly playing "road games". In the long years we worked in the professional sports world as a chaplain, the players often complained about "road weariness". Especially in Basketball and Hockey, where there are so many road games and often trips "back to back", players would complain and say they were exhausted. Playing in Philadelphia one night and the next in Houston, was draining and fatiguing. And since they were playing a game on someone else's turf (arena or stadium), they had all the challenges of hostile fans and, on occasion, "hometown calls" by the referees and umpires. Right now, my referee friend Frank just cringed!

Okay, back to the metaphor of road trips and traveling. Here's some really good news – God loves to make appearances when we are traveling! God specializes in road trip appearances. Have you ever noticed how often "God showed up" when someone was traveling? It is actually rather amazing and encouraging to see how often He did this in scripture. There are too many to mention in this chapter, but let me just point out a few, and make some comments about those appearances. How about Paul (then Saul) on the road to Damascus? God stepped in and not only appeared to him, but saved him, and gave him a new commission as an apostle for Christ. (Acts 9) How about the two disciples on the road to Emmaus? These two men were so saddened and confused over Christ's crucifixion, and Jesus took time to appear to them and speak words of comfort into their lives. He filled them both with hope and joy. (Luke 24) Then there's Jacob on the road back home to Canaan, and being in mortal fear of meeting his brother Esau. God shows up again! And this time He changes his name and gives him hope as well. Time does not permit me to speak of Balaam, Gideon, Hagar, Moses (burning bush), Philip and Elijah (when fleeing Jezebel).

In each of these incidences, God was "on the road with them". Road weariness is real, and sometimes it's unsettling, but God is right there in the midst of the road trip. Jesus reminded us that He will always go with us – all the way until the end of the age (Matthew 28:20). I've often been encouraged and taken solace in the fact that God never leaves us or forsakes us (Hebrews 13:5). His presence will always go with us (Exodus 33:14), and "He is the God of the nearby and the far away" (Jeremiah 23:23). But today, I take encouragement with the added thought that "God loves road trips!" That's where He most often shows up.

As we're "on the road" let's keep our eyes out. It may just be that you'll have a road encounter with the Divine. It could happen. Damascus, Emmaus, or Jabbok were all planned stops by God. So, too, are the cities and towns you live in. In your travels, keep your eye out for God. And you know what? One of these days He might just make a simultaneous road encounter with all of us to take us on up to our real home. It could happen, just be sure you don't get so busy with your travel that you miss His times of intervention and encouragement. Makes the trip worth the while.

# 30
# SADNESS IN LEAVING

There is sadness often times when one has to leave somewhere. The reasons for sadness are plentiful and varied. Sometimes there's sadness in leaving home to go to college, leaving home for good as you reach early adult years, moving away from friends, family and familiarity, the sadness from leaving a restful, beautiful vacation spot to head back to the grind of work, and the sadness that comes from retiring and leaving the work and activity that you've enjoyed all your life. Then, there is perhaps the greatest sadness, the sadness when one is forced to leave a homeland and never to return.

There have been many forced exodus of homeland. One of those times was the mass exodus of the Irish during the horrific "Potato Famine" in the mid-1800s. It was a horrible time, where more than a million people died of starvation and malnutrition. Because of the famine, many Irish fled to America, leaving their beloved Ireland behind (the Irish will tell you that the English also had something to do with their "exile"). But it was a sad moment in history, to leave Ireland. More than a million and a half people had to leave. That would sound staggering and unbelievable, if we have not already witnessed this plight many times in our lifetime. People and people groups being forced to leave their homeland. It seems like we've seen this happen scores of time with several countries in Africa. A dictator takes over, and mass annihilation and carnage takes place. People are either forced to leave, or else escape with their lives. The situation as I write this in Northern Sudan is an illustration of this sad phenomenon. Sudanese people in the north fleeing to the south. And speaking of forced evacuations from a homeland, has anyone suffered more than the Jews? We've all seen pictures of the sad faces of those who have had to leave their beloved homeland.

There is sadness when leaving home for the initial reasons I mentioned in this chapter. And there is unparallel sadness when it is a forced leaving. But I want to share with you one of the most unusual "sadness in leaving" situations that I've ever read. This sadness is a conundrum, it's paradoxical, and it doesn't make sense. When there should have been the greatest joy in leaving, there was instead an element of sadness and longing to stay. The event I speak of is when Jesus was getting ready to leave earth and head "home".

The event is depicted in John's Gospel, chapter 13. Here is how it begins, "Jesus knew that the time had come for him to leave this world and go to the Father." Now, just stop and think for a minute what that meant; it meant going back to His Eternal Father (Christ was and is, the Eternal Son). One whom He had never been separated from – since before space, time and matter were created. It meant having His glory restored (John 17:5). It meant being surrounded by innumerable angels who He had created, falling prostrate at His feet in joyful worship. It meant the end of His earthly suffering and the consummation of redemption for fallen man. You would think that there would not be an ounce of sadness on His part. Now, right at this point, you might be tempted to say, "yes, but there was the excruciating agony of the cross facing Him. And didn't Jesus even pray that if it was the Father's will, He be delivered from this?" Good point, but somehow, in the midst of all that, Jesus actually had "joy" in facing the cross. Remember Hebrews 12:2, "Who for the joy set before him endured the cross..."? But Jesus was filled with sadness for another reason when He was about to leave this earth, or better yet, as the text will show us, leave those He loved. Here is how the passage continues in John 13; "Having loved his own who were in the world, he now showed them the full extent of his love." Here are some other translations of that verse; "Jesus loved his own who were in the world; he loved them to the end." "He had always loved those who were his own in the world, and he loved them all the way to the end." In Jesus' closing words to His men in the Upper Room, there is a touch of sadness, a tinge of regret in having to leave them.

Hold on for a moment, this is amplified a little bit later as he walks away from the upper room. Now, with his apostles listening, He prays for them and in front of them. Here is part of His prayer, "Father, I want those you have given me to be with me where I am..." (John 17:3) Can't you hear the pathos, the sadness, the reluctance to leave His loved ones? Though heaven, God the Father, and all the glories of heaven were awaiting Him, he is sad to leave (physically) His disciples. Think about this; not only was the unfathomable glories of honor awaiting Him in heaven, but look around at those men! He didn't want to leave them? I mean, there are John and James who were always fighting to be first and the greatest. There was Philip and Andrew doubting where Jesus could find enough bread to feed the multitudes. There was Thomas, who would doubt His resurrection. And, of course, there was Peter who would deny Jesus – with Jesus watching and listening! How astounding! How encouraging!

Jesus' sadness in leaving, even on the verge of going back to heaven, was predicated on His great love for His men – and women! He would (physically) be leaving Mary and Martha, Mary Magdalene, His mother, the women who waited on Him and ministered to Him (Luke 8:3). He would be leaving Nicodemus, the 72 disciples ((Luke 10:1), Mark and so many others who loved and followed Him. He wanted to be with them, he wanted them to be with Him!

I don't think we'll ever grasp how much our Amazing Savior, Creator God, wants us to be with Him – and he with us! It's not the angels that He longs for – and misses - it's us! We are the Peters, Johns, Andrews and host of others who are weak, frail, inconsistent, and you name it. He knows all this, and He wants us with Him.

Sadness can be expected when one is leaving a place or a people, but sadness from the Savior who is going back to His throne and finally leaving this world who rejected Him (John 1:11)? That does not make sense! But praise God it is true. Even now in glory, Christ awaits for His dear children to all join Him, so that we can be together forever. He has Cherubim, He has Seraphim, and He has mighty angels surrounding Him in joyful worship. But He longs for you. His gaze is scanning the crowd waiting for you. No wonder the Psalmist said; "What is man that you are mindful of him…you made him a little lower than the angels." (Psalm 8:4-6; Hebrews 2:6-8). We think of the day our sadness will turn to gladness, but just think of the incredible gladness of our Savior when all His children are safely home with Him. Mystery of Mysteries, he wants to be with us!

# 31
# SILENCE PRODUCED DOUBT

Not too long ago, I had an Assistant Pastor tell me of his frustration with the Senior Pastor he served with and under. It seems the Senior Pastor was not a communicator and felt relationships were challenging. So much so, that at one point, he (the Senior Pastor), had not talked or communicated with his assistant in several weeks – even though their offices were only a short distance apart. That's rather hard to comprehend, but as you can imagine, it's even harder to experience. It bred all sorts of thoughts in the mind of the assistant; "Did I do something wrong? Is he angry with me? Does he not like me?" Silence like this can not only affect "staff relationships", it obviously can affect marital, family and friendship relationships. But one of the most powerful areas affected by silence is our relationship with God. Perhaps no other area of our walk with God has a greater potential than silence to produce doubts.

As believers and followers of Christ, we are called to love, worship and serve a God we've never seen or heard. That's a challenging relationship! I know you might be quick to rush ahead and say, "But we have the Holy Spirit, we have the Word of God." All true, but, like in any relationship, you'd probably covet a "two-sided" conversation. And maybe there are times when you wished for an "old testament" experience of God speaking directly to you. You know, from a burning bush or a rumbling mountain – or even in a dream. What would His voice sound like? Loud - you know, the type "that breaks cedars" (Psalm 29:5), or the type whispered in a cave (I Kings 19:12)? Would it be short and commanding "Go to Nineveh" (Jonah 1:1) or reassuring and explanative like when God explained to Abraham His plans for him (Genesis 17)? Whatever it was like, you would think that would mean that people who "heard" from God in the Bible, never struggled with doubts.

I think you know the answer to that! In fact, here's a thought, perhaps the people who did hear from God struggled more with doubts than we do. Okay, hold on a second, let me explain myself. What is more challenging and difficult to deal with, having never heard from or talk to someone, or having talked and heard from them and then they stopped? Maybe a somewhat confusing question, so you may want to go back and read it again. Is it harder having never heard from someone or to have someone stop speaking to you?

I wonder if some of the people in the Bible who heard from God, but struggled greatly at times with doubt, reveal to us an important dynamic in our relationship with God. Most of us center our thoughts on when a person in the Bible heard from God, but do we ever think about when they didn't? You might be surprised to find out that many of the people whom God spoke to, He only spoke sparingly. It was not the norm, and oftentimes there were long gaps between His communication with them. For example, take Solomon, how many times do you think God spoke directly – audibly, to him? You may be surprised to know it was only twice during his lifetime (I Kings 11:9). A careful study of audible encounters with God, and even by those who heard Him a few times, will show that God never had normal constant dialogue with them. Instead, their lives were characterized by long "gaps" of not hearing from God. Moses, Abraham, David, Noah and a host of others are examples of this. Remember Elijah? God spoke to him at least 3 or 4 times during his life, but listen to the opening words of I Kings 18:1; "After a long time, the word of the Lord came to Elijah…" How long was it between God's words to him? A long time!

Think of this, once you heard from God (audibly), that's like the "pinnacle" of experiences with God. I mean, nothing after that will ever compare – unless it's another audible experience with God. Several years ago my wife Bev and I were scuba diving, something we really enjoy. On one of our dives we saw a whale! Unbelievable! Afterward, our Dive Master said, "You might as well pack it up and never dive again; you'll never have an experience like that again." I wonder if that's what an encounter with God is like – except multiplied one hundredfold?

Do you think hearing audibly from God once would be enough? Hardly! It would create greater desire to hear from Him. But, even more, it would create an assumption that God would "speak" again to us. The OT and NT saints must have wondered, "What went wrong? What have I done? Is it over?" I think God gives us a glimpse of what not hearing from God does to your confidence in Him. In the book of Esther, Mordecai asks Esther to go and talk to King Xerxes, who just happened to be her husband. But Esther replies that she hasn't talked to the king in 30 days, and she doesn't know how he will respond to her coming into his presence – it might even result in death! I'm sure the men and women in the Bible didn't fear death when they hadn't heard from God "in a long time", but they certainly struggled with their faith as to why they hadn't heard.

So, what makes God remain silent for a time? More importantly, why does He choose to remain mute in regard to our relationship with Him? It's not only that we've never heard "audibly" from Him, it's that we have times when He seems to withdraw His presence and assurance through the normal means in our life – a word in scripture, affirmation through circumstances or removal of a problem. These times have the potential to "stagger" us in our faith. The New Testament writer of the book of Hebrews knew of this potential in our lives. "Do not cast away your confidence" he writes (Hebrews 10:35). What was the answer for the saints in the Bible? How did they deal with their doubts when God "stopped talking". What is the answer for the believer today when God seems to break off communication?

I believe that the answer is, beginning to grasp how important, pleasing and honoring faith is to God. God loves faith, and especially faith that is not prompted by outward circumstances or favorable acts – or even communication. Faith that is simply centered on who He is, is extremely pleasing to God (Hebrews 11:6). We'll have all of eternity to hear and see God, but the sacrifice and worship right now He is pleased with, is that which is prompted by faith. God has designed our whole lives this way. Paul writes in II Corinthians 5:7, "We walk by faith and not by sight". And in Romans 1:17 he writes, "Our faith is a faith from first to last."

Somehow, Peter grasped the significance of this in his first letter to his Jewish audience. "Though you've not seen Him [or heard Him], you are filled with an inexpressible joy." (I Peter 1:8) When God seems to stop "speaking to you", it's not because He's angry, that He doesn't like you, or that you've done something wrong. It's because He loves unprompted worship and trust, and He's giving you an opportunity to win awards here that you can't in heaven. "Do not cast away your confidence, because it will be greatly rewarded" (Hebrews 10:35). The saints of the Bible had to realize this – "He hasn't

129

stopped talking to me because He's displeased with me." And we need to realize this too. God's silence isn't a sign of disapproval and displeasure, but of delight as He sees you trust in Him without prompts.

# 32
# IT'S SNOWING DUCKS!

How would you like to be Colorado State Trooper Gary Eshelman on a cold snowy fall night in 1977? Officer Eshelman was driving the I-70 corridor in Colorado when an early snowstorm hit the Colorado Rockies. As Eshelman approached the Eisenhower tunnel from the western side, the snow suddenly became heavier, and to his surprise a large object came fluttering down in front of his car. He quickly came to a stop, and got out of his car. There in the middle of the road was a duck that had died when it hit the hard icy road. As he reached down to remove the duck, he heard a "thudding sound". Walking over to the side of the road, he found another duck that had hit the road, this one with its wings all encrusted with ice. It was still breathing, so not knowing what to do, he put the duck in the back of his patrol car. Before he could start to back up, he heard other thudding sounds.

Getting back out of the car, there were other ducks hitting the ground. The ducks were interspersed with the falling snow. Eshelman once again reentered his vehicle to radio the Denver Central Control Center. As he did, he heard a "quacking

131

Bruce McDonald

sound" in the back of his car! The duck had revived! Eshelman got a hold of the dispatcher, and said these rather immortal words, "Well, you've heard it said that it is raining cats and dogs, well, it's snowing ducks out here." When Eshelman drove through the tunnel, he found out it was snowing ducks on the other side. In all, Eshelman retrieved thirty two ducks! Twenty six of them survived. The sudden snowstorm and rapid drop in temperature had caused the south-bound ducks' wings to ice over and send them plummeting to the ground. I'm sure that was a night State Trooper Eshelman will never forget!

If you hadn't heard that story, you'd probably never have believed it could snow ducks! So, if that is hard to believe, could you believe it could rain quail? When wandering through the wilderness the Israelites complained to Moses that they wanted meat to eat. Moses told them God would supply meat for them, but they thought that was incredulous. And, even though they had seen God supply water from a rock and had daily seen His provision through "raining down manna each day", the thought of enough meat for them was beyond their belief. "When he struck the rock, water gushed out, and streams flowed abundantly. But can he also give us food? Can he supply meat for his people?" (Psalm 105:20) But God did supply, and He caused meat – quail, to rain down from the sky; "He rained meat down on them like dust, flying birds like sand on the seashore. He made them come down inside their camp, all around their tents." (Psalm 105:27) At first even Moses was staggered that God could do this (Numbers 11:31-32), but then, by faith, he believed and told the Israelites God would do this. But still, the Israelites doubted.

I wonder, what is it that we have put "limits" on God for? Raining quail or snowing ducks? I'm sure that those illustrations seem rather absurd, especially in our day and age. I mean, after all, does God really do such big and unusual things today? There are probably many of you reading this chapter

132

who would say that God has no limitation. But perhaps most of us, at least deep in our hearts, would believe that God really doesn't do much of the miraculous today (okay, now I got your attention). The thinking goes something like this, "This is the age of grace, the church age, and God no longer does miraculous things." I know, we walk by faith – this is essential! And we don't walk around demanding signs from God, this is important to remember. But here's the thing, in seeking to trust God without outward signs and any form of showiness, we must not seek to diminish God or His capabilities. And for that matter, His desires.

God is still the God of the impossible – "Is anything impossible for me?" – (Jeremiah 32:27), and He still can do far more than we can imagine – "God is able to do immeasurably more than all we ask or imagine." – (Ephesians 3:20). Faith in God is preeminently faith in Who He is. But we must never separate what He can do from His Person. You know, of course, that faith is supremely pleasing to God (Hebrews 11:6), but sometimes we need to examine what that faith looks like. Is it faith in our faith or faith in an Almighty God who has no limitations (except to do that which is contrary to His nature)?

What would cause a believer to doubt God's infinite ability? Well, as mentioned above, perhaps couching our doubts in the thought "that God really doesn't do the miraculous today". Or it may be that we have felt He didn't come through when we had a specific need, so therefore He can't do it or doesn't desire to do it. For some, it may be that the present situation is overwhelming and we measure God's ability by the present circumstances. In (what seems like) these closing days of our present age, it may be that we need to revisit the greatness of our God. Perhaps the reason we don't see the miraculous much today is because we have failed to believe that God really can do what is unimaginable and impossible for us. Our lives should have the testimony of something miraculous, that is, something that can't be attributed to our own self-efforts.

Could there still be some victories out there that God wants you to experience? Could there still be some mountains removed and trees uprooted that have stood opposing you (Matthew 17:20 & Luke 17:6)? Have we believed the Devil's lie that God is either incapable or indifferent? Are there things right now facing you personally, or in your family, or in your church that we've surrendered to our and other's capabilities? Have we quietly given up on God? Can God really do the incredulous? Was the Lord really serious when he said through the Apostle Paul that we "could know His incomparably great power for us who believe, that power is like the working of His mighty strength, which He exerted in Christ when He raised Him from the dead and seated Him at His right hand in the heavenly realms." (Ephesians 1:19-20)? We're not asking God to rain down manna on us or to snow down ducks on us, but we are asking, "Lord, I have heard of your fame; I stand in awe of your deeds, O Lord. Renew them in our day; in our time make them known." (Habakkuk 3:2)

Maybe, for some of us, we need to confess our lack of faith, however it was disguised, in an All-Powerful and an All-Loving God, and begin to again believe He is able! What do you think? Will you join me in this? Will you pick back up that "impossible thing" you have laid down, and call on a God who can do far more than you or I could ever imagine? "You are the God who performs miracles; you display your power among the peoples." (Psalm 77:14) Perhaps the world has yet to see the man or woman who truly believes in an awesome working God. Could that person be you?

# 33
# THERE'S SOMETHING DEAD UNDER
# THE HOOD

Okay, not the most glamorous and attractive title I've given a chapter! We recently had a rather interesting adventure, and it had to do with a car rental on one of our trips. We were in meetings in Michigan and had rented a vehicle from the Detroit Metro Airport. A few days into our meetings a mouse ran across the gas pedal. Thankfully, I had just stopped to head into a meeting. When I saw it, I pointed it out to my wife Bev, who was sitting in the passenger seat. She promptly exited in a manner befitting "The Man of Steel." In other words, "faster than a speeding bullet!" Along with her exit was a rather shrill scream! It took a little while, but we eventually got the little rodent out. Bev showed her bravery by getting back into the car after the meeting.

Then, a few days later, we pulled up to a restaurant and got out of the car. Bev went to the back hatch (an SUV) and lifted it up, and saw, to her horror, another mouse! She screamed again, but this time with anger and determination she "swatted it out of the car"! Alright, now we knew that we had a real

135

mouse problem with the car.. After checking further, we discovered they had a nest in the back spare tire compartment! We don't know how they got in there, especially since we hadn't even been to Disney World! Okay, may take you a minute to get that one.

That was a while ago, and we can look back on it laughingly now. But on that same trip, I had two different people tell me about recently having a dead animal in their car, and that the smell was horrible. One of them was my brother, and both people ended up paying significant money to not only find the animal, but to remove its smell. Not a pleasant experience. I hope you have never had that happen. You certainly would not want to drive around with the smell of something dead in your car! You'd want to get rid of it, even if it cost you a good amount of money. But what if money was tight, and what if you determined to just ignore it and hope eventually, either the smell would disappear or that you'd become used to it and not notice it any longer. I'm told that people who live near paper mills or turkey farms (two powerfully pungent smells) eventually become used to the smell and it doesn't bother them anymore.

Without thinking of an appropriate transition, what would it be like to have something dead in your spiritual life, not under your car hood, but inside your soul? Is that possible, and if it's possible, could a person actually become accustom to it and move on with their life? Scripture talks about people who believe they're alive in Christ, but they're spiritually dead (Revelation 3:1; Ephesians 2:1-4). I think we'd agree that there are people who think they're saved, but they're actually lost. They're not spiritually alive, but spiritually dead. But is it possible for a believer to be dead inside? Perhaps a better question is, "Is it possible for a believer to have something dead inside?" I believe it is, and I believe that I have witnessed it on several occasions. By making that statement, I'm not trying to convey that "I would ever be above that happening to me." But what I am saying is that on many occasions I have encountered this in others. This often happens because I am in a ministry, along with my wife, that gives us the privilege of listening to and hearing people's stories in their ongoing walk with Christ. Particularly, our ministry is to those who are in vocational Christian ministry (notice I didn't say "full-time Christian ministry, because we all are in full-time Christian ministry).

If I may, let me share with you a couple examples of something that can cause death in the life of a believer. Perhaps by sharing them in the context of "Ministers of the Gospel – Pastors and Missionaries", you can more freely read this without too much conviction. Of course, that won't help the ministers who read this chapter! And, truthfully, I know these two examples speak to each one of us.

Okay, here it goes. Here is some "insider information" for you. There are at least two assumptions or attitudes that can happen in a minister's life that if not dealt with, can cause something to die in us. And if these are not dealt with and taken care of, a life of ignoring it and becoming accustomed to "this dead thing" can result.

The first is the subtle thought or attitude that if I serve God then there ought to be some reciprocity involved. No minister would actually come out and say "what's in it for me?", and no minister would want to be known as "mercenary." In other words, "I'm in this for some remuneration". But having said that, there definitely can be a feeling that, at the least, "God should honor those who honor Him" (I Samuel 2:30). The honor a minister (missionary, pastor or other vocational minister) may expect would not necessarily have to be elevation and notoriety, or even a comfortable life. But at the least, a life that shows "some benefits for giving one's life for Christ". And those benefits usually (in their thinking) have to do with the absence of certain difficulties and heartaches. In

Bruce McDonald

other words, no failed marriages, families or ministries, and perhaps we could also include failed health and finances. Even though we teach this is part of the Christian life (I Peter 4:12; I Thessalonians 3:3), we feel we have some type of exemption clause. Okay, I told you this was insider information!

The second assumption or attitude is if I serve God then I will have an inside relationship to Him that lets me know what He is doing, why He is doing it, and when He will do something. I know that was long, so go back and read that important sentence. This second assumption goes underground like the first assumption. No minister would publicly say "God and I are tight," or "I have a relationship with God that's better than yours". Of course they wouldn't! But at the same time, another "perk" for the position (the first was the exemption clause) is that I now have an intimate knowledge of what God is doing and why. I assume my relationship with God is like other relationships, the longer you know someone, the longer you spend time with them, the more you know and understand them. This is true of our relationship with God, but only in a much more limited way. Because no one can fully know the mind of God or fully exhaust what He's doing (Romans 8:33-37), God will always be a mystery. And, truthfully, the more you know Him, the more you realize there is so much more to know about Him. He becomes more mysterious.

So these two very real, at least potentially, assumptions can be in a minister's heart. If they continue, something begins to "die" in that minister (and of course their spouse). And what exacerbates it even more is the fact that the minister "knows" he shouldn't be struggling with these things, and so the problem deepens. Rather than share it openly (because he thinks he shouldn't have these questions), he holds it within. He keeps "performing," but at the same time he dies inwardly.

So what should he or she do? First of all, realize what these

138

dangerous assumptions are. Second, be open and honest with God. He welcomes it and He can take it. And, lastly, find one or more people that you can be honest with. They'll listen and they'll pray for you. They should not let that thing that is dying, or has died, stay under their hood. They need to get rid of it. So, we've talked about ministers, but is there anything dying under your hood? Have you gotten accustomed to it? Realize what it is and remove it.

Bruce McDonald

34
THE PRIZE

Collections are pretty neat. It's fun to have someone show
you their collection. Collections can be a variety of things -
coins, post cards, ball caps, pinball machines (I have a friend
that at one time had close to 150 vintage pinball machines),
rare books, cars, baseball cards, stamps, tea cups, puzzles,
autographs, aluminum foil (okay forget that one), guns, shot
glasses (the girl sitting next to me on the plane just volunteered
as she saw me typing this that she collects them), sea shells –
and I think you get the idea.

But the one thing with collectors is that among their
collections they generally have a favorite, or one that is
especially valuable or rare. I guess you could say I have two
special collections; books and ball caps. I have over 70 ball
caps, and over 5,000 books. The ball caps are from all over –
several countries overseas and special places or events here in
the states. Truthfully, many people have given me these gifts.
And the books I have been collecting for almost 40 years. I
know we live in a day and age where we download most books

140

– I do that too, with many books on my laptop and smart phone, but I still love old books. I love the feel of them in my hands – even the smell of old books. Some of my books are first editions from the 1600s and 1700s. And like every other collector, I have my favorites - both in the ball caps and in my books. You should see my Isaac Watts leather book or my John Bunyan 16th century book. And hats? Each of Golf's Majors is in my home.

Okay, enough about my collections. It would be fun to know yours. But have you thought about God's possessions and the favorites He has? You probably would be surprised to know God has favorites among all He owns. The Bible tells us; "The earth is the Lords and the fullness there of." (Psalm 24:1) Everything is God's – "The cattle on a thousand hills and the wealth in every mine." (Psalm 50:10) God has created all things, and there isn't anything that has been created that He didn't create (Colossians 1:16). But among all He "owns" – like a collector – He has a favorite. And when you find out what this favorite is, it may change your life.

Here's a little known or read verse from a relatively famous chapter in the Bible: "By His own choice He gave us new birth by the message of truth so that we would be the first fruits of His creation." (James 1:18) Don't rush by that verse like we normally do when reading James 1. The verse and statement of fact in 1:18 is so powerfully important that the evil one would have you not stop and think about it. This verse tells us that we are "God's first fruits", but what does that mean? If you are somewhat familiar with your Bible, you may know that first fruits were something the Israelites were to give to God - whether crops, livestock or family. Normally, when we think of first fruits we think of something that came "first." The first of the crops, the first of the animals and the first born in your family. But first fruits means more than that. In a very specific way, it meant "the best". The best of the crops, animals and, figuratively speaking, the best of your family (all the firstborns loved to read that line!). So, go back and read the above verse – God chose us, and gave us new birth, so that we would be "the best" of all He has. I like the way the God's Word Translation puts it; "God decided to give us life through the Word of Truth to make us His most important creation." Wow, are you kidding me? His "most important"? Think about that, God made everything, and among everything He made – you are the most important!

One of the greatest truths in scripture, and sometimes one of the greatest omitted truths for the believer, is our identity in Christ. We are unique among all of God's creations. More special, more favored, more loved, than all He has made. Certainly above all He has made on earth, including animals. But more staggering is the fact that we're more special and loved than the angels themselves. In fact, in the entire spirit world, there is none that hold the place of love and honor that we hold. Not Seraphim or Cherubim, angels of any order – nothing, absolutely nothing, has our high, valued position. And grasp this, nothing is loved as much as us by God! We are the only ones that God would have His Son die for – it wasn't angels He died for, we are the only ones created in His image. Angels and animals weren't, we are the only ones who will reign with Christ. We are the only ones who will judge with Christ--we'll judge angels. We are the only ones who will have glorified bodies – bodies like Christ's. We are the only ones He has invited to sit on His throne with Him – not angels. We are the only ones who have been united with Christ and made the dwelling place of God.

No wonder John says; "Behold what love the Father has lavished on us that we should be called the children of God." (I John 3:1) No wonder the Psalmist could exclaim; "What is man that you are mindful of him…you made him lower than the angels, and yet crowned him with honor and glory." (Psalm 8:1)

Oh dear friends, you have not realized how special you are to God. You are the "apple of His eye" (Psalm 17:8), you are the one to whom Christ said "greater love has no man than this, that he lay down his life for his friends" (John 15:13). No wonder Satan hates you so much – because God loves you so much. Satan knows if he touches you, he touches that which is most dear to God.

When we're in heaven we'll finally grasp how great God's love is for us. We'll finally grasp that in the entire universe – we, yes us, are His favorites. Think of it, the God (Father, Son and Holy Spirit) who has always existed, who has no needs, chose to create us (remember James 1:18) so that we could be the most special of His creation (collection). Oh, how He loves to show us off to the rest of His creation. No wonder He said to Satan when all the angels were gathered before Him; "Have you seen my servant Job?" Spoken like a proud papa, spoken like someone who loves to show you his precious possessions and to point out His favorites. That's you dear friend, and nothing you can do will change that – not your sins, not your mistakes, and not your doubts. You are His. He created you, He died for you, and He now fights and defends for you. Pretty good stuff, wouldn't you say?

# 35
# BACK OF THE PLANE

Do you like being in the back of the plane? Those of you who fly know it is no fun to be in the back of the plane. This is a bummer for several reasons. First, you are generally the last one on the plane (zone 4 or 5). Second, there is the possibility that all of the overhead cargo with be gone. Third, you are the last one to be served from the beverage cart. Fourth, it is the bumpiest place on the plane. And fifth, you are the very last one off the plane.

We took a flight recently, where, for some unknown reason, the airline "bumped" us out of our seat (near the front) to the very last seats on the plane. Which reminds me of another reason the back of the plane is no fun - you have a wall behind your seat and you can't recline your chair! And, right now, one of my best buddies, who always flies first class, is feeling vindicated for looking from the first class section and calling all of us back there "the unwashed masses"!

So, what was my attitude? Was it, "wow, I am so glad I can

be in the very back. That way, others have an opportunity to sit up front"? Hardly! I felt sorry for myself (at least temporarily), and felt I "deserved" to be where I was first assigned. I was reminded once again that in my heart - thanks to the fall - is an ugly spirit of entitlement.

The truth of the matter is, we all have too much of the "old man" in us. Take this little test right now: What is the first feeling you have when someone takes the close parking spot you wanted? Someone else gets the promotion or recognition you felt was coming to you. Someone else is asked to speak and you feel slighted. Someone else takes the last shot in the game. Someone else gets invited to a gathering that you had hoped to go to. I think that's probably enough illustration. None of us likes to be in the back of the plane.

There was only one person (ever) who constantly looked for seats in the back of the plane, and that was Jesus Christ. You remember the amazing passage in Philippians 2, "Do nothing out of selfish ambition or vain conceit, but in humility consider others better than yourselves. Each of you should look not only to your own interests, but also the interests of others. Your attitude should be the same as that of Christ Jesus, who being the very nature God, made Himself nothing taking the very nature of a servant...he humbled himself." Jesus Himself said; "Just as the Son of Man did not come to be served, but to serve." (Matt 20:28)

Serving others and exalting others above ourselves is hard. But, by the Spirit of God, it can be done. By God's grace, I have seen and know many Christians who are "back seat" believers. In fact, one of the greatest servants in my life is Dave, who I jokingly used in the illustrations of calling the back of the plane "the unwashed masses."

In our old natures, we have a competitive spirit to be first, to be honored above others. But in our new man (I Cor. 5:17), controlled by the Holy Spirit, that focus of competition should be non-existent. But here is some good news - we are called to be competitive in one area. And that area is "out-honoring" others. Listen to what Romans 12:10 says; "Be devoted to one another in brotherly love. Honor one another above yourselves." In the Greek, the idea is to compete with each other to out-honor the other person.

The apostle Paul gives us a picture of a man who profiles a "back seat Christian." He speaks of Timothy in the following way: "I have no one else like him, who takes a genuine interest in our welfare. For everyone looks out for his own interests." (Phil 2:20-21) Like Timothy, like my friend Dave, like our Master, the Lord Jesus Christ, let's be believers who desire to go to the "back of the plane."

# 36
# THE CALL

What would it be like to hear audibly – and clearly – from God that He wants us to serve Him? How special would that be? To actually have God speak to us and reassure us that we are indeed His special chosen ones. Have you sometimes desired to be those Bible saints who heard from God, and especially heard from Him a special call? How about Abraham? Genesis 12:4 simply says; "So Abraham left Haran as the Lord had told him." Wow, that must have been reassuring and clarifying! Or how about the Apostle Paul? That whole "road to Damascus" thing! To have your name called out twice and given specific instructions about your life and calling (Acts 9:1-19).

I'd like to remind you of several other Bible characters who heard similar – audible – calls (Noah, Jonah and David are a few that come to mind). But the truth of the matter is, that though there were definitely people who heard God's voice to surrender to a call, they were the exception and not the rule. It's true, the vast majority of Bible Characters that parade across scripture did not hear audibly from God. In fact, once the New Testament arrives, we see this happening less and less.

So what's my point? I think that most of us, if not all of us, desire to have the assurance that we personally have God's call in our life. And more than that, that we are "hand-picked" by God. Ministers and missionaries are the ones who are thought to especially have this "call". Everyone assumes this. But if you talk to these servants of Christ, they too will often say that they struggle with whether they have a call or not. But it is not just so-called "professional Christian workers" that should be haunted by a call from God. It is every single follower of Christ. And we are called – or more importantly – you are called. We all believe that as Christians, we are justified by God, and this is true and important. But Romans 8:30 says: "That those He called He also justified."

If you throw out our calling, you'll have to throw out our being justified (being made right with God). I Peter 2:9 reminds us; "You are a chosen people...to declare the praises of him who called you out of darkness." Then Ephesians 4:1 challenges us to "live a life worthy of your calling." The Apostle Paul addresses the Corinthian believers and reminds them; "Think of what you were when you were called." The Bible reveals, and specifically makes it clear, you are a called person. You may not have ever heard an audible call (this would fit most, if not all of us), but your calling is sure, nonetheless (Romans 11:29).

There is an initial time in every believer's life that he or she hears and heeds the call of God to salvation (Ephesians 5:32 – called out of darkness into light), and puts their faith in Christ. Make no mistake about it, that call was individual, not universal (though it applies to all who are called). And God spoke into your heart just as importantly as He did into Abraham or Noah's heart. You are loved, called and commissioned by God.

But then too, every day of our lives here needs to be the daily and moment by moment yielding to God's call for the moment. That is just as important as God saying; "Leave Haran...Build an Ark...Cross the Jordan or Go into Damascus." We need to be people whose ears – our inner ears and our hearts – are attuned to the voice of God. "God, 'What is your call to me today?'" It may be overseas, it may be to a specific vocation or location, or it simply may be to yield at that moment to the perfect and pleasing will of God. There are no "big moments" of surrender to God, and then "little moments" that are inconsequential. Every act of hearing and heeding the call of God is pleasing and honoring to God. This day, be assured you are called by God – most definitely! But also remember to yield to God's call daily.

# 37
# THE CHAMPIONSHIP RING

I finally saw the ring. I had heard for much of my life about "championship rings". It seems most famous in football – The Super Bowl Ring. But Basketball, Baseball and Hockey also give rings to the championship team. The one I saw, felt and tried on was one from basketball. It was a NBA championship ring. Scott Williams was the owner (and wearer), and he had received it playing for the Chicago Bulls. Pretty cool moment! I had not seen Scott wear it before, which is pretty common among players. All the rings, in each of the individual sports, are quite large. And, not just large, but very ornate (some think gaudy). When the San Francisco Giants won the World Series last year, they were given rings decorated with 77 diamonds. So, most players don't wear their rings. Can you imagine trying to reach into your pocket and get your keys out while wearing that size ring?

Some players have multiple rings; Bill Russell in Basketball won 11 championship rings. In baseball, Yogi Berra leads the way with 10 World Series Rings. In football, the honor goes to a former NFL Executive, Neal Dahlen. Neil has 7 Super Bowl Rings. A side note here, for Hockey players, they have a "bonus". In addition to their rings, they have use of the actual Stanley Cup for a day (ask someone else, who knows hockey, to tell you what they normally do with that cup).

Athletes covet and long for that "championship ring". For many, it is the primary driving force in their lives. So much so, through free-agency and trades, they seek to put themselves in a position to leave their team (if their team is not championship caliber). But what about all the drive that is put into obtaining that ring? What happens when they finally achieve that goal? They finally slip that ring on their finger – quite the moment, but how long does it last?

We've recently heard stories about athlete's selling their ring for a large amount of money, because they needed the cash. It seems more and more athletes are selling their rings (still very small compared to those who keep theirs), and some people have realized that they can make a profit by buying and selling the athlete's rings. Tim Robbins is one such man. He owns Championship-Rings.net. Robbins says that fans will spend $5,000-$50,000 for a ring. And some have gone much higher. My point is, "The shelf life of Championship rings, as far as bringing satisfaction to someone, is very short." This not to say there are not people out there who enjoy their rings – there are many of them. But the achievement of winning a ring does not bring about the joy, satisfaction, and fulfillment that they imagined. Even with those who keep theirs, they usually (understandably) end up in either a "safety deposit box" or else in some other secure place.

The bottom line is, like anything else in life, this does not bring the satisfaction and fulfillment that one hoped for. Have you heard of JeRod Cherry? JeRod won three Super Bowl Rings with the New England Patriots. During a Youth Christian Conference he donated his ring to an Orphanage in

Cambodia. The ring was then raffled off for $200,000 to build the new Cambodian homes. Now that was fulfilling!

It's pretty easy to look at someone like an athlete and scrutinize them and see pursuits of something that's not lasting, but really, are we any different? It may not be a Super Bowl Ring, but it could be something else we have "longed for and desired". Some achievement or recognition– or possession that we thought would bring a sense of fulfillment. But the truth of the matter is, only Christ satisfies. Jesus warned us, and reminded us, of the futility in seeking fulfillment anywhere but Himself; "Do not store up for yourselves treasures on earth, where moth and rust destroy, and where thieves break in and steal. But store up for yourselves treasures in heaven, where moth and rust do not destroy, and where thieves do not break in and steal. For where your treasure is, there your heart will also be." (Matthew 6:19-21) Our "treasures" don't last. Ask former Yankee Whitey Ford, himself a recipient of 6 World Series Rings. His diamonds have fallen out of his ring, it happened so long ago, he doesn't have a clue where and when it happened. Once again echoing Christ's words; "Provide purses for yourselves that will not wear out, a treasure in heaven that will not be exhausted." (Luke 12:33)

But some of us have had the diamonds drop out of our dreams. Set your goals, hopes and expectations on Christ. He alone is the one who doesn't disappoint us. There should be a difference in us and those of the world. As the Lord speaks to my own heart about this, may you and I have the same spirit the Psalmist had when he said; "Whom have I in heaven but you? And earth has nothing I desire but you" (Psalm 73:25).

38
# THE COMFORT OF LOVE

"His disciples stared at one another, at a loss to know which of them he meant. One of them, the disciple whom Jesus loved, was reclining next to him." (John 13:22-23)

Sadly, I do not remember much of my childhood. Especially compared to Bev, who remembers things from when she was 3 years old! I am not sure why I can't remember much. I try, but there is kind of a black hole there. Sure wish I could remember more. But I do remember a handful of events and experiences. One of the moments I remember with my English mother was a comment she made after reading her Bible. She looked at me and said, "You know, I believe that the Apostle John used the phrase, or expression, 'The disciple whom Jesus loved' because he could never get over the fact that Jesus loved him." It is funny that those words have stuck with me all these years. She went on to comment that only John uses this expression of himself of the gospel writers. John didn't even use his own name in the account listed above (the

"Last Supper" meal with Jesus in the upper room). Just, "The disciple whom Jesus loved".

My mother and her father have left me with something wonderful. My mom was always in awe of God's love for her. Like John, she never doubted it, but also like John, she couldn't get over it. Her dad, my grandfather, was a man who could never get over God's forgiveness of his sins. So much so, that he has that one word "forgiven" on his tombstone. My mother doesn't have "The woman God loved" on her tombstone, but she could have. I desire to be like John and my mother, that when I think of myself, I first of all think of being a man that Jesus loves. I believe as Christians that we sometimes struggle with this most elemental truth of the believer – that "Jesus Loves Me" as the old children's song says. Somehow in our walk with God, and even in our service for God, we forget, and somehow press along with a sense of duty or performance. That may sound rather harsh, and perhaps it is, but I do believe that we do not stop long enough to allow the thought of God's extravagant love to wash over us.

Maybe right now would be a good time to stop and think of this amazing love. Let scripture remind you of this great truth. "For God so loved the world that He gave His one and only Son…" (John 3:16) "This is how we know what love is: Jesus Christ laid down His life for us…" (I John 3:16) "Greater love has no man than this, that a man lays down his life for his friends…" (John 15:13) "But because of His great love for us, God who is rich in mercy, made us alive with Christ…" (Ephesians 2:4) "God demonstrated His own love for us in this: While we were sinners Christ died for us…" (Romans 5:8) Dear friends may we see ourselves first and foremost as people (that is, individuals) that Jesus loves. May it define us and compel us. Most of us are familiar with the name John Wesley, the great evangelist of the 1700s. But perhaps you are not as familiar with his brother Charles. A great evangelist in his own right, but known mostly for his great hymn writing. Many of his songs populate our song books. Below is one that we should take with us today, and all the days of our lives – like my mother did!

*"And can it be that I should gain an interest in the Savior's blood? Died He for me, who caused His pain, for me, who Him to death pursued? Amazing love, how can it be? That Thou my God, should die for me? Tis mystery all, the Immortal dies! Who can explore His strange design? In vain the first-born seraph tries to sound the depths of love Devine! Tis mercy all, let earth adore; let angel minds inquire no more. Amazing love, how can it be? That Thou my God should die for me?"*

# 39
# THE CROWN JEWELS

The week before I write this I was in London with Bev and some dear friends of ours. We took this couple over to the Tower of London to see, among other things, the Crown Jewels. Bev and I have been there on a couple of other occasions, but I never cease to be amazed at all the jewels, crowns, and swords (other items too) that are housed there. I must admit to you, I am not into jewelry, diamonds, gold, emeralds and rubies. They do nothing for me. But, there is something there that really astounds me, and that is the crown. There is more than one, but the main one that the Queen wears is amazing. That day, as I stood there staring at it, I thought about the crown that Christ will wear. The Queen's crown in comparison to Christ's will probably look like a dirty baseball cap! Psalm 132:18 says, "The crown on His head will be resplendent." Webster's says that resplendent "means to shine with brilliant luster". Can you imagine what brilliance His crown will have?

In one of King David's battles, he fought against the

Ammonites, and when he defeated them, he took the crown from their king. The king's crown was gold set with precious stones, and weighed 75 pounds! The record (II Samuel 12:30) says the people set it on David's head – ouch! But what a massive crown, yet it was pittance compared to Christ's crown! By the way, Christ's glorious crown is made up of jewels as well. Do you know what those jewels are? They are the believers who have faithfully served Him. Malachi 3:17 (KJV) says we will be jewels in His crown - Wow! And the way we live affects the luster of His crown. Now that is an amazing thought!

That day in the Tower of London got me thinking about Christ's crown, and the fact that you and I have the opportunity to add to the luster and brilliance of that crown. I know what you are thinking, "but there are so many believers, that will be too many jewels". God has a solution for that – Christ has "many crowns"! Revelation 19:12 says, "On His head are many crowns". You have heard of or seen people here on earth that have large wardrobes. Can you imagine the palace that house all of Christ's crowns? O dear friend, how fitting that the King of kings should have such crowns, and so many. His precious, glorious and beautiful head is deserving of all the crowns, and of all the crown jewels. Isaiah put it well; "In that day the Lord Almighty will be a glorious crown, a beautiful wreath for the remnant of His people." (Isaiah 28:5).

# 40
# THE DANGER OF PRESUMPTION

Recently I experienced a period of questioning and concern (some people would have called it anxiety!). I made some decisions, and spent some restless hours (some people would have called it worry!) over something that not only did not come about, but that was not true. I wondered at the time why I did not have peace or experience a measure of grace for what I thought to be true. Looking back now, I see that it was because God only gives grace for things we are actually going to experience and peace when we are in the midst of something. Grace and peace are not promised for imagined things. Tough lessons to learn!

Have you been there, or are you there right now? I wonder how much time and needless energy we spend on worrying about something that either is not true, or will not come to pass. On the one hand, we say that we believe God will give grace and peace for whatever situation we face. But then on the other hand, we worry, fret and plot as if He will not. Pretty disturbing! It seems like it is an age old problem, and that it did not start with us. Let us look at a few examples from scripture.

Abraham got into trouble because he "presumed" that "God was not in this place" when he lied about Sarah being his wife (the second time he did this). When Abimelech asked him why he lied, Abraham said "Surely there is no fear of God in this land." But he was wrong, and he presumed something to be true that was not. He imagined something to happen that did not. (Genesis 20:11) Abraham's son Isaac would years later make the same assumption and lie because he thought he might be killed and his wife Rebekah taken by another Abimelech. History repeated itself! (Genesis 26:9) Saul assumed (or imagined) that David would try to take his life, so he spent the next several years of his life plotting to kill David.

Our imaginary foes are some of our greatest enemies. How many nights of sleep are missed, how many ulcers developed, and how many rash decisions are made because we assume or presume something? Probably more than we care to admit. Maybe that is why David prayed; "keep back thy servant from presumptuous sins". (Psalm 19:13 KJV) There are no benefits to presuming something, and worrying about a situation before it ever comes to be. We dishonor God when we do this, and we only bring problems to ourselves.

What are some "preventatives" for presumptuous sins? Here are a few: First, bring your thoughts under the Holy Spirit's control (Psalm 139:23-24 II Corinthians 10:5). Second, only think about things that are true (Philippians 4:8; Ephesians 6:14). Third, spend extra time reading God's promises (II Timothy 2:15; Psalm 119:116). Fourth, talk over your fears and concerns with godly friends (Psalm 119:63; Proverbs 15:22). Fifth, think the best and don't be a pessimist (Jeremiah 29:11; Proverbs 13:12).

There is hope in the battle with fear, anxiety and presumption. We can confidently place our lives in the hands of our Almighty God. Our Father cares for us (Psalm 103:14). He will not allow anything to come into our lives that does not pass through His hands (I Corinthians 10:13), and He will give peace and grace for any REAL thing that comes our way. (John 14:27; II Corinthians 12:9)

# 41
# THE END OF THE WORLD

Well, are you ready? It's certainly been talked about a lot lately. And I'm sure you all remember the hype back in 2012 that this would be year we see the end of the world as we know it. And how could so many people be wrong? Okay, Harold Camping was wrong about 2011. He thought Jesus would come and take certain people back to heaven on May 21, and then the world would be destroyed on October 21. But that was just one man. However, in 2012 we had several, including an entire civilization, warning us that the end of the world was that year. Not only current ones, but people of antiquity.

In the 1500s Nostradamus predicted that in 2012 there would be mass destruction, the ushering in of WWIII, and a great and fiery star (comet) would crash to earth. But way back before that, the Mayans, who developed an intricate calendar, had the world ending on December 21, 2012. Well, actually, their calendar just ends that day – after 5,126 years. That's how old their calendar is, and they have it abruptly ending on December 21 of 2012. Not to be outdone, even the North

Bruce McDonald

American Indians (Native Americans) predicted that the year 2012 would be a difficult and dangerous times. And then there are our current prognosticators, the New Agers. They long predicted 2012 would be a monumental "shift in consciousness". In the Islamic world, predictions abound that the Mahdi, or the Twelfth Imam, would appear either that year or the next. Certainly his return was imminent.

So......we all know what happened in 2012 – nothing! But what does this year hold? If the Apostles and Disciples were alive on earth today, they would certainly have believed that 2012, or even this year, is this time Jesus is coming back. Don't believe it? It's true. Hey, they all thought Jesus was coming back in their day.

There is much debate today on when Jesus will come back. We have even developed a system of doctrine to describe when Jesus will return (Eschatology). It includes more than the Return of Christ, but His Return is the central theme. We have terminology like "Pre-Tribulation, Mid-Tribulation, Post-Tribulation, Pre-Wrath, Premillennial, Postmillennial, and Amillennial" to help clarify what we believe. But, simply put, though the New Testament writers were given information (revelation) on end time events, they still believed that Jesus could, and would, probably come back for them in their day.

Paul wrote in I Thessalonians 4:15-17 and I Corinthians 15:51-52 about the Lord's Return (Rapture) and included himself when he said "And we who are still alive and left will be caught up together with them in the clouds." Paul even wrote to young men and women to think about celibacy (remaining single) because "The time is short" (I Corinthians 7:29). Peter thought the Lord was coming back soon "The time is near is when all things will end" he writes in I Peter 4:7. And the Apostle John thought the days in which he was living were the last days; "My dear children, these are the last days" he writes in I John 2:18. Both Paul and Peter picked up our

162

Lord's words in Matthew 24 & 25 when He said we should look for Him as a "Thief in the night". Peter in II Peter 3:8 & 10, and Paul in I Thessalonians 5:1-8 uses the same term. Whether you believe in the Imminent (can come at any moment) return of Jesus or not, you have to admit the disciples and writers of scripture did.

Now, that brings us to the book of Revelation. Do you realize that Jesus Himself said He was "coming soon" eight times? You can check it out for yourself (Revelation 1:1, 3; 3:11; 22:6, 7, 10, 12, 20). So, no wonder the writers of scripture and the early church looked for His imminent return – and believed with all their hearts he was coming soon. So if they were alive today, they definitely would believe this "was the year".

Now in case you are wondering, I am Pretribulationist and Premillennialist, and I also strongly believe in the Imminent return of Jesus. So, yes, I believe He could come back this year. I also believe the Lord says much about "end time happenings" and what the world looks like at that time. It sure seems like those things are happening, or beginning to happen. But Jesus' return (the Rapture as opposed to His Revelation or Second Coming at Armageddon) is not dependent on anything. But here is the  question that has always intrigued me, "Why did Jesus repeatedly give the impression that His coming was soon?" This is especially true in the book of Revelation. I mean 8 times He says He is coming soon? What does that mean? It has been almost 2,000 years since He left earth for heaven.

Perhaps Jesus proclaimed it this way for several reasons. First, the idea of "soon" can also carry with it the idea of "suddenly" or "quickly". In other words, when Jesus comes – it will be quick, no delaying. For some, when Jesus comes it will be "too soon". Second, another reason, undoubtedly, is that the blessed hope (Titus 2:13) gives assurance to those who are suffering and in great straits that Jesus could come back at

Bruce McDonald

any moment to rescue them. Third, his promise of "at any moment" is meant to instill in us a desire to live in the presence of His possible return (I John 3:3), and to not be ashamed at His coming. Fourth, the promise is certainly for those who would be living at His actual return.

So, yes, this year could indeed be the year that the "soon" becomes an actuality. The Lord doesn't need Nostradamus, the Mayans, or anyone else to announce His coming – or to strike fear in anyone's heart as to "the end of the world". For the believer, it is "Let not your heart be troubled...I am coming back for you." (John 14:1-2) We don't look with dreadful anticipation at the end of the world, but with hopeful expectation that this could be the year he comes for His Bride. "When these things begin to take place, stand up; lift up your heads, because your redemption is drawing near." (Luke 21:28)

# 42
# AN ETERNAL FLAME

There are so-called eternal fires burning in different parts of the world today. Here in the states, you have one for former President, John F. Kennedy, and you have one that burns for The Unknown Soldier (the one at Washington Square in Philadelphia, not the one at Arlington Cemetery). Several cities in countries throughout the world have "eternal flames." Last summer, I visited one while I was in Sarajevo, Bosnia. The eternal flame goes back a long ways – all the way back to the Old Testament Tabernacle, and then eventually the Temple, where the Menorah (the elaborate candle stick holder) burned continually. Even before that, in Delphi, a flame burned continually. The flames, of course, are not eternal, but they burn continually for a long period of time. There is, however, a flame that burns continually, and it, too, is a memorial for undying love. That love is God's love, and that flame burns brightly and continually for you.

God wants you to know about this "eternal flame", and God wants you to understand how it can never be extinguished. Let me share a wonderful verse with you. The verse is found in Song of Songs. We usually do not spend much time in that Old Testament book, because much of its romantic imagery seems somewhat archaic and foreign to our modern thoughts. While I believe that much of the book can be interpreted literally, and describes an amazingly intimate and romantic love between a husband and wife (even godly arousal), I also believe that much of the book presents symbolism and allegorical pictures and teaching of Christ's great love for His bride – the church.

With that in mind, listen to these words of love from Christ to you; "Love flashes like fire, the brightest kind of flame. Many waters cannot quench love; neither can rivers drown it. If a man tried to buy love with everything he owned, his offer would be utterly despised." (Song of Songs 8:6-7) Wow! Talk about an amazing love. These word put to shame our greatest poets' thoughts on love. Have you noticed that there are times in our lives where we wonder if our sins – many waters – have drowned God's passionate love for us? "Certainly", we say to ourselves, "this time my sins have quenched His love". Have you thought that? Are you thinking that now? Have circumstances led you to believe that you are under God's disapproval, or that your sins have caused His love-flame to flicker out? It's easy to believe that isn't it? But God's love can never be extinguished. He has said; "I have loved you with an everlasting love." (Jeremiah 31:3) He has reminded you that He loved you at your worst; "God demonstrated his own love for us in this: While we were sinners, Christ died for us." (Romans 5:8) God loved you before you even had a thought to love Him; "We love because he first loved us." (I John 4:19)

What manner of love is this? No wonder the Apostle John exclaimed; "How great is the love the Father has lavished on us!" (I John 3:1) Dear friends, I am not making light of our sins, and the fact that they do grieve God. But those of us who love God – by His grace – always feel we sin more than we want to, never that we can sin as much as we want to. And when we sin, yes, even repeated ones, we find that God's unconditional love burns just as brightly as before. No wonder Solomon, in a picture of God's extravagant love, says; "If a man tried to buy love with everything he owned, his offer would be utterly despised." You can't buy love like that, and you can't earn love like that. It can only be received.

This day, this night, as you grapple with whether God still loves you extravagantly, O please hear these words – "Many waters cannot quench love." No, never! The cross forever reminds us that there is an eternal flame that burns brightly for us. The Gospel of John records these words as Jesus faced the cross; "It was just before the Passover feast, Jesus knew that the time had come for him to leave this world and to go to the Father. Having loved his own who were in the world, he now showed them the full extent of his love." (John 13:1) Please don't ever forget that, Jesus' love for you burns brightly, and it can never go out. Not many waters, not many sins, not many failures, not anything! He has promised.

# 43
# THE FEW

The title for this chapter comes from a bestselling book by Alex Kershaw. Kershaw has written many bestselling books, including *The Bedford Boys*, which was made into the movie, *Saving Private Ryan*. The book, *The Few*, is the amazing, moving story of the young American pilots who left America to go and fly with England's RAF during the early days of the Second World War. When these young men left, they had to leave secretly. America had declared "neutrality", and it was actually against the law for any pilots to go to England to fly in the war. There were fines that would be leveled, and also long-term imprisonment.

Nevertheless, these young men escaped through Canada, rode by train across that great country, and then boarded ships to cross the Atlantic. Their bravery, however, did not come from escaping the country at great cost. But their bravery came at the great cost of flying what amounted to certain death missions. These young twenty-some year olds flew the British Spitfires against the overwhelming odds of the German

Luftwaffe (the German Air force).

The battles in the skies above the English Channel, and then eventually over England and London itself, was horrific. At times there would be less than 400 Spitfires battling against a thousand Messerschmitt (German fighter planes) and hundreds of German bombers. The Spitfire casualties were staggering. Hundreds of English pilots lost their lives, but those pilots were fighting for their country. What of the American pilots who fought in the skies above England – long before The United States entered the war? They volunteered – in some cases begged – that they could fly to help defend England against Germany.

Names such as Hugh Reilley, Art Donahue, Eugene (Red) Tobin, Billy Fiske (an Olympic Gold Medalist), Philip Leckrone, Andy Mamedoff, and Vernon Keough fought for the RAF and made up the "Eagle's Squadron." Newspapers in America reported their exploits, and a country looked to its leadership in Washington to see when we would enter the war and join these valiant pilots. It did not happen until we were attacked by Japan in 1942.

But, during those early war years, when it looked like Germany would defeat and overrun England, these brave pilots paid the price to keep England free. During the terrifying nights of bombing, pilot after pilot would head up into the skies to try to drive the German planes back to France. The losses kept mounting up for the RAF. The Americans were soon being shot down, and the loss of life was innumerable. Winston Churchill, on August twentieth, nineteen forty, said these now famous words; *"Never in the field of human conflict was so much owed by so many to so few."*

The next time we celebrate Memorial Day, we should all stop and think of those who paid the great price for us - to keep our freedom. In all our wars, valiant soldiers have answered the call and paid the ultimate price. Thank God for our military, and the young men and women who have served so faithfully.

But as we think about Memorial Day, remember that it's also a time for those of us who know Christ to think about those saints who have fought for our faith, and many who have given their lives. Men and women who would not go away silently in the night. Those who have fought for Doctrinal Purity, those who have insisted on a high view of Christ and the Scriptures, and those who have taken the gospel of Jesus to a darkened corner of the world. Some have been martyred; others have been ostracized and looked at with scorn. The battles may not have been in the skies over the English Channel or out in the oil fields of Iraq, but they have been fought in classrooms, in pulpits, in Congress, in foreign jungles, far flung fields, crowded cities and in the press. We should be encouraged, but also emboldened.

Our example is those that have gone before us. Hebrews 12:1 says; "Therefore, since we are surrounded by such a great cloud of witnesses, let us throw off everything that hinders and the sin that so easily entangles." God cries out to us; "Who will rise up for me against the wicked? Who will take a stand for me against evildoers?" (Psalm 94:16) Will we be inspired by these heroes? Will we be grateful for these valiant Christian soldiers? But more importantly, will we step into their ranks and join the cause. To be brave and mighty for Christ. Lieutenant Colonel John McCrae (MD) wrote these immortal words in 1914:
"In Flanders Fields"

*In Flanders Fields the poppies blow, Between the crosses row on row, That mark our place; and in the sky, The larks, still bravely singing, fly Scarce heard amid the guns below.*

*We are the dead. Short days ago, We lived, felt dawn, saw sunset glow, Loved and were loved, and now we lie in Flanders fields.*

*Take up our quarrel with the foe: To you from failing hands we throw The torch; be yours to hold it high. If ye break faith with us who die We shall not sleep, though poppies grow In Flanders fields.*

This day, let's join the "few." Let us be those who reach high to catch the torch from failing hands. Like Isaiah of old, let us say; "Here am I, use me!"

Bruce McDonald

# 44
# THE FULFILLMENT

Have you ever anticipated something, and it seemed like it would never get here (if it was something good)? You wait and wait, you plan and visualize, and it seems that the day or event is such a long way off. But then it comes, the day or event is here; you cannot believe the time has already arrived. And, usually, you cannot believe it has already passed. We cannot stop time, and it indeed does march on, and each event or hoped for activity will come.

Bev and I find this to be true so often. As I've mentioned before, we travel frequently, and oftentimes overseas. We have looked forward to various trips and ministries that have now come and gone. Many of the meetings are planned as far as three years in advance. They seem so distant, will the day ever come? A I write this, we have already taken two trips out of the country this year, and Lord willing, still have trips to Russia, Greece and the Philippines scheduled for later this year. They have been planned for quite some time, and now they are rapidly approaching. How can it be?

One of the trips we took for meetings was last year during

the spring. We went to Brazil where Bev grew up as a missionary kid. She had not been back for 20 years. We anticipated the trip for two years, and thought the day would never come. But it did, and it has come and gone. In fact, we have since taken another trip to Brazil (a different part of the country) this past January!

Why do I share this? Because we sometimes forget that our most longed for and anticipated day and event will come. I am speaking of course about the Rapture. Jesus will come back for His Bride, it will happen. And then it will be past! But in this case, we won't look back and feel sad the event is past, but we will rejoice as we enjoy each new day of eternity in unbelievable fashion (see Ephesians 2:7). Let me share with you a passage that reminds us that this great day will come. It is found in Ezekiel 12:23,25,28, here is what it says; "The days are near, and the fulfillment of every vision...For I am the Lord; I will speak the word that I will speak, and it will be performed. It will no longer be delayed, but in your days...Thus says the Lord God: None of my words will be delayed any longer, but the word that I speak will be performed, declares the Lord God." These words were spoken to Ezekiel about the fulfillment of God's judgment on Israel (Judah) that had been prophesied for a couple of centuries. It was about to happen, and it did happen. These words can be lifted from that context and applied to our present day. All the prophesies, all the warnings, and all the words of hope will come true. More sure than our trip to Brazil!

I know we all grow weary, I know that we all push to the back of our mind the return of Jesus, but it is still the "blessed hope" (Titus 2:13), and we should never lose sight of it. You may think, "Well, others down through the years have thought that, and He didn't come." Ah, but just you saying that is another indication that the time is near. II Peter 3:3-10 tells us that people will begin to say and think, "Nothing has changed, he isn't coming back soon," and then He will return.

Bruce McDonald

This day or night, whenever you are reading this, perhaps you should think about His return. It is OK to long for the Rapture. The Apostle Paul tells us that we should encourage one another with these thoughts and words (I Thessalonians 4:18). As you think about it, and anticipate its' happening, remember, soon, perhaps sooner than you can imagine, that the moment will occur, in "a flash, in the twinkling of an eye" (I Corinthians 15:53). Even so, come quickly Lord Jesus!

# 45
# THE GLAMORIZING OF TRIALS

We all love good stories, and it seems, the more ups and downs, risk and thrills, victories and defeats, the better the story. As believers, we love to recount the stories of many Bible heroes. Joseph coming through the times of betrayal and imprisonment to being second in command in Egypt. Daniel surviving deportation and eventually the Lion's Den, to being head of all the Wise men in Babylon. Esther and Mordecai escaping the plot of Haman to become rulers in Persia. The list goes on and on – Hezekiah facing overwhelming odds against an Assyrian army. Sarah, Rebecca, Rachel and Elizabeth coming out of barrenness to have children. Abraham, Isaac and Zachariah waiting years for a promised child, and then suddenly the son is born. Wow, good stuff! And even our heroes down through history have had times of defeat and triumph. We especially like those whose stories are stories of overcoming great odds or finally receiving vindication. Ah, stories are great!

But, wait a minute, just what was that time like in those heroes' lives when they were going through those trials? Did

Bruce McDonald

they like it? How did it feel? Were there moments of doubt and despair? Did they wish they were not going through that time? Did they doubt God? Were mistakes made and faith weakened? You probably know the answer to those questions.

Let's be honest – nobody wants trials! No one seeks suffering, heartache and confusion. They make good stories in the retelling – after they are over, but they are painful during the trials. Somehow we forget this, we think that because trials are our lot in life (God has designed it so), and that trials will produce something (God's desired affect), that we will "enjoy them". Far from it! Even the godliest saints struggled with the seeming purposelessness of trials. They are not called trials for nothing! Trials hurt, trials confuse, and trials stretch our faith. Think about some of our Bible heroes as they were in the midst of trials.

For instance, let's consider Joseph. Think how he must have felt as his brother's grabbed him, fought with him, yanked his cloak off, threw him down into a pit – and then sold him by force to mercenary slave traders. Years later, his brothers in recalling this event said; "We saw how distressed he was when he pleaded for his life." (Genesis 42:21). And don't think for a minute that his time in prison was a wonderful and pleasant experience as he wondered what God was doing.

Or think about Mordecai and Esther as they waited for the dreadful day when they would all be put to death – no wonder Esther sobbed before the king. Jeremiah struggled mightily as he was in the midst of trials and said; "I remember my affliction and my wandering, the bitterness and the gall. I well remember them, and my soul is downcast within me." (Lamentations 3:19-20) And don't forget David' s plea and cry (one of his many); "Why, O Lord, do you stand far off? Why do you hide yourself in times of trouble?" (Psalm 10:1) In the New Testament the Apostle Paul speaks for many of us when he said this about his trials; "We do not want you to be

176

uninformed brothers, about the hardships we suffered in the province of Asia. We were under great pressure, far beyond our ability to endure, so that we even despaired of life." (II Corinthians 1:8) If you have not read C.S. Lewis' book "A Grief Observed", then you have missed out on hearing how this great man of God struggled with his faith in times of deep suffering.

Why have I written all this? It is to remind you and me that trials are trials. They are not glamorous. But hear this, neither are they purposeless. Trials hurt – that is the nature of trials – but God is in the trial. Though at the time it does not seem like it, that trial is the safest place to be. God has not abandoned you, it does feel like it – that is part of the trial – but He is there, and He is doing a work for your good and His glory. Romans 5:3-4 and James 1:2-4 remind us that something good is being produced in us that only the fires of trials can produce. And God's great comforting promise of Romans 8:28 assures us that, though the trial may be bad, the result will be good.

So how can we endure trials and suffering? How can we even "welcome them?" First, by recognizing – and admitting – that this trial hurts. It is confusing, and it does not seem like a good place to be. Don't glamorize them, nor let someone else try to glamorize your trials. Remember that others have felt – and are feeling – the same way. Second, keep in mind that trials are everyone's lot (I Corinthians 10:13; I Peter 4:12; I Thessalonians 3:3). You are not being punished – and more importantly, you are not being abandoned by God (Psalm 46:1). He is there for you, and even if His presence seems to be withdrawn, it is not. And third, it will produce and accomplish something. Trials are never wasted. Believe about God in the dark what you believed about Him in the light. Trials are not glamorous, but neither are they purposeless. Trust Him now.

Bruce McDonald

# 46
# THE GOD OF MORE

It seems we live in a world of "less". Not that we are not blessed abundantly living here in the United States. Compared to most countries our existence borders between abundance and extravagance. But, having said that, it seems like much we are offered today is "less". We have an expression, "Less bang for your buck". Prices of food go up, amounts received go down. Objects and items that are purchased escalate in cost and shrink in size. Without being cruel, but definitely bordering on sweeping generalities, even services offered tends to become less. Though this event hasn't happened in recent times, some of you may recall the "less" event that happened in the classic Christmas movie, *A Christmas Story*. The dad won the "special grand prize", but his joy was soon turned to shock and disappointment (though he hid it well in the movie) when he opened the large crate and found "a women's leg lamp". I believe it is safe to say that we live in a world of less.

When you think of God, what type of God do you think of? Is God a tight-fisted, miserly God? Wow, "where'd that come from?" Okay, that was a pretty bold and shocking question. None of us would say that – none of us. But, really,

178

when you and I think of God, what comes to our mind? A God whose fingers we need to pry open? A God who needs to be harassed and hounded until He relents and gives us what we desire? Just stop for a moment, and allow your mind to entertain the question; "How generous do I think God is?" Our arch-foe, the Devil, loves to whisper into our minds that God is a miser, keeping the best for Himself, and giving us the scraps. He has done it from the beginning. Remember his words to Eve; "God knows that when you eat of it your eyes will be opened and you will be like God…" (Genesis 3:4) His insinuation is very clear – God is a tight-fisted miser.

He has used this lie down through the ages, you can see it across the pages of scripture; "Abraham, God is withholding a son from you", "Achan, God doesn't want you to have wealth", "Gehazi, God won't take care of your financial needs", "Judas, Jesus will never help you obtain wealth" and "Demas, the path God has for you is one of hardship and obscurity." Satan never stops with his accusations that God is a God of less, and that to trust and follow Him will always end up in failed promises or disappointing rewards. Though not putting a name and face to it, perhaps you are struggling with thoughts such as this.

God is a God of more, amazingly so. If you have never taken time to study "The mores of God", I would encourage you to do it. I have never seen it before, but I began a personal quest to see this side of God. Here is a very brief sampling: God is not only the God of Grace, but of more grace (James 4:6). God not only enables us to be conquerors, but to be more than conquerors (Romans 8:37). God not only reconciles us to Himself, but to be more than reconciled (Romans 5:10). God will not only do all we ask, but He will do immeasurably more than we ask (Ephesians 3:20). God is not only majestic, but more than majestic (Psalm 76:4). God is not only awesome, but more than awesome (Psalm 89:7). God not only will give good gifts to His children, but more than good gifts (Luke

11:13). God will not only give back what you have given to Him, but He will give you more than you gave (Luke 6:38). And maybe one last one (there are many more), heaven will not only be eye popping and jaw dropping, but more so (I Corinthians 2:9)! Our experience in heaven will not be like Oliver Twist who approached the Orphanage Director and said; "Please sir, I want some more." No, no, no, a thousand times no! Heaven will be so much more than we could even imagine. God will always be unfolding for us "more" treasures of His grace (Ephesians 2:7).

Perhaps in closing, a look back at the heart and generosity of God displayed to Solomon will encourage all of us. "That night God said to Solomon... 'ask for whatever you want me to give you.' Solomon answered... 'give me wisdom and knowledge'... God said to him, 'Since you asked for wisdom and knowledge...I will also give you more wealth, riches, and honor, more than any king who has lived before you or will live after you." (II Chronicles 1:7-12) God is the God of more, not less. He bids us come to Him; "Open your mouth wide and I will fill it!" (Psalm 81:10)

# 47
# OUR GOOD SHEPHERD

As I write this, there is currently a movie showing in theaters across America called, *The Good Shepherd*. It is supposedly an account of the beginning of the CIA. I haven't seen the movie, but the title has got me thinking. All believers know that God the Father and Jesus Christ His Son identify themselves as our shepherd. The Psalm 23 and John 10 passages are the most common, but several other places in scripture identify God as our Shepherd (I have found over 15 references to God being our Shepherd).

I was struck recently by one particular passage that addresses God as a Shepherd. The account is found in Genesis 48:15. This is the story of the last days of Jacob, and at this point in the story, he has gathered his twelve sons around him to hear his last words. Verse 15 says "The God before whom my fathers Abraham and Isaac walked, the God who has been my shepherd all my life to this day, the Angel who has redeemed me from all harm..." Any cursory reading of Jacob's life will reveal a life that seems anything but "led of God". If there is one Old Testament character that seems to be a total recipient of God's grace, it is Jacob.

I am amazed at the most unlikely times God appears to Jacob to comfort him, and remind him of the blessings God intended to pour out on him. His character is definitely a "head-scratcher"! But, you know what? Despite his rocky life, and the fact that God chose unconditionally to bless him, we find him in Faith's Hall of Fame. The account used there to reveal Jacob's faith (Hebrews 11:22) is his words at the end of his life. Jacob evidently looked back at his hard and difficult life – and saw God there all the days of his life! That encourages me. There are so many times when I stagger in my walk of faith, and feel like I am growing in my Christian life at glacial speed. So much of my life – and yours – doesn't seem to make much sense. If God is my Shepherd, then where are the green pastures and quiet waters? Isn't that what our Shepherd is supposed to do? What is the deal with rocky crags and barren heights?

I think in our more sane moments, times when the conflict and travail ease, we looked back and say "oh yeah, God was there too". The truth of the matter is that God has not promised to always lead us in pleasant places, but He has promised to be with us "all our days". This old guy Jacob, or should I say Israel, has something to teach us. God who is our Shepherd is the God who is there. And we do not need to wait until the end of our lives to recognize that. Several years before this account in Genesis, Jacob said, "He has been with me everywhere I have gone" (Genesis 35:3).

You know what, that is great news. Perhaps right now you are in the midst of trials and confusion. Where is God leading? Is He still here, did He abandon His plan? God is there, he is YOUR Good Shepherd. The key is just to stay close to the Shepherd. Hear the swish of His garments, the clack of His staff on the rocks, and hear His singing to you (Zephaniah 3:17). He is there, and He will be with you all your days.

# 48
# THE HEART OF ROBERT THE BRUCE

When I was a young boy, my mother told me I was named after Robert the Bruce of Scotland. I always thought that was neat, and on occasion would read up on him. I knew he was Scotland's greatest emancipator, and the most revered of all Scottish heroes. I particularly loved reading the story of his hiding in a cave (a true story) from the English. While there, he noticed a spider jumping along one wall of the cave. He noticed that several times the spider's web broke and the spider would go back again and try to "make the jump". Almost transfixed by this, Bruce began to count the number of times the spider attempted to jump to a certain part of the wall. In a very monumental moment in his life, Bruce looked up towards heaven and said, *"Lord, I've tried to liberate Scotland from England 6 times, and have failed each time. This spider has sought to jump this small chasm 6 times. If he makes it on the 7th, then I will once again go out and seek to defeat the English."* The spider made it on the 7th time, and Bruce kept his word (later recounting that event to others). That's a wonderful story about perseverance, but a more powerful story follows after the end of his life.

Robert the Bruce eventually defeated the English, who were led by King Edward I on June 24, 1314 at Bannockburn, Scotland. The long desired "freedom" that William Wallace had desired, was now guaranteed. Bruce served as King of the Scots from 1306 until his death in 1329. Shortly before dying, this unbelievably valiant warrior asked that after his death, his heart be removed so it could be "carried in battle against God's foes". And after that, buried in the Holy Land next to the Holy Sepulcher, to have his heart resting near where Christ had lain for three days.

Shortly after he died, his heart was surgically removed and placed in a small silver casket. One of his nobles, Sir James Douglas, put the casket on a chain and slipped it around his neck. He carried Bruce's heart into battle. Sir Douglas is famous for many reasons, but chief among those, are his words as he went into battle. While in Spain, on their way to the Holy Land, the Scottish army was attacked by the Moors. As Douglas and several of his soldiers were being cut down, Douglas took off the chain and casket and hurled it at the Moorish army, shouting, *"Now pass thou onward before us, as thou wast want, and I will follow thee or die."* In other words, "Oh, heart of Bruce, lead on!" Douglas and others died in that battle, but the rallying cry won the day. One of the other Scottish knights, Sir William Keith, picked up the casket containing Bruce's heart, and took it back to Scotland. There they buried Bruce's heart at Melrose Abbey in Roxburghshire. It has lain in that area (it was reburied in 1998) since that time. Today a grave stone marks the sight of the burial. Inscribed on that stone are these words, *"A noble heart can know no ease without freedom."*

What courage and what valor the memory and heart of Robert the Bruce inspired in his men. If you visit Scotland, you'll find he is venerated in a way that is beyond any hero here in the America. As I thought of Robert the Bruce, and the fact that he is still held up today, I thought of our liberator and hero, Jesus Christ. The Captain of our Salvation, the King of

Glory, has inspired us to deeds that are impossible. His inspiration has led countless millions to lay down their life for His cause. It is still happening today. He also defeated an enemy that was thought impossible to defeat. He too defeated a usurper, one who was seeking to extend his rule over our lives. He defeated the Devil – "He disarmed the powers and authorities, he made a public spectacle of them, triumphing over them by the cross." (Colossians 2:15) He defeated the flesh and the world. He went to the very gates of hell and put His feet on the neck of death. But unlike Robert the Bruce, He came back from the dead. He is alive and more triumphant then he was before.

Because of His victory, we don't need to "throw His heart at the enemy". Oh no, instead He rides out to lead us in triumphal victory. "But thanks be to God, who always leads us in triumphal procession in Christ." (II Corinthians 2:14). Have you felt overwhelmed lately? Have defeats begun to pile up? Oh dear friend, don't forget "one who is greater than Robert the Bruce". His name, His atoning work, strikes fear and terror into the life of our enemy. When you're weary, think of His victory, "Fix our eyes on Jesus, the author (champion) and perfecter (completer) of our faith…Consider him…so that you will not grow weary and lose heart." (Hebrews 12:2-3)

Sometimes we believe the lies of the enemy, we believe "he is winning", but he has already lost. And we go out to fight a battle that has already been won. We too, in one sense, have our hero's heart close to our chest. With courageous abandonment, we go out in the spirit of our emancipator. His great heart fills us with bravery to do valiant deeds. "With God we will gain the victory, and he will trample down our enemies." (Psalm 60:12) Oh, heart of Christ, lead on!

"Lead on, O King Eternal"

*"Lead on, O King Eternal, we follow-not with fears!*

185

Bruce McDonald

*For gladness breaks like morning, wherever Thy face*

*appears; Thy cross is lifted over us, we journey in its light:*
*The Crown awaits the conquest, lead on O God of might."*

# 49
# "THE HEROISM OF THE ORDINARY"

That was the title of an article I read while recently in Jackson Hole, Wyoming. The article was in a small paper called; "tetonjournal.com". It was a reprint of an article that Margaret Manning of the writing team of Ravi Zacharias International Ministries had done. I would encourage you to go online and read it.

But the title really gripped me – and got me thinking. You see, most of the people I know are ordinary. Oh, I confess, I do know some, and have met some, that many of us would consider far from ordinary. They seem to be luminaries that God has raised up for such a time as this. But, for the most part, my friends and acquaintances are ordinary people – like me! Since most of us qualify for being considered ordinary, and truthfully, the Body of Christ seems to be made up of ordinary people, where does our heroism come in?

Many years ago I stood in a vacant auditorium at D. L. Moody's Birthplace in Northfield, Massachusetts. The Northfield Conference grounds had been a very famous place in Moody's day, and also for many years after that. I stood behind the pulpit – no one was there, and imagined speaking to those humongous crowds that used to fill the auditorium. As I looked down on the surface of the podium, I noticed that there was a list of names of the "famous" speakers who had spoken there. For those of us in ministry, it was like a "who's who" of great men of the faith. There was Moody's name, of course, but also such names as G. Campbell Morgan, Philip Brooks, R. A. Torrey, Henry Drummond, and F. B. Meyer, to name but a few. As I stood there, I wondered and prayed, "would God use me like those men? God, would you use me like those men?" Well, the obvious answer to that question and prayer, was no. I would not be used like those men. Time and history has proven that in my life, I am an "ordinary man".

So, I believe, that most of you, at least I think, can identify with me. So where does our heroism come in? I mean, if it will not be through notoriety, great influence or monumental contributions, how can we be heroic in the ordinary? The skinny of it is, being faithful to our station and call in life. I know I have been using the term "ordinary", but you know that this is just a term our world uses, and a term that we often misapply. It has been said that "There are no little people in God's program". That is true, but it is also true that there are "no ordinary people" in God's program. You see, our calling and station in life is designed and handcrafted by God. I know He gives us liberty to move about and choose vocations and occupations. These, of course, include mother, housewife and homemaker, but each one of us has giftedness and desires God has wired in to fulfill His purpose for us. God is into detail and design. He planned you to do certain "good works" (things that help advance His Kingdom) far in advance of your birth (Ephesians 2:10). He has been actively involved in your geographical and vocational moves (Acts 17:26). He has given you certain unique and specific gifts (Ephesians 4:7-8). And He means for each experience – good and bad, to be part of a process in conforming you to His Son's image (Romans 8:29).

You may have heard it said that God is concerned more with the depth of your life then He is the breadth of your life. God will take care of the breadth-that is in His sovereign hands. The busy mother, the hard working single girl, the waste management man, the guy in the small cubicle, the pastor in a small rural church and the missionary who has labored unnoticed for years. They – you, are important to God. You do remember, of course, that the criteria for God's approval, has always been faithfulness. "Well done, good and faithful servant." (Matthew 25:21) So dear friend, remain faithful, whatever your station or lot in life. Be all that you can be for Christ.

Former NFL Coach and now author, Tony Dungy, challenges us to be "Uncommon Christians". But we can be uncommon by remaining faithful in all we do. In the 1980s, my wife Bev and I had the immense joy of meeting Geogi Vins. Georgi was a former Russian pastor who had been imprisoned in Siberia for his faith. He suffered horribly for 13 years. He had finally been released, and was the guest of honor at a conference where I was one of the speakers. He requested a time that he and his wife could meet with Bev and I. Late one evening we met, and it was an experience I will never forget. Near the end of the evening, Georgi looked at me, and then said through his wife (at that time he could not speak much English); "I have something to say to you, Bruce." I leaned forward and listened intently. He then took out his Russian Bible, opened to I Corinthians 4:2, and quoted to me the verse as I looked at it; "Now it is required that those who have been given a trust must prove faithful." He stared at me for a few moments, and then said, "That is my challenge to you." Just reading about this, you can imagine how I felt at that moment.

Friends, I am not Georgi Vins, nor will I ever be, but I pass along that challenge that still rings in my heart and ears, "Be faithful". Most likely none of us will reach the stature and

notoriety of Geogi Vins, but we can be heroes – not in an
ordinary way, but as ordinary people. "The Heroism of the
Ordinary", I like the sound of it – and so should you!

# 50
# THE HUNDRED YEARS WAR

Right now, here in America, people are genuinely concerned, and some angry, with how long our wars last. In recent years it has been Iraq, the first Desert Storm, and our most recent involvement. Then our time in Afghanistan, and before that Viet Nam, and before that Korea, and before that…well, you get the idea. I do not make light of our servicemen's involvement in the horrors of war. Though I believe there are oftentimes "just causes" of war, and that everyone of our soldiers are heroes for their sacrifice and valor, still, everyone of us wishes war "would end" sooner, rather than later. The family, friends and loved ones – not to mention the military personnel, would all want war to end now, no matter what war. They obviously desire for the war to end in victory, but to end nevertheless.

That makes me try to imagine what it would have been like to experience war all the days of your life. If you lived in the years 1337 to 1453 in England or France, you would have experienced the horrors of war during your entire lifetime. Though that period is 116 years, historians call the

Bruce McDonald

French/English war, "The Hundred Years War".

Can you imagine that? Granted, there were some times when there was a very brief respite of peace. But, for the most part, the war continued on. The Hundred Years War took an unbelievable toll on lives. (And, in addition to the wartime casualties, the Black Plague hit France and England, and a third of all the people living in France and England died,) The beginnings of the Hundred Years War actually started almost 200 years earlier. In 1066 William, Duke of Normandy (also called William the Conqueror), invaded England and conquered it. He set himself up as King of England. But a problem was created when he did this, because though he was "King of England," he was also Duke of Normandy (in France). Thus, a "vassal" of the King of France (are you following this?). This situation did not sit well for either side, for obvious reasons. It came to a head in 1337 when King Philip VI of France attacked Normandy (and other surrounding southwest territories in France) to dispel the English – even though they had ancestry in France. Thus, the war was started and lasted 116 years. By the way, some notables during that long war were Joan of Arc and Henry V. Okay, enough of a brief – very brief, history lesson.

So why bring The Hundred Years War up? Because, have you ever thought of this, that you and I are in our own "hundred years war". Granted, most of us won't live until we are 100, but we will experience "war" all our lives. I am not talking about with another country or with a radical religious group, but I am talking about our war with our archenemy, Satan and his legion (innumerable) of followers – fallen angels. The Bible makes it abundantly clear that we are in a fight – and it is not with unsaved people! It is with Satan and his demonic hordes. The Bible pulls no punches on this; "For our struggle is not against flesh and blood, but against the rulers, against the authorities, against the powers of this dark world and against the spiritual forces of evil in the heavenly realms." (Ephesians

192

6:12) And this war is constantly continual. Unlike the Hundred Years War, we have no brief respites of peace and safety. But it is not that the enemy wishes to let up. It is "a forced break" that God imposes on him, and gives us in His kindness. But Satan and his hordes desire to never let up. Think of it, they (or he) never think; "You know, they are having a bad day, this really wouldn't be fair today." Or, "You know I have been going kind of heavy on them recently, perhaps I should try someone else." Or even, "Wow, this person is pretty godly, I should leave them alone." Don't you wish! The Bible reminds us that Satan "prowls around like a roaring lion looking for someone to devour." (I Peter 5:8) One of the definitions for the Greek word 'peripateo", translated here as "prowl", means to be "preoccupied" with a task. Constantly intent on accomplishing a purpose.

Speaking of "lions", think of the "animal likeness" of our enemy. He is called a "bird that snatches away seed [Word of God]" (Mark 4:4, 15), as a "wolf that disguises himself as a sheep to come and wreck havoc." (John 10:12; Acts 20:29) A "serpent that is cunning and dangerous". (Revelation 12:9) And, of course, "a great dragon that is terrifying." (Revelation 12:9) Add to this, that he has at least one third of all the created angels (unless God has created new ones since Satan's fall) at his beck and call (Revelation 12:4).

During the Hundred Years War, one of the main things that happened was the development of weapons and warfare tactics. The beginning of the war, weapons were pretty much standard and ancient. But during this long war, the longbow and crossbow were developed, the firearm and canon were invented, and the very nature of how attacks were carried out evolved from so called heavy cavalry (horses and riders weighted down with heavy armor) to light infantry.

I think, too, we have a parallel in our spiritual warfare – Satan has been doing this a long time! He has grown and developed in his tactics. He knows what is best to carry on this warfare. Does he need the weapon of discouragement? The weapons of lust, greed, worry, fear, laziness, pride, doubt, indifference or anger? Whichever works best, he uses. We need to be alert and mindful of his many weapons of war; "In order that Satan might not outwit us. For we are not unaware of his schemes." (II Corinthians 2:11) But, and this is so very important to know, unlike the Hundred Years War, we know how this one ends - it ends in glorious victory for Christ - and you in Christ. "But thanks be to God! He gives us victory through our Lord Jesus Christ." (I Corinthians 15:57).

Knowing and planning on something is half the battle. We are at war! It will never end during our lifetime. But God has made provision for this battle. We have His armor (Ephesians 6:10- 18), we have His promise of His presence, help and victory. We are "more than conquerors through him who loved us." (Romans 8:37) Let us never lay down the sword and shield. Even though "the battle belongs to the Lord" (I Samuel 17:47), we must still fight (II Timothy 4:7).

In 1919, at the end of the First World War, the League of Nations was formed to prevent any further wars – it, of course did not succeed. Then, at the end of World War II, the United Nations was formed to prevent any further wars. It too failed, as has any human attempt to stop war. Our war with the spiritual enemy will never have an "armistice day" until that one day –O let it come soon, when King Jesus, both literally and spiritually, causes "All wars to stop and military training will come to an end." (Micah 4:3) I am sorry that you and I have been born in the midst of the Hundred Years War", but with alertness and God, we will win the victory! (Psalm 18:29)

# 51
# THE INCOMPREHENSIBLE GOD

It seems like quite frequently I am faced with something that is "beyond me". Whether it is trying to figure out something about my computer while my sons and daughter try to explain it to me, or maybe something in the stock market or business world that Bev wants me to look into. It may be a foreign language I am trying to grasp or how the electrical wiring works in my house. There is a plethora of things that seem incomprehensible to me.

That being the case, it seems strange that I would attempt to "figure out" the Almighty! I have noticed that one of my regular pastimes is scrutinizing God. The ancient book of Job contains these words by a man named Zophar; "Can you fathom the mysteries of God? Can you probe the limits of the Almighty? They are higher than the heavens-what can you do? They are deeper than the depths of the grave-what can you know?" (Job 11:7-8) Still, there is something in me that wants to figure out God. The admonition in scripture is to know our God. That can be found several places, and it is a desirous pursuit. However, seeking to know God, and trying to figure

Him out are two different things.

Our faith is strengthened when we know our God – that is, who He is. God has revealed much about Himself, particularly His heart. But He has not revealed everything about Himself, not even close! We live in an age where we want to know everything. We have access to so much knowledge, and it is expanding at an incredible rate. I read recently that it is estimated that we now have only 3% of the information that will be available by next year. What a thought! But for some reason, not knowing God fully, and what He is up to, is disconcerting. God remaining a mystery is somewhat unsafe for us; we do not like it, because we lose some element of control.

C.S. Lewis in his book *God in the Dock* tells how we, as Christians, have reversed our concept of God. That the ancients viewed themselves as before a holy God/Judge, and they were in the dock (a dock is an enclosed stand that the accused stood before a judge – particularly in England). They needed to give account of their actions and motives. Modern man, says Lewis, has changed that setting to make us the judge and God standing before us in the dock as the accused. He needs to give an answer to the charges and questions we direct towards Him. And if we are satisfied with His answers, we may even acquit Him! Don't misunderstand me, we do have serious questions, and God does want us to come to Him with our concerns and heartaches. But we must also understand that we will never be able to grasp all that God is doing. Romans 11:33-36 says, "How unsearchable are His judgments, and His paths beyond tracing out." God can be trusted, not because He can be figured out, but because He is good.

The incomprehensibility of God is something we should embrace. He is a God of wonder. We live in a wonderless society – we know too much. But we can never know the mind and workings of God. Yes, we can know His heart, praise

God, but the rest remains a wonder. Go ahead and search out the matter – that is ok. Proverbs 25:2 says; "It is the glory of God to conceal a matter; to search out a matter is the glory of kings." But as you do, keep in mind that "the secret things belong to the Lord". (Deuteronomy 29:29) We cannot know everything about God, but we can trust and love Him.

# 52
# THE INSPECTED LIFE

1 2,000 gallons! I could not believe my eyes when I opened my water bill. I have had bills as high as 4,000 or even 5,000 gallons, but that had been when we had lots of company. But we had had none this past month (outside of some occasional dinners), and I had been gone for a week! What happened? I immediately thought that my water meter must be broken. After checking with some people, they said that this was highly unlikely. Each person said to me "you must have a slow leak in one of your toilets." At first, I thought, "that can't be possible. I do not hear any water leaking, and I think I would have noticed that." But they all urged me to check it out. One water specialist said; "most toilets leaks and you cannot even hear it." He went on to tell me that a small water leak can cause you to lose up to 600 gallons a day. Wow! Who would have thought?

That got me to thinking about my personal life. I oftentimes keep my eye out for "the big sins", or the noticeable areas of my life that would reveal backslidings. But, more often than not, it is probably the slow, little sins – either of omission or commission – that cause me not grow, or worse yet, to commit some sin I will need to confess. To switch metaphors, it is like a slow leak in a dam that you do not notice until it is too late. Solomon wrote, "It is the little foxes that ruin the vineyards". (SS 2:15)

What might a "small steady leak" look like in our lives? Perhaps it is skipping our time alone with God. Maybe, at the beginning, it is becoming a little sporadic, but then missing altogether. Another thing might be finding it easier to miss a church service now and then, or perhaps drop out of a church/growth group. Then again, maybe not just sins of omission, but commission. We start to watch things we shouldn't watch, and we are not as guarded. We listen to conversations or say things we shouldn't say. All seemingly "little things", but they begin to accumulate, and we suddenly find ourselves faced with sin "full blown". I wonder if it might be good right at this moment to ask the Holy Spirit to reveal if there have been any "little sins" happening in our life. Perhaps take a pen and paper and think and pray it through, and write down what God might reveal to you.

Are there some leaks? I think so. When I found that I had a water leak – I found out the hard way – I asked others who had had similar problems, I then checked with "experts", I searched to see where the leak could be, and then I did something about it. I think that would be a good formula for us. Surround ourselves with others, make ourselves accountable. Check with others who have gone down the Christian life before us. Sit under, and surround yourself with godly people who perhaps know more than you, or at least seem to have God's stamp of authenticity on their lives. Search your life, and hold it under the magnifying lens of God's scripture. And then, by the grace of God, do something about it. Make the necessary changes, confess sins, and reinstitute godly practices. Are little sins serious? Absolutely! My" little leak" caused my water bill to jump from $55 to $399. A costly mistake. But little sins can lead to even greater consequences.

By the way, one other analogy from my experience this week. When I began a thorough search for the problem, I found out it was not a leaky toilet, but a water hose that was dripping. When we sense sin, or experience the result of sin, we may be surprised to find that it was not in the "little" area we thought. So all the more reason why it is important to live "the inspected life".

# 53
# KNOWLEDGE THAT IS DESIRABLE

Usually, the idea to know something is positive, especially if what you are trying to know is good, or at least not evil. Most of us who love God have a desire to know about God, and to know His Word. In fact, for many of us, that would be a mark of being an evangelical - the exaltation and pursuit of God, and the dependency on the sufficiency and authority of scripture. If the truth were known, we would wage some significant wars proclaiming and defending those two priorities.

A haunting thought is that even if these two important passions are operative in our lives, we still may be distant from God, or at the least, not intimate with Him. Knowing about God and knowing how to handle scripture properly are important, but not the most important things (see the Pharisees). Greater than knowing about God, is knowing God. Greater than knowing how to handle scripture (principles of hermeneutics, exegeting a passage correctly, implementing the best Bible study techniques taught in our Seminaries and Bible Colleges), is knowing how to learn to let the living Word of

God speak to us.

In my travels, and in many of my experiences, I am meeting more and more ministers and missionaries who have been doing Bible Studies and teaching about God for years, but they have somehow lost connection with the Head. I have had more than one pastor tell me this year that he does not have his own quiet time, but just uses his study of the Word of God in preparation for meetings to be his time alone with God.

Years ago, C.H. MacIntosh reminded us *"that when Jesus said, if any man is thirsty, let him come and drink, he didn't say let him come and draw"*. Drawing for others is good, but if our souls are dry, we will not have much to offer someone else. A relationship with God is just that, it is entering into a vital living relationship with Him. God wants us to know Him, not just about Him. He desires this, and He knows it is crucial for each of us in our walk of faith.

Take some time and reflect on these passages – Jeremiah 9:23,24; Ephesians 1:17; Philippians 4:11. Knowing our God is essential, Psalm 9:10 reminds us that those who know their God will increase in their trust in Him. And how do we know God? We know Him through many means – His creation, His Spirit's inner working and teaching in our lives, through the lives and lips of others, and through trials. But the greatest way is listening to Him in scripture. This is not a familiar path I am challenging us to walk down; I do not mean "technically and mentally" learning things about God. What I mean is coming quietly, and prepared, into His presence. Praying and asking God to reveal Himself to us through His Word, and what He wants us to know at that precise moment.

Here are some practical suggestions:

1.   Find a place to be alone.
2.   Quiet your heart first.

3. Ask God to speak into your heart.
4. Read the intended passage (short or long) several times, even out loud.
5. Use your journal, and write down any thoughts that God puts in your mind.
6. Speak back to God what is necessary – confession of sin, grateful thanksgiving, spontaneous praise.

When was the last time any of us had "holy heartburn"? Like those disciples on the road to Emmaus, may we get back to knowing our God intimately, and hearing from Him regularly, so that our hearts are aflame for Christ. I pray that Jesus would never have to say to me "…have I been among you all this time without you knowing me?" (See John 14:9)

# 54
# THE LESSON OF THE SNOWFLAKE

The other day we had about three inches of snow fall on our home up in the Rocky Mountains. I went out early to clean off our deck, but as I was sweeping (the snow at that elevation and low humidity is very light and fluffy) the snow away I noticed the strangeness and beauty of this particular snowfall. Snow has often looked pretty, but this particular snowfall seemed more unusual than most. I could actually see the individual snowflakes piled in the snow. It was as if someone had taken a large assortment of pure white pick-up sticks, separated them slightly, and piled them together. It was amazing! I could actually see through the layers of snowflakes. I ran inside and asked my wife Bev to come out and look at the snow. She did, and like me, was totally enthralled by what she saw. For the rest of the time I was sweeping the deck, I would stop and stare at the snowflakes piled up on the railings and steps.

I know we all have heard that there are no two snowflakes alike, and knowing that made this particular snow event all the more amazing. William Matthew wrote; *"And here comes the snow…A language in which no word is ever repeated."* Cool way to put it! A gentleman by the name of Wilson Bentley (1865-1931) was the first man to use modern devices to study the snowflake. In fact, he spent most of his life in this pursuit. His findings confirmed that, indeed, there are no two snowflakes alike. He wrote of his study; *"Under the microscope, I found the snowflakes were miracles of beauty, and it seemed a shame that the beauty should not be seen and appreciated by others. Every crystal was a masterpiece of design, and no one design was ever repeated."* Bentley published many wonderful photos of the snowflake. Most recently, Kenneth Libbrecht did a masterful work entitled simply, *Snowflakes.* It is published by Voyageur Press, and I would highly recommend you purchasing it. The photography is stunning and in many ways, "mind-blowing".

It is not just snowflakes that God has chosen to be unique – one of a kind, but also every human being that has ever lived. Snowflakes are wonderful, and they have much to teach us of our Creator God (Psalm 19:1 & Revelation 1:20). And in some specific ways, even the snowflake causes praises to raise to God; "Praise the Lord you…hail, snow and clouds." I believe that snowflakes should cause all of us to stop and ponder "the individual design" that God has worked into human beings. Never has there ever been another you, and never will there ever be another you!

Dear friends, I hope you believe this. First of all, that you are indeed unique and one of a kind, but that, also, you are a priceless work of art. No, really, I am serious. Please don't think that that is some platitude, it is not – you are!

There is much discussion and debate as to why and how snowflakes stick together. Words and terms such as; sintering, electro static attraction and hexagonal symmetry are used in attempts to figure out the how and why of snowflakes. But God's greatest creation – you, is explained in Psalm 139: 113-14; "You made all the delicate, inner parts of my body and knit me together in my mother's womb. Thank you for making me so wonderfully complex! Your workmanship is marvelous!" You are not just a conglomeration of random particles and molecules coming together to produce a human being. If you look up a technical definition for snowflakes in the dictionary, you will find this: "Snowflakes are conglomerations of frozen ice crystals that fall through the earth's atmosphere. They begin as two snow crystals which develop when microscopic super cooled cloud droplets freeze." Right! But this does not take into affect that God has His individual hand on each flake. It is the same with you, only more so. It is true that genes and DNA come together in your mother's womb to help shape you.

But never forget God is there as the Master Geneticist, shaping you to be the "you" He has designed. Earlier I quoted from Wilson Bentley, the scientist who did the early work with snowflakes. He had become so amazed, and to some degree, enamored with snowflakes, that he wrote these lines; "*When a snowflake melted, that design was forever lost. Just that much beauty was gone, without leaving any record behind.*" Oh dear friend, that is you. God brings you on the scene unique, and when you or I leave, there is not another us. God throws the mold away! If you are living in a part of the country or world that has snow, go out and take a look the next time it snows, and study the snowflake. If you don't have snow – pull up a picture of a snowflake on the internet. Or better yet, go buy Libbrecht's book *Snowflakes*. Be amazed at God's creativity, but also be encouraged that He has shown that wonderful creative individuality in you! "And God looked over all he had made, and saw that it was very good." (Genesis 1:31) Amen!

# 55
# THE LONG HARD WALK

His name was Slavomir Rawicz. He accomplished something that defies human logic and ability. In 1941 he was with the Polish army when he was captured by the Russians and taken to Moscow for imprisonment and interrogation. After the communist were unable to get him to confess to his alleged crimes, he was sentenced to 25 years imprisonment in Siberia. After a long train ride of over three thousand miles, he arrived in Irkutsk, in southern Siberia. From there, he, along with several hundred other soldiers, were chained together and made to march hundreds of miles north into upper Siberia. They traveled through winter, often in sub-zero weather, at last reaching Camp 300, just 400 miles south of the Arctic Circle. Most of the hundreds did not make it, either by dying at the hands of the Soviets, or from the toll of the death march.

As horrendous as that march was, once Rawicz reached the prison camp, he began to make plans for an escape. A ludicrous thought – since there was no place to escape to! But escape he did, and he did something that no one else on earth had ever done, and something that was thought to be humanly

impossible. Rawicz walked from Northern Siberia to India. A
journey of a staggering 4,000 miles. He walked through Siberia
in the dead of winter, while hiding from the Russians. He then
walked all the way through Mongolia, and in southern
Mongolia, he encountered the massive Gobi Desert. He
somehow survived the brutal heat by day, and then the frigid
weather by night. He continued his walk on into Tibet and
traversed through that country until finally coming to the great
Himalayan Mountains – in the middle of winter! He somehow
made it over the mountains and eventually walked all the way
to India, where he was finally rescued by some English
soldiers. He made this impossible trip with basically little
clothing and a small amount of food when he escaped from
prison. The walk lasted one year, and each night of his journey
he reckoned as his last. What he survived on would turn most
of our stomachs. No one had ever made such a difficult and
lengthy walk, especially in the part of the world he was fleeing
from. He went on to write the book, *The Long Walk*, which
details this arduous journey.

Have you noticed that the Christian life is often compared
to a walk? There are a few passages where Paul, and then the
writer of Hebrews, refers to the Christian life as a race. But, for
the most part, it is characterized as a walk. Now, why is that? I
mean, isn't walking easier than running? Well, evidently not!
Listen to what Isaiah 40 and verse 31 says; "They who hope in
the Lord will renew their strength. They will soar on wings like
eagles; they will run and not grow weary, they will walk and not
faint." Did you get that? Running will make us weary, but
walking can cause us to faint. Evidently, walking is the harder
of the two. I think I understand why, and do you know what
the reason is? Because walking takes longer.

Let me share from a personal experience. For years I was a
runner, I ran for exercise (along with basketball) for 28 years. I
loved it, and it fit my schedule. I could run even when I was
away in meetings (my wife Bev ran all those years too). It was

quick – I wasn't quick though – and could be done at just about any time. But three years ago I had knee replacement (because of running), and was told not to run. So, now I walk or hike. Because I love to exercise, I do it every day. But here is the problem. I find I need to walk a lot farther and longer (time-wise) than when I was running. If I walk 4-6 miles a day, it is time consuming. It just can't be done quickly. I think that is why God likens our Christian life to a walk – it is a time consuming life. The Christian life is not to be lived as a sprint! It is a slow, hard, and long walk. I know there are exceptions, as some people are called home to heaven early, but I believe the norm is that God has us in a walk, not a sprint.

Have you noticed that Jesus walked everywhere? I don't just mean that he lacked transportation; I mean that we have no picture of Jesus running anywhere. Do your own study and see how often the New Testament talks about Jesus walking somewhere, even in His post-resurrection appearances (Luke 24:15). And think about the admonition for us to walk a certain way. This parenthetical remark; I know that the Greek word for walk can sometimes mean our whole manner of life. But there is a reason the Holy Spirit uses the metaphor of walking.

Now back to the admonition of how we walk. Here are some commands; "Walk in the footsteps of faith" (Romans 4:12). "Walk in the light" (I John 1:7). "Walk in obedience" (II John 1:6). "Walk in the truth" (III John 1:3). "Walk in newness of life" (Romans 6:4). "Walk honestly" (Romans 13:13). "Walk by faith" (II Corinthians 5:7). "Walk in the Spirit" (Galatians 5:16). "Walk worthy of our calling" (Ephesians 4:1). And, one last one, "Walk worthy of God" (I Thessalonians 2:12). I could give several others, but I think those are sufficient. The point being, we are in this walk for the long haul.

In a sense, we, too, are escaping from the prison of this world of sin, to become the man and woman God wants us to be. And as we head – not to India – but to our Celestial City, we find the walk hard and long at times. We wake up each day and continue the journey. Sometimes over rugged mountain peaks in the dead of winter, and other times through hot, blistering deserts. But, by God's Holy Spirit and the provisions along the way, we make this journey, this walk, that each day brings us closer to home. The wonderful news is that God is there in the mountains, out in the desert and with us each step of the way. It is a long, hard road, so expect it to be. But the journey will be worth the destination.

# 56
# THE MERCY RULE

If you have had kids who played sports when they are little, you may be familiar with the "mercy rule". It usually has to do with the amount of runs the other team is ahead, and calling the game early to save further embarrassment. Sometimes, like in baseball, it will be "per inning," and not allowing the other team to score more than 10 runs in one inning. Both rules are in place to keep the losing team from being totally embarrassed. It really is not a bad idea, and perhaps it should carry over into the adult world. There are certainly some times we could use that rule!

But, with that said, have you ever thought of the fact that God is the one who initially instituted the "mercy rule"? His is a little different. His is not to save embarrassment, but to keep people from getting what they deserve. Early on, the scripture states the incredible truth; "For the Lord your God is a merciful God". (Deuteronomy 4:31) A wonderful truth, but at the same time, an understatement. Further on in the Bible, God's mercy is called "great" (Psalm 5:7). In trying to grasp the greatness of God's mercy, the psalmist says; "For as the

Bruce McDonald

heaven is high above the earth, so great is His mercy…" (Psalm 103:12) Mercy is high, because it reaches all the way up to heaven, and into the throne room of God. God is "rich in mercy" as Ephesians 2:4 puts it, and His wealth of mercy is inexhaustible. James says "The Lord is full of compassion and mercy" (James 5:11). Mercy and grace are often contrasted. It has been said, and I think this is a good way to put it, "That grace is getting what we do not deserve, and mercy is not getting what we do deserve".

In some ways, we do not, or cannot, ask for grace (there are exceptions). Grace comes to us out of God's sovereign purpose and love. Mercy is something we cry out for; "God be merciful to me a sinner". God loves to lavish grace on His undeserving and unsuspecting children. But, in mercy, God loves to respond to His children's cry of repentance and asking forgiveness. God rushes to show mercy to those who genuinely repent. He obviously does this also for an unbeliever when he cries out for forgiveness and salvation.

Perhaps sharing a few examples in scripture of God's mercy might help. The first one has to do with King Ahab. He was the most wicked of Israel's kings. About him it was said; "There was never a man like Ahab, who sold himself to do evil in the eyes of the Lord." (I Kings 21:25). The list of Ahab's sins is mind-boggling. He married wicked Jezebel, and he participated, or at least approved of the murder of God's prophets. He disobeyed God by not putting the King of Syria (Ben-Hadad) to death. He approved the murder of Naboth, and he promoted false worship throughout Israel. And yet, at the end of his life, he repented and cried out to God for forgiveness, and God heard him and forgave him (I Kings 21:25-29).

A second example is God's impending judgment on Nineveh as revealed in the book of Jonah. When Jonah finally arrived at Nineveh and preached God's judgment, the people,

212

from the king down, repented, and God chose to withhold His wrath and show mercy – much to the consternation of Jonah!

The list could go on and on. David shown mercy in his sin with Bathsheba. Jonah showed mercy in the belly of the great fish. God showing mercy time and time again to the Israelites in the book of Judges. Why do I share this truth that many of us have heard for years? Because we forget how merciful God is! Jesus is called a "merciful high priest" (Hebrews 2:17), and we need one!

God's mercy is important in two ways for us. Number one, we must never forget that God longs to show mercy to the lost (II Peter 3:9). No one, absolutely no one, is beyond the mercy of God if they cry out in repentance and ask for forgiveness. Paul settled this once for all, when he wrote in I Timothy 1:15-16 that God forgave him, the worst of sinners, so that we would forever remember the truth that no one is beyond saving.

The second truth is this, that God longs to show His children mercy. He waits for us to cry out in repentance, and acknowledgement of our sins. And He rushes to show mercy. Romans 5:9-10 tells us that God desires to do this "much more" for His children.

As you read these words, maybe you are struggling with forgiveness of sins (or better yet, the truth of forgiveness of sins). Maybe you are wondering can God use me anymore, have I sinned beyond His gracious forgiveness? Has He had enough of me and my sins? O dear friend, God longs to show you mercy, He longs to exercise the "mercy rule". He waits to hear from you, and then He will rush with forgiveness and renewed commissioning. Jesus' words to Peter about forgiving seven times seventy (Matthew 18:22) were not just an admonition for us, but a revelation of God's character. We must forgive others, but we must first remember God's willingness and desire to forgive us. He longs to show mercy, He is waiting right now for you to come to Him and ask for it. Then you and I can say along with the psalmist; "Praise be to the Lord, for He has heard my cry for mercy." (Psalm 28:6). Thank God for the "mercy rule"!

# 57
# THE MISSING JEWEL

I lost something, actually something very valuable. I was somewhat aware of it, but somehow let some time pass before I really got serious about finding it. Before I tell you what I lost, let me tell you about a 67 year old English woman by the name of Joan Spiers, who also lost something very valuable. Joan lost her valuable certified diamond antique wedding ring. It was not just the value of the ring, which was considerable, but the sentimental value as the ring was given to her by her late husband.

Joan lost her ring two years ago down a hotel toilet. After she lost the ring, a waste firm was hired to retrieve it. They emptied the entire 12,000 gallon septic tank, sifting through all the waste carefully, but could not find it. They then inserted a camera inside the pipes to see if the ring was lodged somewhere. This also met without success. They even sent someone in with a metal detector, but to no avail. When they were all done, they emptied the sewage into the Thames Water Site.

Two years past, and the same waste firm was hired to clean out one of the sewage works channels. It was then that the ring was found by an honest worker. He remembered seeing a photo of the ring two years earlier and brought the ring back to Joan. That was quite a moment.

For some reason, wedding rings seem to be one of the more valuable things that are lost. My wife Bev has lost her wedding ring twice in the years we have been married. Thankfully, both times it was found. Our daughter-in-law, Wendy, lost her wedding ring (worth considerably more than Bev's), but sadly never found it.

I, personally, don't have a diamond wedding ring. However, I am glad the ring Bev gave me on our wedding day is still on my finger. I've not lost that, but I had lost something even more valuable than a diamond wedding ring. I lost Personal Worship. It's embarrassing for me to write those words for others to read, but I'm afraid it's true. You see, it's embarrassing because I often teach and do seminars on "How to have Personal Worship Times", or "Why Personal Worship Times are important for you and God". But I lost it, that is, I lost my personal worship time. Not my devotions, quiet time or bible study, but my time where I singularly and solely focus on worshipping God through singing, praise and scripture. Not quite sure why I lost it, or even when I first began to lose it. I would be cognizant of it at times and determine to do something about it, but then time would slip away.

There were probably a few "reasons" it happened to me. One very practical one was that I have been having significant problems with my throat and voice. This has been going on for quite some time now. I have actually completely lost it many times, and at other times, it has become weak and raspy. So suddenly I couldn't sing worshipful praise songs to God. Very frustrating!

So it could have been that initially I had some very real physical limitations to private worship. But, undoubtedly, there were some other contributing factors to my lack of private worship. I believe that these can be hindrances and obstacles for all of us. Here are a few that seem to challenge each of us; 1) Busy Schedules 2) Physical and Health Issues 3) Substituting Studying for Worship 4) Unanswered Prayers and 5) Indifference. If private worship is lacking in your life, you might want to look again at those possible reasons to see if one fits you. I might add another reason that private worship may be lacking in our lives, and that is that we don't believe it is that important.

Is private worship important? I believe it is immensely so. John 4:23 records Jesus' words telling us that "The Father is seeking those who will worship him in spirit and truth." In many ways, private worship is the forgotten gem, and for many, the missing gem. It is far more valuable than the costliest diamond. In researching costly diamonds I found several in the "millions", with the rare "Pink Diamond" valued at 10.8 million dollars. But who can put a price on private worship? Psalm 29:2 says, "Worship the Lord in the splendor of his holiness."

I have had the joy – and the great responsibility, of serving Christ for many years now. I love to serve my Savior, and find great joy and passion doing that. But, though God is pleased with my service, He desires worship and praise first. They're not automatically the same. I came across this verse recently, and it was part of what God used to get me to realize I had lost my personal worship. It's in Zephaniah 3:9. Here it is: "Then I will give all people pure lips to worship the Lord and to serve him with one purpose." Did you notice the order, to worship and to serve? Even in glory that will be the priority and arrangement.

Have you "lost it"? Is the Spirit of God prompting you to

realize you've lost it? Are you desirous of "finding it"? Allison Berry also lost her diamond ring. Her diamond ring was valued at $70,000, and she was determined to find it. Hers also was lost down a toilet (slid off her finger while flushing the toilet), and this time at an expensive restaurant. So, she hired "Mr. Rooter" to retrieve it. They stuck a camera down the toilet and through the pipes. It was seen three feet under the ground and five feet along the pipe. They "jack-hammered" the floor for 1 ½ hours and worked for another 8 hours and retrieved the ring. Allison said; "Forget diamonds being a girl's best friend, plumbers are a girl's best friend!"

Allison was pretty serious about finding her gem. I wonder, are we? Have you lost it? Do you want to find it? Are you willing to go to great lengths to retrieve it? We will worship God joyfully throughout eternity and around the throne – let's start practicing for it right now! Here are some suggestions: 1) Search your heart and life – is the worship gem missing? 2) Confess it to God. 3) Search for it with all your being. 4) Then take the following steps: a) Look up "worship and praise passages" (for example Revelation 4 & 5; Isaiah 40; Daniel 2 & 4; and a plethora of others). b) Grab your hymn book and your I-Pod or Smart Phone, CDs or whatever you use to listen to and sing along with Christian music. c) Stand, raise hands, kneel, sit, walk run, ot whatever you do, and join your whole body, soul and spirit in worship and praise. Go ahead, it's private and nobody's watching. Have a "rehearsal" for that future day. Worship, and watch service flow.

# 58
# THE MUSHROOM AFFECT

Okay, here is the truth up front, I don't like mushrooms! I know, I know, there are many of you right now ready to rise up in defense of mushrooms (like my wife, daughter, and daughter-in-laws). But, really, have you ever thought about mushrooms? I mean they are nasty looking, grow in damp places, and how is this for the technical definition of a mushroom; "A fleshy, spore-bearing fruiting body of fungus." There, I rest my case! I mean, a "fungus!" Yuck!

I hate to give press to the subject of mushrooms, but I continue on. There are about 5,000 different types of mushrooms, and of those 5,000, one hundred of them can cause sickness. Of the 100, there are about 12 that are lethal. Now, here is a somewhat discouraging note for me, most of the varieties of mushroom are found in the Great Lakes Region (I'm originally from Michigan). More than two thirds of all varieties of mushrooms are found in this area.

So, we got a fleshy fungus that can kill you. Anybody else picking up on this? I have a new favorite author. Not just because of some of the books he wrote, but more importantly, his thoughts on mushrooms. Alexandre Dumas (he wrote, among others, *The Three Musketeers* and *The Count of Monte Cristo*) once said; "*I confess that nothing frightens me more than the appearance of mushrooms on the table, especially in a small provincial town.*" Now, I wish I could stop right here, because I feel like I could "rest my case" against mushrooms. But, sadly, I have found something good, in fact, something rather wonderful about mushrooms. Sigh!

Do you know what the largest living thing in the world is? It is a mushroom! The particular type of mushroom is a "honey fungus" (Armillaria ostoyae). The largest ever recorded was found in Malheur National Forest in Oregon. It covers 2,200 acres and is between 2,000 to 8,000 years old! Most of it is underground, and to quote; "in the form of a massive mat of tentacle-like white mycelia (roots)."

Now here is where I must give mushrooms their due, not because of taste (my opinion), but because of the beautiful picture it portrays. You see, the honey fungus for a long time, was thought to be several independent mushrooms. Literally all over the 2,200 acres. But then it was found to have "one root system". They all were connected to the same root! So, though on the surface there were many mushrooms, they all were connected under the ground.

I often like to say that "God has a variety hour". Meaning that God is into variety, and that He is not into "sameness". You are unique, and God has designed you that way. But here is the completing thought, that though God's Body has variety, we are all connected. The connecting "root" is Jesus Christ. We are different – especially on the surface – but we all belong to each other (that is, those in the Body of Christ).

This is a major truth we sometimes forget. The Apostle Paul reminds us in Romans 14:7; "None of us lives to himself alone and none of us dies to himself alone." You see, we are all "connected together". Switching metaphors for a moment, and moving away from a connecting root to a corporate body, Paul writes; "The body is a unit, though it is made up of many parts; and though all its parts are many, they form one body. So it is with Christ…Now the body is not made up of one part but of many." (I Corinthians 12:12, 14)

Now, back to the "root metaphor." Jesus is called the "Root" in Isaiah 11:10, Romans 15:12, Revelation 5:5, and Revelation 22:16. This picture represents a couple things. First of all, He is our root. Our life – spiritual life – comes from Him. If we were not connected to Jesus, our root, we would be dead (and we are, apart from Him, Ephesians 2:1). A corollary thought could be, if we don't stay connected to Jesus in our abiding, our fruit will dry up.

But the second picture represents how we cannot be disconnected from one another. We are different and unique from one another. We have our own calling and giftedness, but we never lose the "family connection". We are tied in with each other, we are not "independent" – a favorite word for some of us! Again, Paul writes in Galatians 6:10; "Therefore, as we have opportunity, let us do good to all people, especially to those who belong to the family of believers."

Friends, we are "the largest living organism in the world" (the body of unsaved is not "spiritually living"). We are massive – probably much more than we realize. And we are all connected to the same root, Jesus Christ. So let's remember this. There are over 5,000 types of mushrooms, but there are many thousands of individual Christians (and many in their own little movement). But we are all connected at the deepest point, the Root, Jesus. Okay, so I admit, there is something good about mushrooms. They give us a great picture of how we are united with Christ – but I still don't have to eat them!

Bruce McDonald

# 59
# THE POWER OF WORDS

Perhaps no writer of scripture portrays the power of words like James, the Lord's half brother. Proverbs says more, but James says it succinctly and graphically. If you have not read James 3:1-12 lately, you ought to read it. What a world of disaster the tongue (our words) can create. A great reminder and an important warning. No wonder Ecclesiastes puts it bluntly – "Let your words be few" (Ecclesiastes 5:2). James gave us these familiar words – "Everyone should be quick to listen and slow to speak" (James 1:19). Wars have been started, families divided, and irreparable harm have all come from our words.

Having said the above, there is still something positive to be said for words. The right choice of words, and the right timing in the use of them, make for some of the most powerful and healthy impact we can have in anyone's life. Hebrews 10:25 tells us to "encourage one another", and certainly the thought is to use our words. Most of us like to quote Proverbs 25:11, "A word aptly spoken is like apples of gold in settings of silver". What a wonderful picture! God is called the God of encouragement (see II Corinthians 1:1-7 and II Thessalonians 2:16,-17), and He oftentimes desires to encourage us through the words of others – apples of gold. There are several accounts in scripture where someone came alongside another to speak words of encouragement into their lives.

That happened to me recently, and it came from an unusual, or should I say, unexpected, source. I had been home from the hospital for a few days after my knee surgery when our dear friends, Ryan and Julie, came over. They themselves are a continual source of encouragement and blessing to Bev and I, but God chose to use someone else in their family to speak words of encouragement.

Ryan and Julie have two daughters, Jessica and Katie, who were 6 and 8 at the time. Julie came back over with the girls because she said Katie had something special for me. When they arrived, Katie presented me with two drawings she had done. The first was a picture (brightly colored) of me on crutches and her standing next to me – we are both smiling! The other picture was of a rainbow with the name God underneath it. Great pictures and ones that made me smile. But she wrote words on each of them – "Hope you feel better" and "Take care". The most important words she wrote were "love Katie". Talk about melting your heart! There is even more though, she also typed (eight years old) two Bible verses on the drawings – Hebrews 11:27 & 12:1-2. I have to confess I thought I could throw away my crutches at that point and take off running! How powerful are words of love and encouragement! God spoke to and through Katie that day – and continues to do so, since I have her pictures and words on my refrigerator.

What if we, as adults, decided to let our words be used of God to encourage others? What a world this would be, even in the church and in our homes. Proverbs 12:18 says "The tongue of the wise brings healing", I experienced that from Katie.

Bruce McDonald

# 60
# "THE ROAD TO AWE"

That was the title of an article in a magazine my wife purchased. The magazine was *Sunset, living in the west.* The article was on visiting Glacier National Park. It gave suggestions for touring the park, and seven destinations to see while you're there. It was a fun article to read, and I must admit, of all the National Parks our family has seen, we rate Glacier at the top. It truly is an awe-inspiring place to see and visit. Now, many of you reading this chapter do not live in the west, and even for those of us who do, the drive is quite far. So, you may not ever experience this awe-inspiring place. But I have good news for you, you can experience an even greater "Road to Awe". The believer in Christ has the great privilege and benefit to have a life lived on the road to awe. Let me remind you of some unbelievable stops on our way to our final destination.

First of all, we are literally on the road to awe. Our final destination – heaven – will be the grandest place of awe in the universe. We are on our way there, but we have the unimaginable joy of journeying on a road right now that is filled with awe-inspiring moments. Sadly, we can travel this

224

road and not take time to notice awe-inspiring moments. Like a visitor to Glacier who has their head down, reading a book while they're traveling through the park on the "Going-to-the-Sun-Road", or someone on a cell phone the entire time they are passing beautiful "Lake McDonald" (no kidding). We, as believers, can miss so many awe-inspiring moments. And the truly amazing thing is, we, as believers, can see and appreciate so much more than those who do not know our Savior/Creator God. God has literally "littered the landscape" with awe-inspiring moments. Let's think of these.

The "Road to Awe" is characterized by God's Creation and His Salvation. In regard to creation – God has made it all! "It is I who made the earth and created mankind upon it. My own hands stretched out the heavens; I marshaled the starry hosts." (Isaiah 45:12) There it is – everything was made by God; this earth, mankind and all the stars and planets of the heavens. So, as we travel this road to Awe (heaven), we are reminded that the road we are on is a road filled with "present awe". The mountains, the grass, the trees, the flowers, the lakes and rivers, the large oceans, and the quiet ponds, are all works of the Creator God. The rain falling, the snow falling, the sun shining, and the wind blowing, are works of His hands. Stop…not only smell the roses, but stoop down and look at their intricate design. Gaze at mountain peaks, dig your toes in the sand, and skip a rock across the water. Marvel at the Creator and His creation. Look at His wonders in the stars, get lost in the vastness and the orderliness of His sprawling universe. Lie in the grass, or sit in a lawn chair, and just stare at the stars, try counting them! Turn your eyes to His crowning creation – mankind! Especially women! (I had to say that because my wife will read this)

But, in all seriousness, what beauty and variety He has made. Get lost in a child's giggle or the touch of a loved one. Look at the variation of God's creative work among humanity, the colors, size and uniqueness of each individual. Learn to "savor moments", to see what your eyes were designed to see. All of creation points to a God who has made all things well, but, also to a God who has made all things for us!

But the greatest awe-inspiring moments come when we behold His work in salvation through the wonder of the cross. Stop and gaze at the Atoning work of Christ on our behalf. Let your breath be taken away by His substitutionary death for us. His suffering on our behalf. Our justification (made right with God) through His finished work on the cross. Our reconciliation because Christ has met the holy demands of God for sins to be paid for. The stunning fact of all our sins forgiven. Oh dear friends, this is our most awe-inspiring moment on our road to Awe. As we stop our hectic, distracted life on this road, and lift our eyes to the cross, we agree with the Old Testament writer Micah, who said; "Who is a God like you, who pardons sin and forgives the transgression of the remnant of his inheritance." (Micah 6:18)

Friends, why not right now, metaphorically speaking, "pull the car over, get out of the car, walk out into that field, and look all around you. See His creation and His salvation, be filled with awe – right now – and then say in agreement with the Psalmist; "All heaven will praise your great wonders, Lord, myriads of angels will praise you for your faithfulness. For who in the heavens can compare with the Lord? What mightiest angel is like the Lord? The highest angelic powers stand in awe of God. He is far more awesome than all who surround his throne. O Lord God of Heaven's Armies! Where is there anyone as mighty as you, O Lord?" (Psalm 89:6-8) Friends, to miss the sights and spectacular scenery of Glacier National Park is one thing, but to miss the awe-inspiring sights on our road to Awe is quite another. Enjoy and be in awe, on the road to Awe.

# 61
# A CARD CARRYING MEMBER

Fraternities, secret societies, orders, and clubs all have their required membership. Not sure if you have belonged to any of the four that I listed. There are an abundance of fraternities and sororities, somewhat secret in nature. They all love to have their "Greek Insignias". There are also many service and civic clubs in existence today. They range from the Kiwanis, the Knights of Columbus, the Rotary Club, the Shriners, the Lion's Club, Toastmasters International and the Elks. Then you have your more secret clubs or societies-like the Masons. Speaking of secret orders or societies, here are the top ten most secret orders or societies in America (most of these are International as well): Skull and Bones (Yale's Secret Society, with both President Bush's as members, The Freemasons, Rosicrucians, Ordo Templis Orientis, Hermetric Order of the Golden dawn, The Knights Templar (not the original ones from the 12th century, but a branch of Masonry), Illuminati (you have to go back to 1776 to join them)\, The Bilderburg Group, The Priority of Sion (not really, just a made-up one of author Dan Brown in The Da Vinci Code!), and the Opus Dei Priests. There you go, in case you were looking to join a secret group!

Of course, in all these, you have to be "chosen" or "invited" – no applying. I was tempted to put that wonderfully secret society The Raccoon Lodge, but I resisted. You remember the Raccoon Lodge of Brooklyn, New York right? Its most famous members were Ralph Kramden and Ed Norton. Otherwise known as Jackie Gleason and Art Carney of The Honeymooners. Okay, go ask your parents or grandparents on that one!

Well, it may be that you've never joined, or have been asked to join a club, society, order, or for that matter, even a sorority or fraternity. But I want to let you know that you are already in a rather large "club", and you probably didn't even know it. The club doesn't have secret handshakes, signs or other cryptic greetings. And you can't find any official bylaws or "rites" to be a member. However, having said that, there has probably been more written on it than any other society or club. And you do have your own "handbook". You probably think I'm talking about being a "Christian", and actually I'm not. No, the club or order I speak of is one that we sometimes try to deny we belong to. But, deny it as you may, you and I are card carrying members of this order. The order doesn't have a neat sounding title like Lions, Elks or Knights, no; it's actually a rather humbling title for our group. So, are you ready? Your order – and mine, is that of "Sinners".

Ouch, that hurts! But you say, "Wait a minute, I'm not a sinner, I'm a saint. I've been washed in the blood of Christ, My sins are forgiven, and I am now a new creation, all things are made new." Well, that's good, and it's certainly Biblical. And that is what your IDENTITY is, and you and I should always remember that. However, having said that, you still have a lifelong membership in the "Sinners Club". In fact, you weren't asked to join it – you were born into it. And while you're on earth, you "can't leave it".

So our identity is that of a child of God, but in current practice and actuality, I'm still a practicing (card carrying) sinner. I wish it were different, but it's not. Sin was not eradicated from my life – the penalty was – when I trusted Christ as Savior. I'll belong to this club, this order (maybe better yet, disorder) as long as I'm earthbound. But, and here's the purpose of this chapter, your and my propensity to sin, can still work for God's glory, and bring us the measure of freedom we desire while still here on earth.

To help understand this, I want you to recall an event from the life of Christ. It's a wonderful story, here's what takes place: Jesus has just called Matthew (Levi) to follow Him. This story is found in three of the Gospels – Matthew, Mark and Luke. After Matthew leaves everything to follow Jesus, he throws a large banquet for Jesus. For this banquet, he also invites many of his friends – tax collectors, and other so- called riff-raff.

Here is how Mark records it; "Later Jesus was having dinner at Levi's house. Many tax collectors and sinners who were followers of Jesus were eating with him and his disciples." (Mark 2:15) Did you catch that? "Sinners who were followers of Jesus". No need to try and sanitize this, it is what it says – many sinners who were followers of Jesus. Notice, not people "who had been sinners", no, "people who were sinners". You may ask, "How can this be, how can sinners be followers of Jesus?" Well, do you know a follower of Jesus who is not a sinner? Who does not sin at some time, in word, thought, deed and attitude? Either sins of omission or commission? But this actuality, or confession, does not have to lead down a path of discouragement and bondage. I said the realization of our "card- carrying sinner's membership" can actually lead to greater glory for God and greater freedom for ourselves.

First of all, as many of you are already thinking – and

perhaps concerned that I haven't brought it up - there is victory in Christ Jesus, and Christ's coming not only paid for the price of sin, but also made available the potential to have victory over the power of sin. Revelation 1 puts it succinctly; "To him who loves us, and has freed us from our sins." And we know that all the passages of Scripture that admonish us not to sin, mean that God has made provision that we don't sin. John writes under the inspiration of the Holy Spirit that "we might not sin" (I John 2:1), but before that he says; "If we claim to be without sin, we deceive ourselves…if we claim we have not sinned, we make him[God] out to be a liar." (I John 1:8, 10) That's pretty clear. So yes, Christ does want us to sin less and less, and He has made provision through His atoning work and the presence of the Holy Spirit to help us, but sadly – we still sin.

Can you identify with Jonathan Edward's words from his journal? *"On January 12, 1723 I made a solemn dedication of myself to God, and wrote it down; giving up myself, and all that I had to God; to be for the future, in no respect, my own, to act as one who had no right to himself, in any respect, and solemnly vowed to take God for my whole portion and felicity; looking on nothing else, as any part of my obedience; engaging to fight with all my might against the world, the flesh, the devil, to the end of my life. But I have reason to be infinitely humbled, when I consider how much I have failed of answering my obligation."*

We sin – more than we want to, but God's grace is more than sufficient; "Where sin increased, grace increased all the more." (Romans 5:20) We sin – more than we want to, but Christ died for us when we were deep in sin; "Christ died for the ungodly." (Romans 5:6) We sin – more than we want to, but God's forgiveness of our sins, past and present, point to His amazing grace, and reveal a glory this is incomprehensible; "How great is the love the Father has lavished on us." (I John 3:1)

The truth is, you and I will never get out of the "sinners

order" while we are still here on earth. We'll always be card carrying members, but Jesus has always been called the "the friend of sinners" (Matthew 11:19). In the Beatitudes, Jesus said "blessed are those who mourn" (Matthew 5:4) and He wasn't just talking about unsaved people. We mourn and grieve over our sins, but we rejoice and are forever grateful, that Christ still loves us and forgives us. There is a difference between trying to stop sinning and trying to stop being a sinner. Learn the difference. You don't have to prove that Christ made the right choice in saving you from your sins.

Bruce McDonald

# 62
# THE SEARCH FOR PURPOSE

One of the more disturbing experiences I've encountered when working for many years with professional athletes, was a phone call from a distraught football player's wife telling me that her husband was contemplating suicide. I rushed over to the house and found the man standing in the backyard. He indeed was considering suicide. When I quickly asked the reason, he shared that he had been listening to the local sports talk radio, and the announcer was having people call in with their "worst" stories of this athlete's playing. The DJ kept up a venomous stream of verbal attacks on this player, and was encouraging others to call in and vent their frustration with this player's ability on the field.

I was shocked, and when the player said to me that he no longer had a reason to live, I realized that his entire reason for existence and his sense of self-worth were totally dependent on his ability to perform on the field. Worse yet, it was dependent on what others thought of his performance. I thought of that experience this past week when I read an issue of Sports Illustrated. A well-known college coach, who coaches a prestigious school, had his son recently resign from the coaching staff. The reason why was that he could no longer take the constant criticism from the media. He was so discouraged, he even despaired of life. Before I move onto an application for us, let me say the pro football player did not make an attempt on his life; he surrendered his life to Christ, and to this day is walking with the Lord.

The above two stories illustrate the struggle we all have with a sense of purpose and significance. It is easy to criticize these two men, but who of us does not struggle at times with these issues? Pastors, missionaries, housewives, teachers, businessmen, students, construction workers, and any other occupation you can think of, has moments when a sense of purpose has vanished. The cause can be any of a number of reasons. Perhaps failure or confusion, trials or lost dreams, or just a lack of affirmation or productivity. The list could go on and on. God does not want us to live purposeless lives. He does not desire that we feel a sense of confusion over our existence. Knowing we have purpose and significance is not the same as always knowing the exactness of our calling. Most of us have times when we struggle with "knowing God's will". But this is not the same as wondering if I should be here at this time, and if I have any significance.

If we are to live passionate, purposeful lives, we must come to grips with the fact that we are important to God, and He has us here for a reason and a purpose. Scripture encourages us in these vital areas. Before the world began God had me in mind (Ephesians 1:4), before space time and matter He chose when I would live, what I would do, and how I would be gifted (Acts 17:26; I Corinthians 12:18; Romans 12:4,5). God did not randomly cast a net into the sea of humanity, and indiscriminately pull out fish (believers) flopping on the shore! He was intentional and purposeful. He had a plan, and He was going to accomplish it (Ephesians 1:11).

If you are struggling with this truth right now, may I encourage you to find your bible and turn to II Timothy 1:9. Read this verse slowly several times aloud, and ask God to speak to your heart about the truth of this verse. "God, who has saved us and called us with a holy calling, not according to our works, but according to his own purpose and grace, which was given to us in Christ Jesus before time began." Do not let our enemy convince you that you are not significant, and that your life has no purpose. You were created in the heart and mind of God, and will one-day share eternity with him.

# 63
# THE SLEEPING GOD

Do you feel sometimes that your life is often spent trying to awaken Deity? Have you cried out to God, only to experience silence? You know He is there, you believe in Him with all your heart, but sometimes you feel He is asleep, and no matter what you try, you cannot wake Him. Perhaps at your greatest time of need – at least, it is in your opinion – God seems to be snoozing.

Right now, many of you are starting to feel uncomfortable. These words are pretty strong, and you don't know if you should keep reading. This might be a good time to share with you a word that theologians sometimes use when trying to explain some of God's words and pictures to us. The word is "anthropomorphism". It is a word that basically means attributing a human characteristic to God. God uses these terms sometimes, such as when he says "He was surprised at something", or, when he says, "He changed His mind about something". Biblical writers and Biblical characters often use anthropomorphic terms in addressing God or describing God. You read about God's heart, mouth, mind, hand or feet.

Oftentimes these are anthropomorphic terms explaining something about God.

So, back to my question, "Do you feel that sometimes God is asleep when you cry out to Him?" Come on now, be honest. If you have felt this way, you are not alone. People in scripture struggled with these feelings. The Psalmist in Psalm 44:23 spoke for many distraught believers, when he cried out; "Awake O lord! Why do you sleep? Rouse yourself! Do not reject us forever." In fact, just a quick glance at the book of Psalm reveals various writers asking God to wake-up four different times. The prophet Isaiah also cried out, "Awake, awake! Clothe yourself with strength, O arm of the Lord; awake as in days gone by, as in generations of old." (Isaiah 51:9) Sometimes, when God chooses to act on the behalf of His children, people respond as if He just woke-up, "Then the Lord awoke as from sleep, as a man wakes from the stupor of wine." (Psalm 78:65)

So, dear friend, your occasional feelings of approaching a Deity who sleeps is understandable. It seems like it at times! God, of course, does not sleep – ever! God knows we will struggle with feelings like this – and sometimes exasperation and downright panic. But he reassures us that He is the ever-vigilant God, a God who never sleeps; "He who watches over you will not slumber; indeed, he who watches over you will neither slumber nor sleep." (Psalm 121:3-4)

A picture comes to my mind - perhaps of a cartoon I saw one time. Where a cat (say, of Tom and Jerry fame) is trying to tip-toe by a sleeping dog, which suddenly wakes-up, because he is a light sleeper. Or perhaps a scene from the Hobbit, where Bilbo Baggins tries to slip by a sleeping dragon – only to have the dragon suddenly awake. I also think of illustrations from my own life. I am a light-sleeper, and once when one of my teenage sons tried to sneak out of the house I heard and saw him, and "woke-up" and made him go back to bed.

Perhaps when you think of a God who wakes up easily, you think of Him as a light sleeper. He is no such thing! He never sleeps or slumbers, He always watches over you. He is El Roi- "The God who sees" (Genesis 16:13). His eyes always watch over you; "The eyes of the Lord range throughout the earth..." (II Chronicles 16:9) And nothing is hidden from Him; "Nothing in all of creation is hidden from God's sight." (Hebrews 4:13) He not only is always alert and able to see everything, but He always hears everything; "The eyes of the Lord are on the righteous and his ears are attentive to their prayers." (I Peter 3:12) He promises to always – and I do mean always, hear you; "The Lord will hear when I call to him." (Psalm 4:3) And this powerful promise that should assure us for all time; "This is the confidence we have in approaching God; that if we ask anything according to his will, he hears us." (I John 5:14)

So, dear friends, our God is really not a sleeping God – He may seem like it at times. From our perspective (anthropomorphically speaking), He may seem to be in a dead sleep. So, we cry out, "Wake-up O God, wake-up!" Like the disciples of old, who were in a storm-tossed boat, and Jesus was asleep (so they thought) in the stern. They woke Him and cried out; "Teacher, don't you care if we drown?" (Mark 4:38) Jesus rebuked the waves – and then gave a gentle rebuke to the disciples; "Why are you so afraid? Do you still have no faith?" A weary and tired Jesus in His humanity did fall asleep in the boat – but in His Deity, He was still vigilant and watching over them. Today, the risen Savior never sleeps or slumbers, He does not need to be awakened. Go ahead and call, he does hear – and see – and you can be confident in that.

Bruce Mcdonald

# 64
# THE SMELL OF OBEDIENCE

The sense of smell is a rather amazing gift God has given us. Think where we'd be without it? I wonder what your favorite smells are? For me, I love the fragrance that a Lilac bush gives off. Roses and Orange Blossoms are some of my favorites too. Even a recently mowed lawn or a fresh cut hay field is a sweet aroma. And, as far as food, I love the smell of bacon sizzling when we are staying at a camp ground, or better yet, the smell of Turkey in the oven during the holidays. Lastly, probably the best fragrance for me is any perfume that my wife is wearing!

The gift of being able to smell things is a wonderful blessing from our Creator. I recently read where the average human has 5 to 6 million yellowish receptors high up in their nasal passage. That's pretty amazing! Of course, when it comes to the ability to smell things, we take a backseat to many of God's other creations. The rabbit has 100 million receptors and the dog has 220 million. A large bear has a brain one third the size of a human brain, but the part that is devoted to smell is 5 times larger than a humans.

It's not just land animals that the Creator has endowed with the uncanny ability to smell, two thirds of the shark's brain is devoted to smell. They can detect the tiniest drop of blood more than a mile away (yikes!). Smell is also not confined to noses and the nasal passages. The moth can smell something 6 to 7 miles away – with its feathery antennas. The snake smells with their tongues, and albatross' are one of the few birds that hunt with their sense of smell, not with their sight like other birds.

I think for most of us, we are most amazed at a dog's ability to smell. A bloodhound can smell the trail of someone days after that person has walked the trail. A dog can even recognize the smell of a certain neighborhood cat – and smell what it had for dinner! Perhaps one of the most amazing things about a dog's ability to smell, is that dogs can be trained to smell certain types of cancer, and be more successful at it than our modern day scanning equipment!

Yes, thank God for our sense of smell. But here's a question, "Does God smell things?" I know that trying to determine what God looks like is a challenge, because many of the terms and expressions God uses about Himself are anthropomorphic – as I talked about in the last chapter. Meaning he uses human terms and expressions to convey certain things. But scripture repeatedly uses expressions like "God saw" or "God heard" and "God smelled". If you just looked at the times the Word of God says something was a pleasing aroma to God, you would find that expression 39 times.

So does God "smell" things, and what things smell "good to Him"? I got to thinking about this the other day. As I write this, I'm teaching an Adult Equipping Class with a friend of mine. During the class, we were teaching on a passage that talked about a certain sacrifice that was a pleasant aroma to God. One of the people in the class raised his hand and asked, "does that mean God has certain smells that He likes?" For example, if the bull that was being burned on the offering smelled like a good steak to God? Wow, I had never thought of that! Then he followed that up with asking if God had any other favorite smells, since we are created in His image. Fun question!

I shared with this gentleman, after telling him I appreciated his thoughts – I really did, that the aroma that was pleasing to God was actually "the smell of obedience". God had instructed the Israelites to offer certain types of sacrifice to atone for their sins (He also instructed them to offer other types of sacrifices). When they obeyed Him, this was a pleasing aroma to God. Evidently, obedience has its own aroma to God. In fact, more than even the smell of the lamb, goat or bull being offered. Samuel reminded King Saul, that "to obey is better than to sacrifice". (I Samuel 15:22) Some years later King David wrote, "You do not delight in sacrifice, or I would bring it; you do not take pleasure in burnt offerings. The sacrifices of God are a broken spirit; a broken and contrite heart, O God, you will not despise." (Psalm 51:16-17)

So obedience, has its own type of smell, and this is God's favorite smell. During the Old Testament period, and the early days of the New Testament, people had the opportunity to offer something sweet smelling to God, and that was their obedience in either performing the sacrifices, or bringing an offering for the sacrifices. Today, we still have the opportunity to offer sweet smelling sacrifices to God, and we can do it daily! Any sacrifice that is prompted by obedience is a pleasing aroma to God. Perhaps some of us are uncomfortable with the word obedience, you feel it is too "Old Testament". Well, for one thing, the word "obedience" or "obey" is mentioned over 250 times in the Bible – including the New Testament. So that should tell us something!

Jesus Himself told us, "If you love me, you will obey what I command." (John 14:15) Hmm… that kind of goes in the face of a spirit that says "God loves me, and it doesn't matter how I live." Evidently, love prompts and produces something in us, and that is obedience. II John 1:6 reiterates this, "And this is love: that we walk in obedience to his commands." It couldn't be any clearer; our love prompts us to obey Him, which in turn is a pleasing aroma to Him. Maybe that's why the New Testament writers use the terminology of "sacrifices" when talking about a life pleasing to God; "Therefore, I urge you brothers, in view of God's mercies [not His stern demands] to offer your bodies as living sacrifices, holy and pleasing to God-this is your spiritual act of worship." And, "Through Jesus, therefore, let us continually offer to God a sacrifice of praise." (Romans 12:1-2 & Hebrews 13:15)

Hey, think about it. What a joy and privilege we can offer up one of God's sweetest fragrances – obedience. It doesn't take a "Rocket Scientist" to figure out where obedience falls for the believer. God has made it clear in scripture what pleases Him, and what does not please Him. And it is a win-win situation. Because He also knows what is best for us, and what things will hurt us. And, by the Spirit of God, we can live this way. "His commands are not burdensome" (I John 5:3) If a moth can smell something 6 or 7 miles away, imagine a God who can smell something from an infinite distance. Let's bring a smile to God's face as He inhales a sweet aroma from our life of joyful obedience.

Bruce McDonald

65

# THE STOPS OF A GOOD MAN OR WOMAN

Most of us do not like stops. Whether it is at a traffic light or someone telling us to stop doing something we enjoy. We like forward movement, and bristle at having to stop when we want to continue. It seems early in life we learned to not like the word, "stop." For some reason, our mothers didn't want us to play with grandma's china set when we were 3 years old! So, we would hear, "stop that right now!" As we got older, we would hear, "stop hitting your little brother." Then, when we became teenagers, it was, "stop making that face or you're grounded!" Stop, stop, stop! It was never our favorite word!

As adults, we have not fared any better at handling the "stop" word. Especially when it comes to charting a course of action we desire to take. Or, to take a spiritual slant on it, we do not like "stops" when we feel we are heading in the direction that God is leading us - or one that we feel would honor Him. I mean, "What is the deal with all these stops!"

Oftentimes, I have felt, and many times I have heard, "This

seems like God's will, but every time I feel there is an open door – it closes! There have been so many stops along the way that I don't know if I'll ever arrive at the destination (spiritual or literal) that I felt was God's call on my life." Why does God allow stops? In fact, why does so much of life seem to be made up of stops?

When I was a young man, and early on in my ministry, I would often hear people quote a verse from the King James Version of the Bible; "The steps of a good man are ordered by the Lord." (Psalm 37:23) None of the other translations translate this verse quite like that, but it was one that was often repeated. I remember the first time (maybe the only time) I heard a different slant on that verse. I was 26 years old and a Youth Pastor at a church in Northfield, Ohio. Our Senior Pastor, Lynn Rogers, was gone on a Sabbatical leave and our interim pastor (actually, pastor emeritus), Earl Willets, was preaching. At some point in his message he said, "Remember, it is not only the 'steps' of a good man that are ordered by the Lord, but also the 'stops' of a good man that are ordered by the Lord." When I heard him say it that day, I thought that was pretty clever – you know, switching one letter in the word. That's about as far as it went in my mind. Little did I know at that time how profound his words were! You see, God is not just the God of the forward moves (steps), but also of the standstill moves (stops). It is hard for us to see any value in stopping. In fact, it is hard to see God at all when we are in "stop mode".

Probably many of you remember the story and events of the Apostle Paul's second missionary journey (with Silas this time). It is found in Acts chapter 16, and the story – at least at its beginning, is filled with "stops". Here is how their journey starts out; "Paul and his companions traveled throughout the region of Phrygia and Galatia, having been kept by the Holy Spirit from preaching the word in the province of Asia. When they came to the border of Mysia, they tried to enter Bithynia, but the Spirit of Jesus would not allow them to. So they passed by Mysia and went down to Troas. During the night Paul had a vision of a man from Macedonia standing and begging him, 'Come over to Macedonia and help us.'" Just in this brief passage you have the Spirit of God "stopping" the Apostles three times from their intended destination. Once from going into Asia, once from going into Bithynia and once from staying in Troas to minister. I'm sure at the time this must have seemed confusing. After all, they were going about sharing the gospel. But God had a better plan (eventually to go to Macedonia and beyond).

I must confess, from my finite human perspective – even when "bathed in prayer", I often cannot comprehend why God orchestrates "stops". Perhaps you are in one now, or maybe you have been in one for a long time now. God's stops are not necessarily "discipline stops", though the evil one would like us to believe this. In fact, they are usually indications that you are in the center of God's will. "Stops" are not wasted times. They certainly can be mysterious and downright confusing at times, but never wasted. God is the Author and Finisher of your life's story (Hebrews 12:1). He has written everyday of your life in His book (Psalm 139:16), and He has included the "stops". History is filled with stories of men and women's attempts to accomplish something, only to be stopped, and then inadvertently discover either something else, or the very thing they were hoping to discover – only in a different way.

I think of my friend Harry. He and his dear wife Lynn surrendered to God's call to go to East Pakistan as missionaries. But the Pakistan government continually rejected their visa applications. It was extremely confusing, so while they waited (in a "stop mode"); they went to Hong Kong to help other missionaries. There they "stayed" for 31 years, starting four churches and being instrumental in starting the China Baptist Theological College. Nice "stop", huh?

Believe it or not, your story is the same. God has ordained (planned in advance) not only your steps, but your stops. Has finances stopped you? Has health stopped you? Has family obligations stopped you? Has outside influences stopped you? Has........you name it, any of a number of things that has caused you to stop your intended pursuit. Be encouraged, God is the One who will fulfill His purposes for you; "I cry out to God Most High, to God, who fulfills his purpose for me." (Psalm 57:2) You know, Earl Willets did have it right; "The stops of a good man – or woman, are ordered by the Lord."

Bruce McDonald

# 66
# THROUGH THE EYES OF LOVE

"You are altogether beautiful, my love; there is no flaw in you." (Song of Solomon 4:7) What a beautiful thing to say! These words came from the lips of Solomon to his bride. Song of Solomon is an incredibly romantic book/letter. Depicting the love, intimacy, and eroticism of married life. It is a "turn on" in many ways. Love and sensual relationship depicted and displayed as God intended. Not Hollywood smut, but all the forms of love as God designed – agape, phileo, and eros.

The above verse is true in a genuine love relationship in marriage. It is how we see our partner. As they say, "Love is blind." But it is actually more than that; it looks at our loved one through eyes of genuine love. Not blind to flaws and inconsistencies, but drunk and immersed in love, so as to color and shape all thoughts and feelings of the loved one. Bev and I have been married for almost 45 years. I have changed in my physical appearance, and so has she (though not as much as I). She is still beautiful, and can still take my breath away. But we have changed. Time does that to all of us. However, in some ways, love continues to grow. It deepens, and richness is added. Yes, I can still read Song of Solomon and have my emotions stirred for Bev.

Though the book is on husband/wife relationships, it can also, in a broad way, depict the love of Christ for His Bride. Though I do not agree with some past commentators and theologians that the book is only about Christ and His church (they seem somewhat embarrassed to believe that God would actually have so much sexual and sensual intimacy in scripture), I do believe there are some wonderful applications and truths depicted in our love relationship with Christ. The above verse is especially one of those. Somehow, amazement of amazement, Christ sees us with "no flaws". How can this be? Is He blind with love? Intoxicated with our relationship to Him? Far from it, He sees us as we really are (Psalm 139:1-5; Hebrews 4:13). He knows our flaws – our selfishness, sins, inconsistencies and failures. So how can He see us without flaw? He sees us through the lens of satisfied justice (Propitiation, Romans 3:21-25), and through the lens of satisfied love (Ephesians 2:4). God has wooed us, paid for our sins, cleaned us up (Ezekiel 16:1-14), and made us beautiful in His sight. Positionally, we are without flaw! We are clothed with the righteousness of Christ. He took our sins upon Himself, and we received His righteousness charged to our account (II Corinthians 5:21).

O dear friend, if we could only comprehend that our Beloved Savior, and His Holy Father, find no flaw in us! Who can ever grasp the wonderful truths of Jude 24 and Ephesians 5:27? Those verses tell us that we will one day be presented to God as blameless, without spot or wrinkle, holy, without blemish, and in great splendor. Wow, and double wow! Solomon loved his bride and saw her without flaw. Bev loves me, and loves me despite my flaws. But Christ loves us with an unfailing and unconditional love that will last through eternity. His banner over us is love (SS 2:4). Go forth today knowing you are loved and covered by the righteousness of Christ.

# 67
# TIME TRAVEL!

We live in an interesting age. Through the marvel of unbelievable technology, we have seen things that sometimes are beyond even the mind's imagination. For example, movies and the amazing special affects they present. Dinosaurs come to life, Giant Apes walk the planet, Space Ships hurdle through space and people disappear and reappear right before our eyes. Even cartoon characters seem real now…and donkeys speak! Probably all of us have seen time travel portrayed in movies. The *Star Wars* and *Star Trek* movies and series have captured our imagination. The *Stargate* film, and other time related movies, make us wish we could travel like that.

As I type this chapter, we are getting ready to make the long trip back to the states from the Philippines. Due to lengthy layovers, our travel time will be even longer than necessary. Our actual travel time – with layovers – will be 28 hours. Twenty eight hours to get home! I wish there was a way to walk through some portal and be home, or maybe even hop in some space ship and travel at warp speed and be there in seconds. Alas, it is not to be! We live in space and time, and at this point, cannot transcend it.

Life is like that isn't it? We cannot fast forward to events we'd like to be at. We cannot fast forward to becoming the person we desire to be or even desire someone else to be. In some ways, life is a slow process towards desired results. Our earthly life is all about limitations and restrictions, in the sense of moving towards something. We are not only bound by the laws of gravity, but we are bound by the laws of spiritual inertia. God wants to take a lifetime to grow and mature a person. Granted the length of that lifetime varies for each person, but, nevertheless, it still is one's lifetime.

God isn't in a hurry. He designed it that way. And what is true for our individual lives, is true for our plans and desires. Ministry "seems" to move at glacial speed, and relationships hurl along at the pace of a tortoise. An event we wish would soon pass doesn't, and we seem to perpetually live in that moment. So what is the answer? We can daydream, or watch movies and read books that place us in a fantasy world where everything works out instantly. Or we can trust God and live in the moment. James 5:7 says, "Be patient, then brothers, until the Lord's coming." The main Greek word that is used in the New Testament for "waiting" and being patient is a word that literally means "to stay under", or "to remain". I believe the idea is to not try to run ahead of God's timing. Accept it, rest in it, and allow God to accomplish what He desires to accomplish. This even includes times of trial.

It does seem hard, and, at times, even frustrating, not to mention frightening. But God is there, in the moment. Interestingly, the key to "abiding" and "staying under" is realizing that one day you will experience time travel. We wait patiently, but as James 5:7 says, we do it in the context of the return of Christ. Christ will come back – or He will call us home – and when it happens, it will happen quickly (Revelation22:7,12,20). In fact, much quicker than a movie's time travel. Ours will be in an instant, faster than the blink of an eye. (I Corinthians 15:52) So you will experience the ultimate time travel!

In the meantime, we accept and adjust to living in space and time. We are confident that no time is wasted time. God is in the moment. Yet even in these moments (in light of eternity), there are answers and fulfillments in God's timing. Luke 18:7-8 reminds us, when God does finally act – it is quickly. So, today, as you have time restrictions, remember that God has so designed it for you and me – for now. But one day…we will be transported to a different time and dimension, far, far away, in the blink of an eye.

# 68
# TIMING IS EVERYTHING

Timing really is everything. From joke telling (do you have a family member who gives the punch line too early?) to catching flights. Maxwell Smart of the old *Get Smart* series (in recent times, made into a movie) used to say "missed it by this much!" Timing is important in sports – running a pass route, it is important in cooking – not leaving something in the oven too long, and it is important in meeting deadlines. We live in a world where timing is essential in all aspects of life.

It is no less true when it comes to our spiritual walk. Many of the stories in the Bible reveal moments when people's timing were not in sync with God's. Remember the time when the Israelites were supposed to enter the promise land? God wanted them, by faith, to leave the wilderness and cross into Jordan. However, because of their rebellion, they waited 40 years too long. We have this interesting – and telling remark from Rahab in Joshua 2; "I know the Lord has given you this land, she told them. We are all afraid of you. Everyone in the land is living in terror. For we have heard how the Lord made a dry path for you through the Red Sea when you left Egypt."

Think of it, they waited 40 years too long (when Rahab made these remarks). God had made the hearts of the people of Canaan melt with fear, so that the Israelites would have had less battles and conflicts – but they didn't believe God. And there were times in the Bible when people rushed ahead of God's timing. King Saul comes to mind. He was the people's choice for King when God wanted the people to "wait" for the man of His choosing – that being David. The results of rushing ahead of God's timing were disastrous (see I Samuel 10-12).

If there is anything that is difficult – make that humanly impossible – it is waiting on God's timing, or responding to God's perfect timing. It seems we either do not respond and act when God wants us to, or we rush ahead and get tired of waiting. We take matters in our own hands. I believe that David – as in King David, has much to teach us on this subject.

The story I want to share with you is an amazing story, and one that, I believe, God would use to teach us much. The story takes place in I Samuel 24, and here is the setting. King Saul knows that David has been anointed by God, he knows that the people love David more than he, and he knows that the Spirit of God has left him (an Old Testament thing). While trying to suppress the Philistines, he is seeking to kill David. David is forced to hide out in the desert, being pursued like a renegade criminal. One day, while Saul and his men are chasing David, Saul enters a cave where David and some of his men are hiding. Let's let scripture take up the story from here. "At the place where the road passes some sheepfolds, Saul went into the cave…David and his men were hiding farther back in that very cave! 'Now's your opportunity!' David's men whispered to him. 'Today the Lord is telling you, I will certainly put your enemy into your power, to do with as you wish.' So, David crept forward and cut off a piece of the hem of Saul's robe. But then David's conscience began bothering him because he had cut off Saul's robe. 'The Lord knows I should not have done that to the lord my king,' he said to his men. 'The lord forbid that I should do this to the lord my king and attack the Lord's anointed one, for the Lord himself has chosen him.' So, David restrained his men and did not let them kill Saul."

Have you thought about David's incredible restraint in waiting on God's timing, and not just God's timing, but God's own provision for this calling? Think of several excuses or "reasons" David could have used. Circumstances: Saul "happened" to walk into the cave where David was hiding. Support: David's men all thought he should do this. Logic: Saul was bad and he was ruining the kingdom. Lastly, Assumption: David was supposed to be king. So how did he restrain himself? How did he wait on God's timing? The answer, and this is important for all of us, was in his faith in what God had planned and what God could do.

While David was hiding in that cave – he wrote a psalm! He really did. It is found in Psalm 57. Here is part of what he wrote (call it his journal); "I call out to God Most High, to God who will fulfill his purpose for me...My heart is confident in you, O God; my heart is confident. No wonder I can sing your praises! Wake up, my heart! Wake up, O lyre and harp! I will wake the dawn with my song." Wow, are you kidding me? Here is David surrounded by his enemies (see Psalm 57:4&6), resting and rejoicing in God! The key, I believe, is that he believed that God would fulfill His purpose for him, and that God was fully able to do it in His own timing.

Here is the lesson for all of us – wait on God, wait for His perfect timing. I know there are times when we move forward in bold faith, but more often, there are times when God says; "I haven't forgotten you, and I am still working out my plan for you. Trust me and wait on my timing." It is hard – humanly impossible, but faith in God - who He is, faith in His ability -

what He can do, and faith in His wisdom and timing, are the key to sleeping well at night and rejoicing in the God who will fulfill His purpose for me. Timing is everything.

# 69
# MAGNIFIED DEPENDENCE

Aren't "just in time" stories thrilling to read about? They get your adrenalin flowing, your heart pumping, and then, wham, the rescue takes place! How about these two that happened not too long ago? A trucker driving a big rig on I-70 collided with a mini-van; the big rig flipped on its side and skidded down the highway. The huge truck lay on its side for several minutes as the driver slowly regained consciousness and tried to escape the truck. Smoke and steam were rising from the rig. He desperately attempted to open the door that was now above him. He couldn't, despite repeatedly kicking at the door. He could smell, see, and hear that his rig was about to burst in flames.

When all hope seemed gone, two off-duty fireman came upon the scene. At the same time, a surveyor who had been working nearby, ran towards the truck. All three men got there at the same moment. The firemen tried to open the door, but couldn't. The surveyor had been working with a sledgehammer, driving stakes into the ground. His sledgehammer still in his hands, he smashed the window of the cab, and the two firemen pulled the driver out. As they were dragging the driver away from the truck, there was a loud, earthshaking explosion, and the entire truck had burst into flames. He was rescued (unharmed) "just in time".

Or how about Lawrence Bishop? Lawrence was hiking in California's Sierra National Forest. After ascending a high peak, he was coming down a 10,000 foot descent. He accidentally made a wrong term and tumbled over the side of the cliff. He was able to grab onto something to stop his fall and slide. He then managed to find a small hole and a rock sticking out, and pressed himself to the side of the steep precipice, holding the rock, and wedging his foot in the hole. He was bruised and sore – and then he waited. One hour passed, then another, and then a day and night, and then on into the next day and night. For 52 hours he clung to this position. But, finally, exhaustion and dehydration set in. He realized he was going to die, either in that position, or when he lost consciousness by falling down the steep cliff. Right as he began to lose final control, two rescuers came scaling across the mountain and grabbed him. They held him in that position as a helicopter flew to the scene to rescue him. He was rescued "just in time".

Man, don't you love "just in time" stories. Don't you love to read about them or to hear about them? Yeah, good stuff! But hey, I wonder what Lawrence Bishop and the truck driver thought? Was that really cool? I'm sure you wouldn't have wanted to be in the smoking cab or on the dangerous cliff? Of course you wouldn't, and neither would I. But you know what, you and I often face "just in time moments". It's part of the Christian life, its part of the design of God. God actually delights in coming through "just in time". Not early, and not late, but just in time. Just a cursory or casual reading of scripture reveals how God has been the God of "just in time" since the beginning.

Take a moment right now to think of some of those times that are mentioned in the Bible. Or if someone is close by, talk between the two of you and see which ones you can come up with. Go ahead, I'll wait… Okay, are you back? Then, let's go ahead with the chapter. Did you come up with Esther, Mordecai and the Jews in the Book of Esther? That's a good one. Just when it looked like they were going to be exterminated, God came through in a really miraculous way. If you haven't read the story in awhile, go ahead and read it again. Some really good stuff there.

But I want to share something else from that story that we often overlook. If you're at all familiar with the story, you'll remember that Mordecai, Esther's uncle, asked Queen Esther to go to King Xerxes and ask him to rescind the command for extermination and annihilation. Esther was at first unwilling, because there was a law that you couldn't approach the king unless you were bidden by him. If you did try to approach him without his bidding you to come, you could be put to death.

Now, here's the thing most of us forget or don't pick up in that passage – Esther had not been asked by the king to come to him in 30 days. Don't miss that, it is an important part of the story, but also an important part of your life's story. The fact that she had not been bidden was highly unusual - highly so. Chapter 4:10-11 makes it clear how much the king loved and adored her. But now, suddenly, she has gone 30 days without seeing him, and she has great concern as to what might happen. Mordecai presses her to talk to the king about this urgent matter, and at any other time, she'd be able to do it, But not now. The prolonged absence of time with the king has suddenly exacerbated the situation.

Don't miss this, because God was behind the scenes causing this – yes, causing this. Esther was suddenly at a point of fearful dependence on God. In fact, you might say "Magnified Dependence" on God. Why didn't God have this happen 30 days earlier? Why didn't God have the king inviting her in during that time? Why does God seem to allow things to get worse when we need Him the most? The story goes on, Esther decides she'll risk it and go to the king. But, first, she tells Mordecai to get the Jews to fast and pray for three days before she goes in. Smart and godly move, but there may also be more in the request. The hope that sometime in the next three days, God might work it so that the king would invite her in. It doesn't happen. She still needs to go before the king in utter dependence on God. God has now allowed the time to go from 30 to 33 days. Wasn't the answer she was looking for!

Dear friends, we live in that "wait period". And, unlike reading these cool stories of people having to wait until the last minute – we're in it! And it's no fun! Can you identify with what Lewis Smedes says? Here are his words; *"We wait in darkness for a flame we cannot light. We wait in fear for a happy ending we cannot write. We wait for a "not yet" that feels like a "not ever"".* Why, why, why must we wait? It makes no sense to us, but then again, we are not all-knowing and all-sovereign. We think that waiting is bad, and it seems especially bad when it goes past the "okay, now I'm really in trouble moment". The truth is that the waiting – and trusting, is actually more valuable to God then the thing we ask for, or the thing we're waiting on.

You see the reason that God comes to us "just at the right time", or from our perspective, "at the last moment", is because that is how long the waiting process takes to accomplish what God desires in us. So, no wonder there are so many admonitions to "wait" on God. "We wait in hope for the Lord." (Psalm 33:20). We think of the "just in time" as the point where God rescues us, or we have the answer we so desire. But, truthfully, the "just in time" has more to do with the end of the waiting time that God was using in us in the process of conforming us to His Son. So, you too have a cool story, not just the deliverance, but the development. Be encouraged!

# 70
# TOO GREAT A DEBT

Right now, many of us are wondering where our economy, and perhaps even our country, is going. Until recently, unemployment had skyrocketed, housing foreclosures were at an all-time high, and the stock market had plummeted 778 points. Congress even overturned the White House's recommended 700 billion dollar rescue plan. Did you get that? 700 billion dollars! Who can even comprehend such a bailout? For that matter, who can comprehend such an immense national debt! I do not have answers for our national and personal financial indebtedness, but I would like to present a debt that is far greater. A debt that can never be humanly resolved. The debt I am talking about is the debt our sins have caused against a holy God.

To help explain this, check out Jesus' parable in Matthew chapter 18. Let me quote part of it for you; "Therefore, the kingdom of heaven may be compared to a king who wished to settle accounts with his servants. When he began to settle, one was brought to him who owed ten thousand talents...And out of pity for him; the master of the servant released him and forgave him the debt." (Matthew 18:23-24, 27)

I know for many of you, this is a familiar parable. But, oftentimes, we look at the picture that follows about the forgiven man not forgiving the servant who owed much less. For right now, let's not focus on that part of the story, but just the part I have quoted. Have you ever comprehended our great debt of sin to God? When Jesus told this story, He used some hyperbole as He often did. He made a man owe an astronomical amount. It was humanly impossible for one man to owe another person that much. A talent was equivalent to 20 years worth of a man's salary, so this man owed 10 times 20 years of his salary. An amount that was impossible to pay. Yet the king forgave him!

What an amazing picture of what our king has done. Our debt of sin to God is incalculable, it is beyond comprehension. Being born with a sin nature is enough to condemn us, but our sins are innumerable. If truth be told, they probably outnumber the grains of sand on the all the seashores of the world. But what amplifies this, is the One whom we have sinned against! The greatness of our sins is understood by the greatness of the one we sinned against.

Our debt was too great – but there was a "bailout". God Almighty became a man, took our sins upon Himself, and died in our place. He rose from the dead for our complete justification. We are forgiven! Colossians 2:13 says, "When you were dead in your sins and in the uncircumcision of your sinful nature, God made you alive with Christ. He forgave us all our sins."

Perhaps right now, you are facing a debt that is overwhelming – my heart goes out to you. I have been there, and there is such a helpless feeling during these times. But let this time remind you that a debt far greater – and with much more severe consequences – has been paid in full. Our sins are huge, but God's grace and forgiveness is greater. "Where sin increased, grace increased all the more." (Romans 5:20)

Our country may have talked about a bailout, but even if the funds had been made available, they themselves would still go further into debt to help Wall Street out. But God never goes into debt, His resources are inexhaustible. "In him we have redemption through his blood, the forgiveness of sins, in accordance with the riches of God's grace that he lavished on us." (Ephesians 1:7) Thank you Almighty God for forgiveness for our debt of sin!

Bruce McDonald

# 71
# IT'S TOO LATE

I still remember the first time I heard my oldest brother
tell me this story. Years ago, he and his wife were working with
the college youth in a church in Lapeer, Michigan. One of the
young men in their group was struggling, at times, with
pornography. He came to my brother, and to show how
serious he was about being free of this "despicable sin", he told
my brother that he had asked God "To hurt him real bad if he
ever looked at pornography again." I don't know how you feel
about that statement. Perhaps you commend the young man,
or maybe you are shocked by such a comment. Whatever you
feel about it, this statement, though well-intended, reveals that
this young man did not understand something very
fundamental and important - that someone was already "hurt
real bad for his sins".

But this man was probably more representative of believers
in Christ than we'd like to admit. For those who love the Lord,
for those who desire to live a holy and pleasing life before
God, we struggle with a serious dilemma, "What do we do
about sins we commit? Especially sins that seem so repetitive?

As devoted followers of Christ, we know that, though we were saved by grace, we do not ever want to use grace as a "license to sin". So, when sin appears and we succumb, we scramble to know what to do. Asking forgiveness and confessing sin again and again seems like...well, it seems like we are not really serious about forsaking that sin.

So, then we seek to show God how serious we are. We are going to do something about it. But, wait, we sin again! So, being serious about it wasn't enough. Thus, in order to deal with this, we actually begin to seek some visible punishment. After all, we deserve it. Most of us are not of the religion that would have us "lash our backs" or have us "carry a wood-splintered cross on our back". Or maybe like Martin Luther, prior to his conversion, "crawl the steps of a large cathedral on hands and knees." So, again, what do we do? I know of one believer who actually asked God "to take him to the woodshed and punish him real good."

But is this pleasing to God? Does God desire that we respond to our sins and failures to live as we desire, and as we know He would have us live, by asking Him to punish us in some way? We need to understand something very clearly; "God doesn't believe in double jeopardy". He does hate your sins, and He will enact punishment on them. However, it's just that He already has! I Peter 3:18 reminds us; "He himself bore our sins in his body on the tree..." Sins must be paid for, but the wonderful truth of the matter is, "That Christ already paid for ours".

I know, I know, that's got to be too good to be true, but it is! Let me illustrate: I recently went in to get my car's oil changed. It came to a little more than $40. When I was paying, the cashier said; "You know your oil change has already been paid for, you received a coupon book with free oil changes when you leased your car". However, I didn't have my coupon

Bruce McDonald

book, and since they had finished changing the oil on my car, I had to pay "again" for the work. It was needless, and truthfully, foolish on my part.

When we sin, we sometimes come to God and say, "I'm sorry, let me pay for that." But it's too late. It's already paid for. No matter how much you feel you should pay for it. You see, your sin and my sin is so great that it demands an eternal payment. All sins will be punished – all sins, but the payment for those sins is an eternal payment. Either Christ pays for them with His infinite eternal death, or a person pays for it forever in a place called hell, cut-off from God. There is no in-between. You can never say, as a believer, "Here let me repay you for that". It can't happen in any way, shape or form.

I know, once again, this sounds too good to be true. I mean, won't there be a temptation to go ahead and sin more? No, absolutely not! A Christian "does not sin as much as they want to, but a Christian sins more than they want to." Paul reminds us that, "God's kindness leads us towards repentance." (Romans 2:4) Sinning less (not sinless) is a result, not of our desiring to be "punished real good", but a result of realizing God has punished "Christ real good on our behalf". The redeeming work of Christ was brought about by an infinite payment for our sins – "For you know that it was not with perishable things such as silver or gold that you were redeemed from the empty way of life...but with the precious blood of Christ." (I Peter 1:18)

Are you fighting a fight that already been won? Are you seeking to pay for something that's already been paid for? You're too late! Christ was already "punished real good" on your behalf. This is what is freeing. This is what is empowering. Praise God I'm redeemed, and praise God that you are redeemed too!

264

# 72
# TOUCHING THE FACE OF GOD

If you have never seen The Kennedy Space Center, it is a must for anyone visiting Central Florida. Entering the grounds, you are immediately whisked away to life "up there". Rockets, Space Capsules, Space Shuttles and Space Stations become your home. You are there, circling the Moon – landing on the Moon, living in the Space Station and looking at earth from Outer Space. While experiencing all these things, it's hard to think of the heavens the same anymore. In fact, it's hard to think of earth the same anymore.

When you first enter the Kennedy Space Center, you see a picture of Leonardo da Vinci, and this now famous quote of his; "Once you have flown, you will walk the earth with your eyes turned skywards, for there you have been, and there you long to return." Wow, that quote literally stops you in your tracks. Isn't that what the writers of the New Testament were trying to convey? Isn't that what Paul said in Colossians 3:1-2? Paul wrote, "Since, then, you have been raised with Christ, set your hearts on things above, where Christ is seated at the right hand of God. Set your mind on things above, not on earthly

Bruce McDonald

things." I like the way Eugene Peterson paraphrases it in his Message Version, "Don't shuffle along, eyes to the ground, absorbed with the things right in front of you. Look up, and be alert to what is going on around Christ – that's where the action is. See things from his perspective."

Quite the way to put it; "Absorbed with the things in front of you". But the truth of the matter is, if you've not been to the heavens, it is hard not to be absorbed with the things in front of you. My good friend, Keith, recently sent me this quote from Randy Alcorn's excellent book Heaven. Keith shares my passion with longing and looking for our heavenly home. Here is the quote he sent me; *"The stronger our concept of God and Heaven, the more we understand how heaven resolves the problem of evil and suffering. The weaker our concept of God and Heaven, the stronger our doubt that Heaven will more than compensate for our present suffering."* How true, and how very important.

The Apostle Paul emphasized the same thing in two passages of scripture, Romans 8:18 and II Corinthians 4:17-18; "I consider that our present sufferings are not worth comparing with the glory that will be revealed in us." And, "For our light and momentary troubles are achieving for us an eternal glory that far outweighs them all. So we fix our eyes not on what is seen, but on what is unseen. For what is seen is temporary, but what is unseen is eternal." If I might asked for your indulgence on one more quote that supports what Paul, and author Randy Alcorn have said. This one comes from J.I. Packard (of Knowing God fame); *"Lack of a long, steady thinking about our promised hope of glory is a major cause of a plodding lack-luster lifestyle."*

So, how do we do it? I mean, how do we gaze at the heavens more? Or, more importantly, how do we "spend time up there", so that, in Leonardo da Vinci's words, *"we long to return"*? Life down here is hard, and oftentimes, so very hard. As I write this, I think of dear friends, family and loved ones

266

that are traversing through deep waters of pain and confusion. What can help them – help me, "find more than compensation" for this present world of evil and suffering? It's learning to "Touch the face of God". We must develop the discipline and passionate practice of "heading to the heavens" each day to see the glories of Christ, and to look back at the earth with that perspective. We can't take the Space Shuttle into space to have a downward look at earth, but we can take the wings of prayer, meditation, worship and scripture into the heavens. We can't be content to shuffle about looking only at life from an earthly perspective – we won't survive. But if we can cast a glance upwards, and then follow that glance with time in the heavens with Christ, we can survive, and yes, somehow in God's infinite care and comfort, find strength and victory. Back in the early 1940s a young pilot, still in his teens, wrote these immortal words;

*"Oh, I have slipped the surly bonds of earth, and danced the skies of laughter-silver wings. Sunward I've climbed, and joined the tumbling mirth of sun-split clouds – and done a hundred things you have not dreamed of. Wheeled and soared and swung high in the sunlit silence. Hovering there, I've chased the shouting wind along, and flung my eager craft through footless halls of air. Up, up the long delirious, burning blue. I've topped the windswept heights with easy grace, where never lark or eagle flew. And, while with silent, lifting mind I trod the high untrespassed sanctity of space. Put out my hand, and touched the face of God."*

The young pilot and poet who wrote those words was Major John Gillespie Magee Jr. Shortly after writing that poem, he died in a mid air collision over Lincolnshire, England in 1941. He was with the Royal Canadian Air-force in World War II. John's parents were missionaries in China, and John was a believer as well. John literally touched the face of God that fateful day of December 11, 1941. One day you too will see God's face, but until that day, take "flight" each day up into the heavens and touch the face of God.

Bruce McDonald

# 73
# YOUR TRUE IDENTITY

Just who are you? When you look in the mirror, what do you see, or better yet, what do you think? Really, seriously, what is your identity? It is interesting to see the way people (like you and I) seek to handle their identity. Some people seek to hide who they really are, and others try to be someone they really are not. That sentence may have seemed to be somewhat cryptic, but go back and read it again; hopefully it will make more sense to you.

Let me seek to illustrate these two polar opposite ways of handling identity. These are two rather "earthy" illustrations, and somewhat comical, but they are revealing nonetheless. First of all, "Some people seek to hide who they really are". Think of our present day "Super Heroes", fictitious though they be, they still illustrate an important point. All the so-called super heroes have one thing in common – "They seek to hide who they really are". For example, who are the following people? Dr. Bruce Banner, Peter Parker, Clark Kent, Bruce Wayne and Don Diego de la Vega? The answer: The Hulk, Spiderman, Superman, Batman and Zorro. These superheroes do not want anyone to know their true identity.

But what about those who seek to be someone they really are not? Let me give another revealing illustration. Barry Bremen...have you heard of him? He has been dubbed as "The Great Imposter". What has Barry done to earn such a bodacious title? Here are some of his great imposter tricks: He donned a New York Mets uniform and snuck into the Major League Baseball All Star Game and stood next to other players during the introductions of the ball players. He was caught after the fact. He also put on an NBA uniform and took warm-ups with other players during a Professional Basketball All Star Game. Again, he was caught, after the fact. He once put on a Football Referee's Uniform, and walked out to the center of the field and stood next to the real referees during the opening coin toss. He even dressed as a Dallas Cowboy Cheerleader and joined the cheerleaders during their game – without them knowing it - and, Barry is six foot three inches tall! One last "Great Imposter Stunt" to blow your mind. He once snuck into the Emmy's (Daytime Award Show for Actors and Actresses) and accepted the award – are you ready for this, as "Best Actress in a Dramatic Role". He "Accepted it on her behalf" while she was still walking to the front to accept the award!

Okay, I think you got the picture - two different attempts to handle identity. One, to seek to deny who we really are, and the other, to seek to be someone we really are not. I wonder, "Where do we fit?" Do I really know who I am in Christ? Do I really know who God made me to be? This is not a moot point or an irrelevant question. If we do not know who we really are, then our "accuser", that is, the Devil, will wreck havoc on our lives. I do not need to hide who I am – that is, be ashamed or embarrassed of the way God made me, or the calling I have. And I do not need to seek to be someone else, as if it would be better to have someone else's gifts, looks or calling in my life. Let me repeat the gist of that sentence again; "I do not need to hide who I am, and I do not need to seek to be someone else". Period! Exclamation point!

Let's just encourage one another with these closing, powerful truths as to who you and I really are. I (you) are; Called (Romans 8:28), Created (Psalm 139:13-14), Placed (I Corinthians 12:18), Gifted (Ephesians 4:8), Loved (I John 4:10), Kept (Jude 1), Indwelt (I Corinthians 6:19), Sealed (Ephesians 4:30), Given a purpose (II Timothy 1:9), Set-apart (I Corinthians 6:11), Commissioned (Matthew 28:18-20), Fought for (I Corinthians 15:57), Prayed for (Hebrews 7:24-25), Never abandoned (Hebrews 13:5) and Given a certain hope (Ephesians 1:18). That, my friends, is what you look at in the mirror - that is what you see and who you are. No hiding it ,and no need to be someone else. This is your "True identity".

# 74
# THE MEANING OF SERVANTHOOD

I believe most Christians understand the call to be servants of the Living Christ. It is clearly emphasized and modeled throughout scripture. Most of the New Testament writers start their letters identifying themselves as servants of Christ, and most often use a stronger word that means "bondslaves". Jesus clearly taught servanthood, and rebuked His disciples when they sought greatness. Most importantly, Jesus modeled it for His disciples, and in turn, for all of us down through the ages.

I don't know about you, but when I think of "service for Christ", I tend to think about ways I can minister for Christ. In other words, when I speak or teach, I am serving Christ, and when I write or give to something, I am serving Christ. My service for Christ is all about Him, and that is as it should be.

However, I read something recently in the Word of God that reminded me of what genuine servanthood looks like. The passage of scripture is found in I Samuel 25:4, and it is the account of Abigail's encounter with David. If you have the time, read this story. But verse 4 really jumped out at me. Here are Abigail's words to David's servants; "Behold, your handmaid is a servant to wash the feet of the servants of my Lord." Wow, did you get that? Not just a servant to wash your feet David, but to wash the feet of your servants. That is the lowest of the low!

I can think of serving Christ, why wouldn't I? He is King, He is my Master, He is my Savior, and I owe Him everything. But serving others? Including the least of the least? Whoa, that is a challenging thought! Remember when Jesus washed the disciple's feet? He said; "...I, your Lord and Teacher, have washed your feet, you also should wash one another's feet. I have set you an example that you should do as I have done for you." (John 13:14-15) Jesus, the ultimate head of the universe, condescended to wash the dirty feet of His fickle followers. Could there ever be a lower condescension? But we are called to have an attitude of "washing the feet of Christ's servants".

Has that been our attitude? I know that this is one of the many areas I struggle in - much to my shame. I want to be a servant, but I find myself enjoying, and at times, desiring, to be served. To be honored and exalted, oftentimes, clamor for my attention. I am sure, that like me, you know people who are servants to the servants. Bev and I have been so blessed in knowing people who serve well. You cannot succeed in trying to out-honor them. Even as I type these words, so many faces come now to my mind. They will truly be blessed and rewarded in heaven, when the last become first.

Here is a challenge for each of us this day, let us look for ways "to wash the feet of the lowliest servants". Ask God to help you in this area. May you and I out-honor others. Warning, if you pray and desire this, then you will be presented with an opportunity. You will also most likely, be tested or tempted by the evil one to exalt or promote yourself. But God can give the glorious victory. And let's remember, when we serve the least of these, we are really serving Christ.

# 75
# UNCOMPROMISING SUPREMACY

It would be ludicrous to say that a moment in a movie, albeit a comedy at that, captures for us one of the most powerful lessons we could ever learn. But the movie *City Slickers*, starring Billy Crystal and Jack Palance, comes very close to making a powerful statement about the Christian life and our relationship with Christ. You may recall the movie, it centers around 3 men, with Billy Crystal being the central character. He decides to "head west" to a "Dude Ranch" to experience life, but, more importantly, to deal with a "mid-life crisis" that his character "Mitch" is struggling with.

Many hilarious adventures take place while the three men are on the ranch, but the trio meets "Curley", who is played by Jack Palance to perfection. Curley is an old, rough and tumble genuine cowboy, and he doesn't like "city slickers". The relationship between Mitch and Curley develops throughout the movie, but one thing that Curley keeps seeking to remind Mitch of is that he must "figure something out" while he's at the ranch. Mitch has no clue, and, at one point, Mitch asks Curley "what's the meaning of life, what's the all important

Bruce McDonald

thing?" Curley holds up one finger, which causes Mitch to ask; "Your finger?" "No", Curley responds, "you need to find that one thing, that one important thing, and live your life pursuing that" (paraphrased by me). This is a lesson we all need to heed, and it was a lesson the 12 Apostles were slow to learn. Let me explain.

In many ways, the Apostles struggled with priorities and pursuits similar to us, but at times they struggled more so than we do. There is an incident in Scripture that really illustrates this. Most of us are familiar with the "Easter Story", that is, the events centered around Christ's betrayal, arrest, suffering, crucifixion and the resurrection. But one event that happens just before the events of Christ's betrayal is sometimes overlooked in its power and portrayal. The event can be found in Matthew's Gospel, chapter 26. Here is Matthew's account of that evening; "While Jesus was in Bethany at the home of Simon…a woman approached Him with an alabaster jar of very expensive fragrant oil. She poured it on His head…When the disciples saw it, they were indignant. 'Why this waste', they asked. 'This might have been sold for a great deal and given to the poor.' But Jesus, aware of this, said to them, 'Why are you bothering this woman? She has done a noble thing for me. You always have the poor with you, but you do not always have Me.'" (Matthew 26:2-11)

Don't miss the power of Christ's words, and we could say, even His gentle rebuke of them. The disciples were caught up in a movement, unfortunately, not in a man. They were caught up in principles of the kingdom of God, but not with the King. What would be nobler than helping the poor? The answer to that, and any noble act of humanitarians, is the exaltation of Christ. There were many noble causes and movements the disciples could have invested effort, money, time and loyalty, but Jesus jarringly reminded them that, these and anything else we might imagine, all must fall secondary to exalting Christ.

274

This speaks much to us today, when it is so easy to get caught up in movements, causes and our own groups or associations. God the Father and Christ Jesus the Son have one consuming passion for us - the exaltation of Jesus and His atoning work for us. The Holy Spirit was serious when He said through the Apostle Paul, "That He [Christ] might be first in all things." (Colossians1:18)

Jesus "jarred" the disciples when He rebuked them and reminded them, there is no greater thing that can be done than honoring Christ. He went on to say that what the woman did for Him will be remembered always, and talked about always. I think it's easy to sometimes forget the passion God has for His own glory. The problem the disciples often displayed was forgetting just "who" Jesus was, and "why" He came to earth.

I believe one of the things that all of us followers of Christ will be shocked about in heaven, is just how exalted Christ will be. Again, the Holy Spirit, speaking through the Apostle Paul, says; "Christ is seated far above every ruler and authority, power and dominion, and every title given, not only in this age, but also in the one to come." (Ephesians 1:20-21) The challenge today for so many believers is to boldly identify with Christ, and to seek to exalt Him above all things. This is especially true here in the United States, and to some degree, in all of Western society. There are many exceptions, praise God, but identifying with Jesus, and exalting Him unashamedly is passé or frightening. There does seem, however, a willingness to "imitate" Jesus in His help to the poor and needy. There is nothing wrong with this endeavor. This is commendable, and Jesus calls us to be His hands and feet. But, and this is very important, it should never be instead of His exaltation, and it never should be above His exaltation – or even comparable to it.

I would encourage you to take the time and read the account of the woman who poured the sweet fragrance over

Jesus' head; I think it would be profitable for you. Shockingly, the disciples criticized this woman that Jesus so highly commended. Is it possible to "get busy for Jesus", and at the same time, not proclaim His name and His finished work on the cross?" Is it possible for us to get caught up in causes or our own 'group" and forget Jesus' preeminence? There is no higher calling then to proclaim and exalt Christ's name – no higher calling. It surpasses even doing good deeds. Digging wells for the thirsty and sick - important; starting hospitals and delivering young women from the "slave trafficking" - important; building homes for the homeless and educating the illiterate – important; proclaiming Christ's name and finished work – "priceless!"

There are many good deeds that should be done, but Curley had it right – there's just "one thing" that should be preeminent, that should control and consume our lives, it is the foundation and source of all we do – exalting Christ. Long after helps and humanitarian efforts are past, Christ will remain, and He is first and foremost in all things. So do "good works", help the poor and do many other things, but never replace these things for exalting and naming Christ. And never put them on par with worshipping and proclaiming Christ

"For this reason God also highly exalted Him and gave Him the name that is above every name." Philippians 2:9

# 76
# UNDECIPHERABLE PATTERN

This chaptert is about secrets. Here is a family secret – Bev's (my wife) handwriting is often indiscernible. She sometimes will ask me what "she wrote" if it's been awhile since she wrote it. It may be an address, it may be a recipe, or it may be directions she copied down. To her defense, she claims it's because she is left handed and the teachers taught her improperly.

So why divulge that? Because I want to share with you some other things that are undecipherable. Usually with Bev's handwriting, if our family gets together and tries to decipher it, we can come pretty close to figuring it out. And, truthfully, if she really wants to, she can make things legible. But there have been certain writings that have never been deciphered. These writings have not been deciphered because of poor penmanship, but because of being in an unknown language. Three of the oldest languages are Egyptian Hieroglyphics, Mesopotamian Pictographs and Indus Script. Of those three, the Indus Script has never been deciphered. The Indus Script was written in the area around Pakistan, and we have 2,500

Bruce McDonald

examples of it-all undecipherable. Besides the Indus Script, there are several examples of writings – clay tablets, scrolls and books that to this day remain a mystery because they have never been deciphered. Here is a list of some: Linear A (Greece 1800 BC), Zapotec (Mexico 500 BC), Merotic (Sudan 300 BC), Isthmian (Central America AD 300), Rongoronga (Easter Island AD 1800), Joycean (Ireland AD 1900), and the Voynich Manuscript (Europe AD 1200). Of these, the Voynich Manuscript is the most intriguing and baffling.

The Voynich Manuscript, now housed at Yale University, is a book approximately 6 inches by 9 inches. It contains 246 pages (at least 262 pages originally), and is filled with drawings, diagrams and sentences. In the book are pictures of unidentified plants, herbal recipes, tiny naked women (sorry) in intricately designed bathtubs, astronomical objects seen through a telescope, live cells seen through a microscope and charts with calendars and Zodiac signs. All this, and undecipherable sentences describing the pictures. For over 800 years, no one has been able to decipher this book. No one can determine the language or the origin of the book. A baffling mystery indeed!

For the believer, there is something far more baffling and undecipherable than the Voynich Manuscript, and that is the ways of God. Romans 11:33 says, "How unsearchable his judgments, and his paths beyond tracing out." And Ecclesiastes 11: 5 says, "As you do not know the path of the wind or how the body is formed in a mother's womb, so you cannot understand the work of God, the Maker of all things." However, the undecipherableness of God's way goes beyond the fact that God is unimaginably wise and complex. The thing that exasperates about the mysteriousness of God's way is that God has no pattern. Go back and read those last two lines again. What frustrates Christians is not that God is often indiscernible in what He is doing - because He is so infinitely complex – this should actually result in praise and worship.

But, instead, it is the fact that He has no discernible pattern that we can recognize, and therefore have some measure of expectation. We want a God who is great, but we also want a God that, to some degree, can be figured out.

Like the Voynich Manuscript and the Indus Script, God's dealings, plans and ways seem completely indiscernible and indecipherable. One time He does things one way and the next time He does something another way. Which way is His "normal" pattern? When Elijah is told to announce to King Ahab there will be a three year drought, God tells Elijah He will take care of him during the drought. How will God do that? By sending him eastward to the Kerith Ravine. There, God would have the water keep flowing and ravens feed him. However, the brook dries up and the ravens fly away. So, now Elijah has a problem. God says "No problem, go westward to Zerapath and I will have a widow miraculously take care of you."

So, if Elijah thought he could see a pattern as to how God was going to take care of him, he was mistaken. One time go eastward, the next go westward. One time ravens will feed you, the next a widow. Think about Moses, he represents all of us in our assumptions about God having a discernible pattern. One time, God tells him to strike the rock and the next time to speak to the rock. Moses, thinking he knows God, strikes the rock again – big mistake! How about the disciples? One time Jesus sends them into town (John 4) to get supplies, the next time He chooses to multiply fish and bread to feed thousands (Matthew 14). If there is any pattern to God, it is that He has no pattern.

I think sometimes we acknowledge that God is infinitely wise, so we can't always know what He is thinking or doing. But we aren't as willing, or ready, to acknowledge that He doesn't always act in the same way. In fact, He rarely does. Perhaps you pray about a financial need and God has an unexpected check come in the mail. The next time that need is there, you look for the same provision in the same way, but instead you find there was an error in your bookkeeping and you really don't owe anything. Or maybe He even has the boss suddenly give you "overtime" opportunity.

The fact that God's working does not follow a pattern can cause needless worry, and sometimes cause us to question God's love and care. We can be like Naaman in the Old Testament. When God chose to heal him, he had him go to the Jordan River and submerge himself 7 times. Naaman was angry, because he thought (assumed) God would have Elisha "wave his hand over his head". God is faithful, and God will provide, but He won't follow a pattern. Perhaps the reason God does this is so that you and I won't look towards the method, or raise our hopes focused on how something might come about. But, instead, we'll look solely to Him, trust Him, and leave with Him the timing and the manner in which He supplies and provides. If God's ways are indecipherable, that's okay, because it is not the method or manner, but the God behind the promise. Have you been looking for a certain way out of a situation? Perhaps God is saying to you, "Look to me".

# 77
# UNHEARD OF

So, do you know of Charles Martel? Is that a familiar name to you, or have you no clue as to who he is? Before I tell you who he was – or remind you of who he was, let me first of all tell you how much of the world today benefits from his life and exploits. We live in a day and age where we frequently hear news from the Muslim world. Most of us are more acutely aware of Islam and Muslim beliefs - especially radical Muslim beliefs since 9/11. And then our attention has been riveted to countries such as Iraq and Afghanistan because of our military involvement. Many of us here in the United States find ourselves reading the stories in the newspapers, or on the Internet, of countries surrounding Israel – Syria, Lebanon, Egypt and Iran. Islam seems to be garnering most of the intention of the international media. But it is not just the Middle East; Islam is often strongest and has its most adherents in Indonesia and the surrounding nations.

When you think of Islam, your mind kind of sees a map of the world where it is most prevalent. I'd like you to imagine that right now, and as you do, doesn't your mind's map stop at the border of Europe? It's true that Islam is seeking to infiltrate parts of Europe, not necessarily through military conflict, but through repopulation and propaganda. But, still, Europe has historically been the boundary line for Muslim countries. Can you imagine if all of Europe was Muslim? Frightening thought isn't it? But why is, relatively speaking, Europe not Muslim? Enter Charles Martel.

Charles Martel lived from 686 to 741 AD, and in 732 AD he accomplished something that Europe, and, to some degree, even the United States (since we came from Europe), has benefited from until this very day. In the early and mid part of the 700s, the Muslim world was seeking to spread its empire, and particularly set its sights on Europe. They were conquering and advancing at an alarming rate. In 732 Abdul Rahman Al Ghafiqi led an army of 80,000 Muslims into Europe. They were a terrifying army, skilled fighters, ruthless, and equipped with the world's largest cavalry. As they entered Europe, they beat back one army after another. They slowly headed into what is now known as Northern France. Europe was on the verge of falling to Islam, except, there was Charles Martel.

Charles held a very non-distinct title; "Mayor of the Palace", but he was a lion at heart. He marshaled an army of 30,000 soldiers - with no horses for Calvary, and met the Muslim hordes at a place called "Poitiers," or some refer to it as "Tours". He soundly defeated the Islamic Army, killing Al Ghafiqiled in the process. He and his army then chased the Muslims all the way out of Europe – never to return again! Historians have called this battle, and this moment in time, the decisive turning point in the struggle against Islam taking over Europe. Historian, Leopold van Ranke, said; *"This turning point is one of the most important epochs in the history of the world."* Wow…did you get that? Europe, and possibly the US, would look entirely different today, if it were not for Charles Martel.

So what's my point? Why take two paragraphs to tell you

about "ancient history"? Because, a man you most likely have not heard of, was used by God (certainly in the big picture of things), to stem the tide of Islam flooding into Europe and forever religiously and politically changing that landscape.

So, if a man who saved all of Europe could be forgotten and slip into "an unknown category" today, it becomes understandable that your life and events may sometimes go unnoticed. For every Chuck Swindoll, Beth Moore, Max Lucado, Elizabeth Elliot, Franklin Graham and Rick Warren, there are people unknown, and, often, not remembered, who have been used of God in life changing ways. I'm serious about this. I have always been fascinated by the unnamed, unknown and unremembered people in scripture. They populate much of scripture, but we tend to think of them as a "by-line", focusing instead on the "big names". Read II Corinthians 8:18-22 to see some "no-names", and read Romans 16 to see names that are "forgotten" now.

Dear friend, you are important. You are integral to God's program. Expansion and exposure are over-rated. It's faithfulness to your own calling and station in life. There are no insignificant people. Take heart in Jesus' words to you, "I know your deeds, your hard work and your perseverance." (Revelation 2:2) And be encouraged as you hear the Spirit of Christ speak through the writer of Hebrews, "God is not unjust; he will not forget your work and the love you have shown him as you have helped his people and continue to help them." (Hebrews 6:10) I'm sorry you are not recognized more – you should be, you have helped others, and you have lived faithfully for Him. Who knows, maybe heaven's historians will one day say, "He or She was used by God to cause the decisive turning point in this person's life, this family's life, this church's life, or maybe even, this nations life." You never know how much your life matters. Unheard of is not synonymous with unused. Thank you for your faithfulness. Great is your reward in heaven.

# 78
# AN UNMITIGATED JOY

The three friends had been scouring the dry river beds for months now. They were down in Venezuela looking for diamonds. Months of fruitless endeavor had finally gotten to Rafael Solano, after digging his hands once again in the dry and dusty pebbles of the old river bed and coming up with nothing. He looked at his friends and said, "if I do this one more time, it'd be the millionth time I've done this. I quit!" His two friends looked at him and said, "Do it one more time, make it a million." So he did, he reached his hand down deep under the pebbles and rocks, and suddenly felt something large. He pulled up the large rock; it was encrusted by smaller pebbles. He brushed it off, and to his and his friends' astonishment, it was a large diamond. He literally shook with excitement and realization. He eventually brought the diamond back to the states, and found out it was the purest diamond ever found. In fact, it still is to this day, and that was back in 1942!

Solano sold the diamond for 2 million dollars, an unbelievably staggering amount at that time. The amount of money would certainly be amazing in and of itself, but added to that, was the fact that "you" found the purest diamond ever. Quite a find!

The purest! It has a great ring to it. Seems like we're always looking for the purest of something. The one sample of something that is not mixed, diluted, or tarnished. As stated above, the purest diamond ever found was the one in Venezuela. The purest gold ever found was actually right here in the United States, and it was found at Dukes Creek in White County, Georgia. It was discovered back in the early gold rush days of our country. Additionally, the purest air is found right outside my door here in Colorado…not really! The purest air is found in Tasmania (some argue, Estonia), and the purest water is found in small town outside of Toronto, Canada. The little town's name is "Elmvale". But even though each one of these is the "purest", they are not completely pure, nothing is.

What is true, generally speaking, in life, is true also in the Christian life. In our deportment, our walk, our conversations, our attempts at life and godliness, and our overall experiences in the Christian life, nothing is absolutely pure – 100% unmitigated. It's just the way things are. The stain of sin has seeped too deep into this world, and we are not exempt from it. This is not meant to discourage us, or to make us feel a sense of hopelessness. Instead, it is meant to remind us that, in this life, nothing will ever be fully as it was designed to be. It is meant to cause us to yearn and long for a place where everything will finally be correct, and there will be undiluted experiences to the fullest.

Perhaps the greatest example of this is our present happiness and joy. Praise God for wonderful times of laughter, fun and joyful experiences. Where would we be without this? Can you imagine a life that never had the break of spontaneous joy and outright exuberant laughter- filled times? But even in these God- given times, our joy and laughter are not pure. In the midst of these joyful and fun experiences, there lurks the

Bruce McDonald

"reality" of life. We may laugh, we may have great fun, and we may be overcome with great joy, but, at best, the experience is temporary. And it's not just that it is temporary, it's the fact that we know that there are still things out there that are disheartening, confusing and overwhelming. These things have not been removed, they still need to be dealt with, or they still need to be honestly faced. Laughter is a gift, and joy and fun are from our Creator. But they're temporary and transient, and they don't "remove" what still is out there.

Life would be tragic if that is all there was, if we simply had brief, albeit, wonderful times of joy and laughter, and then had to "get back to the reality of life". But that is not what awaits the believer in Christ. Life is tough and difficult now, it really is, but God interlaces that with respites of joy and laughter. He gives us brief forays into the rarified air of relief and fun. These are necessary, but these are only "snippets" to tantalize us and prepare us for something greater, something purer.

Here's a wonderful passage of scripture for you to take with you today and in your life. "The Lord of Hosts will prepare a feast for all the peoples on this mountain – a feast of aged wine, choice meats, finely aged wine. On this mountain He will destroy the burial shroud, the shroud over all the peoples, the sheet covering all the nations; He will destroy death forever. The Lord God will wipe away the tears from every face and remove the people's disgrace from the whole earth…" (Isaiah 25:6-7) You might want to go back and reread that passage again. What a day – and it will last forever! There will not only be incredible joy – a feast! A banquet! But something will be removed so we can experience fully, in an unmitigated way, the great joy and fun we're having. The "shroud" will be lifted – forever! No more dying, no more suffering, no more sadness, but, instead, complete comfort and joy. In another passage God puts it this way; "Everlasting joy will crown their heads, gladness and joy will overtake them, and sorrow and sighing will flee away." (Isaiah 35:10) No wonder Jesus' said when He will welcomes us into His heaven, He will use these words, "Well done, good and faithful servant! Come and share your Master's happiness." (Matthew 25:21)

Hey, on this earth, there are things that "are pretty pure"; they come close to being the authentic thing. Clean air and water, sparkling gems and diamonds – purest gold. But even these things aren't completely unmitigated. In this life, we have some incredible experiences – praise God for these, but these, too, are not completely free of small amounts of contamination. God blesses us with many benefits and experiences today – we need these, but these are just the "appetizers." The real thing is still to come. God will throw a banquet, but He will also remove that shroud that is over all the earth. Today, let your thoughts go "to that day", a day of great joy and gladness, but also a day when sorrowful or troubling thoughts will not enter your mind. "You will fill me with joy in your presence, with eternal pleasures at your right hand." (Psalm 16:11)

Bruce McDonald

# 79
# UNREALIZED DEHYDRATION

Okay, weird title, but stay with me for a few moments. I'd like us to think about water for a few moments and our great need of it. There are many times when our senses are heightened to our need for water. Perhaps it's something as simple as a good, hard work-out, and we crave a drink of water. Perhaps it's working hard in the field or garden, or any other strenuous work. It may simply be because of a very hot day or hot environment. It may be because you have not had a drink of water for quite some time. These are all times when we become aware that we are thirsty. But more serious times may make us aware of our thirst, times when it can result in a life and death situation. History is filled with battles of days gone by where a city or a castle was besieged and the attacking army cut off from the water supply. The people inside the city or castle either surrendered or died of thirst. Stories are told of people crossing the desert and running out of water, and then they succumb to death. We need water, and desperate times and circumstances make us more acutely aware of this.

Our hearts have been broken in recent times as we become aware of how much of the world either lacks water, because of elongated droughts, or due to unsanitary drinking conditions. A recent study showed that 1 billion of the world's population lacks safe drinking water. It's staggering to hear this. Even more troubling and saddening, is to hear that 1,000 children will die each day from drinking unsafe water. One thousand! Praise God that the church, ministry groups and believers in general have not only been made aware of this, but many are seeking to do something about it. The list and names of organizations would be too long to list in this chapter, but Samaritan's Purse, Compassion International, World Vision and Living Water are a few that have sought to provide safe drinking water to many regions of the world. My own Mission Agency (again, along with many others), ABWE, has also been active in this endeavor as well. It's something we all should be concerned about and seek to somehow get involved with.

But I want to shift gears here for a few moments. I have been writing about the critical water needs we are greatly aware of. However, just as deadly and dangerous, is water needs we are not aware of. It's actually possible to be in great need of water and not be cognizant of that.

If I may, I'd like to illustrate that from something we see out here in our Colorado home where we live at about 9,000 feet elevation. Our home is blessed with many visitors each year, and many of these stay for several days. One of the first things we tell them is "drink lots of water". I know they get tired of us reminding them to do this throughout their stay with us, but it is necessary and important. At this altitude you lose lots of water from your body. More than twice the normal amount at sea level, and even up to 3,000 feet. At sea level we're told to drink 6-8 glasses of water a day. However, here, we have to drink more than twice that. All sorts of problems can develop – some severe – because of lack of drinking enough water. The main problems can consist of headaches or altitude sickness.

So, we keep reminding them (nagging?) to drink lots of water. Of course the normal complaint we hear is; "I had to keep getting up to go the bathroom during the night!" So you may be asking, "Why do you have to keep reminding them, they certainly are aware of their thirst." Well, here's the interesting thing, they aren't! Because of the dryness up here, you most often don't even realize you're thirsty, or that you need water. You just don't feel thirsty until you get a headache or perhaps something more.

Going without water because you are unaware of your need for it – lack of thirst, is dangerous. But here's the thought we need to consider, "Going without the water of the Word because we are not aware of our thirst, is even more dangerous." Our bodies need water to survive, but here is what most of us forget, "Our spirit and soul needs water to survive." Sickness and death to the body are evident and very noticeable, but sickness and death to the soul and spirit are not so noticeable – at least, not at first. Jesus reminded the woman at the well in John 4 that He could give her "Living Water". He then went on to tell her that if she drank this living water she'd never thirst. (John 4:10-13)

Jesus was certainly talking about the Holy Spirit coming into a person's life – "If anyone is thirsty let him come to me and drink…streams of living water will flow from within him…By this he meant the Spirit, whom those who believed in him were later to receive." (John 7:37-39) But He was also talking about the living and powerful Word of God that the Holy Spirit would illuminate in our lives. In Ephesians 5, Jesus says we have been washed by the water of the Word, and in Revelation 22 the Holy Spirit and the Lord Jesus Christ bid everyone to come and drink of the Water of Life.

So, here is my question; "Are you getting enough water?"

Or, more specifically, are your soul and spirit getting enough of the water of the Word? You may not even be aware of your great need for this, but lack of drinking deep and long and regularly can cause a drought of the soul and spirit. But many don't believe this; they think they can somehow be the exception. Just like people staying at our house may think "I can go without drinking much water", and soon find out how wrong they were, so it is with our drinking of God's Word. How much water (The Word) do you take in each day? It can't be measured in glasses like H2O. Do you go long times without it? Do you just "sip" once in awhile?

The malady is not just for those who have no interest in growing as believers. It can happen to those who love Christ, but have for some reason or another neglected to drink deeply and regularly of the Word. Even ministers and those who vocationally serve Christ can be guilty of this. We can be busy "drawing water for others, but never drinking ourselves".

Recently, we were up in Montana, and we drove by a plastic pipe coming out of the side of the mountain. People were standing there filling their water jugs. Sometime later I stopped by and filled up some of our water jugs. It was amazing! Truthfully, it was the best water I have ever tasted. I wished I lived near by; I'd regularly drink from this natural mountain water.

Hey, just think, not very far from any place in your home is the best drinking water on the planet – your Bible. Pick it up and drink deeply. The statistics for children dying each year of thirst are troubling and horrifying, but the number of believers either dying of thirst or drinking from contaminated waters probably surpasses that statistic. Go ahead, reach for that Bible.

# 80
# GOING UP TOO FAST

Scuba Diving has provided me with many analogies of the Christian life, and I'd like to share one with you that I have been thinking about recently. A few days ago we had two couples over for dinner. During the course of the evening, the topic got around to scuba diving (undoubtedly introduced by Bev and me!). The one couple stated very clearly that they would never want to try diving. They listed the usual reasons that people give who are somewhat uncomfortable in water, especially deep water. I shared with them that divers are not concerned with "sinking deep" and drowning. The concern they have, is that they will go to the surface too quickly. The potential danger is going "up too fast".

You see; when scuba diving, you must ascend slowly, even take a "safety stop" at about 10 or 12 feet below the surface. I won't bore you at this point with diving technicalities, and why you must ascend slowly and take safety stops, but I'll simply say, if you ascend too fast, you will get "the bends", or "decompression sickness". It can even be fatal. So, going to the surface too fast is a big mistake, and has serious consequences. In fact, if you have been diving at a certain depth, you cannot fly for 12 hours, or even drive up a mountain that is above 2,000 feet. It does nasty things to you!

Okay, so much for the "Scuba Diving Lesson", but here is the analogy; "Ascending too fast in our Christian life can be harmful". Here are some numbers for you: 13, 15, 30, 40, and 100. Do you know what they are? They are the years it took Joseph to ascend to second in command in Egypt after his dreams, the years it took David to claim his rightful throne after being anointed by Samuel, the years before Jesus Christ stepped into public ministry, the years before Moses became emancipator after he was led to believe he was the chosen one (see Acts 7:25), and the years it took Noah to build the Ark after God said it was going to rain (see Genesis 5:32 & 7:6). We could add the number 25, which are the years between God's promise to Abraham to have a child and the actual birth of Isaac.

You see, God knows that time is essential to growth and fulfillment. God often gives promises – even hopes and dreams, and then "grows us into them". Quick ascendency has the potential to be harmful, or even fatal. There is a telling passage of scripture in I Timothy 3:6. It states, regarding an "overseer" or "bishop", that "He must not be a recent convert, or he may become conceited and fall under the same judgment as the devil." The "King James" translates it; "He must not be a novice". The Greek word translated "recent convert" or "novice" is a word that literally means "recently planted". A practical way of saying it would be; "a person who is, as yet, unfit for a certain task."

Have you ever wondered why, in some ways, things seem to, at times, go so slowly? Especially when you feel you are following God's leading. It is because God knows that ascending too fast is harmful. And it is not just frustration with not attaining some position or dream early on. It is also

293

frustration with not becoming "the person" we desire to be for Christ. Sometimes, our ascent seems to move at "glacial speed!" Ephesians 4:13 gives the goal and aspiration of all true believers in Christ, that we "would attain mature manhood and the measure of the stature of the fullness of Christ." It is not only our goal, but God's as well (Romans 8:29).

If you have been feeling levels of frustration lately in regard to "things not coming together" as you hoped, or something not happening that you have anticipated for quite some time, remember God knows that you can go "Up too fast". God's timing is perfect; He will bring about His perfect will in His perfect timing. "What I have said, that will I bring about; what I have planned, that will I do." (Isaiah 46:11) "Though it linger, wait for it; it will certainly come and will not delay." (Habakkuk 2:3) You may be in a "safety stop" right now, but just wait; God will soon have you break through to the surface!

# 81
# WAITING TOO LONG

Living up in the Colorado Rockies is wonderful, and I thank God regularly for this gift of being in a part of the country – actually, the world – that is so beautiful. As I've mentioned before, we live at almost 9000 feet, and the views are breathtaking. You might think that because we live so high in the mountains we get "pummeled" with snow. However, that is actually not true. We do get some good snow storms now and then, but not regularly. This area of our country is called "high desert", and the humidity here can be extremely low – like in 10%! When it does snow, the blazing sun can melt it rather quickly.

That leads me to share a problem, or better yet, a challenge about living at this altitude during the winter. Because of the bright sun we have, the snow will begin to melt soon after it falls. The snow, which at first is very powdery, can quickly turn to water running across and under the snow. That would be a blessing, but because the daylight is somewhat shorter (the sun dips behind the mountain peaks around 3:00 PM), the dry air begins to rapidly freeze the running water. When that happens,

Bruce McDonald

there is a smooth glaze of ice covering everything.

The real challenge comes when those of us who live here must quickly sweep the snow away before the cycle of melting and freezing begins. I say "sweep" because the snow up here is very powdery and can be whisked away with a broom. That's nice, and it sure saves the back and time. It also makes the snow blower work better on the driveway (500 feet of driveway!). But if we wait, or are gone at the time, and the sun comes out, the snow will turn wet and heavy. And then once the sun lowers, the melting snow will turn to ice. Then, instead of a broom, you have to use a shovel and ice scraper. Even places where our dog has walked on the snow (Much worse where humans have walked) are hardened. The steps especially can become perilous. So, acting quickly before the freeze sets in is imperative. I know, because I just experienced this yesterday!

So, all this to say, there is a spiritual application I would like to make here - one that, unfortunately, is like the ice melt/freeze scenario I mentioned. Sins must be dealt with quickly. If not, there can be a hardening of heart. Promises must be kept, or they will soon be forgotten. Action must be taken, or opportune times will pass. Little sins must be quickly confessed and forsaken, or they will grow to larger ones that can become besetting sins.

I have thought of this as I have worked hard to chip up ice off our deck and driveway. If I had acted sooner, it would have been much easier and faster. The Bible is filled with warnings and reminders of being immediate in our response to conviction and leading. "Today, if you hear his voice, do not harden your hearts." (Hebrews 3:7) I wonder if I might leave a challenge for each of us (me included). It is this, is there something you have been putting off? Then, do it now. It might be one of the following:

1) Confessing and forsaking a sin
2) Going to someone and asking forgiveness
3) Confronting someone in love
4) Starting that spiritual discipline you have been putting off
5) Giving that money you have promised to give
6) Helping that neighbor you have thought about
7) Spending more time with your family
8) Breaking off that flirtatious relationship
9) Stop gossiping
10) Volunteer to help at church

In all these areas, if we wait too long, it will get harder, and the price could be more than just an added hour or two on the deck and driveway. George Whitefield once said, *"The greatest prayer someone can pray is this; 'Make me willing to be willing"*. Why not pray that right now, and follow through with God's enablement.

Bruce McDonald

# 82
# WELCOME HOME TROOPS!

As I write this, I've see that sign a lot lately. Since we travel much, whenever we come home to Colorado the sign is posted above the gate as we depart from the plane. I know that it is in other airports as well, but the military presence is huge in the Colorado Springs area. One of the bases, Fort Carson, annually has the most troops in Iraq or Afghanistan. Occasionally, we get to see family and friends gathered together to welcome home their husband, wife, father, mother, son or daughter. As you can imagine, the greeting is quite emotional, and often, overwhelming. This is especially true if the family member has been gone for a long time, or has been in a part of the world that is dangerous.

A couple days ago, I got off the plane here in Colorado and noticed that sign again. This time, I stopped and stared at it for a few moments. The thought came to my mind; "Is there a sign like this in heaven?" When we leave here and arrive in glory, will there be a large banner like this? You may think that sounds rather far-fetched, but let's think about this for a moment.

First of all, the Bible says that when we enter heaven, we will receive a rich welcome. Here is how Peter puts it; "You will receive a rich welcome into the eternal kingdom of our Lord and Savior Jesus Christ." (II Peter 1:11) What does that "rich welcome" look like? The welcome referred to here, is a welcome that was given in New Testament times to Olympic heroes and to military commanders. In fact, on some occasions, a new road, and even a new gate (opening in the wall), was made just for that individual who was returning home. The welcome would be lavished abundantly on the conquering hero, and the citizens and leaders of the city made sure that the recipient knew of their heart-felt thanks.

So, there will be a "welcome", but there will also be the final arrival "home". How special must it be for our returning soldiers to come home? How wonderful that feeling must be. It probably is twofold. First, to be home with family and loved ones, and second, to be away from the conflict and constant danger of being in "harm's way". What will it be like for us, to finally be home? Home, a place where we have never been before! And heaven IS our home. Jesus said; "I am going to prepare a place for you." (John 14:2) And Paul wrote; "Our citizenship is in heaven." (Philippians 3:20) The Apostle John recorded hearing a voice in heaven in his glimpse of the future, and that voice said; "Now the dwelling of God is with men, and he will live with them." (Revelation 21:3) So, one day, you'll be welcomed home to heaven.

The welcome is telling, the home is encouraging, but the reminder that you are part of God's troop is essential. Welcome home troops! If you look up "troop" in Webster's Dictionary, the second definition is simply "soldiers". And that is what we understand it to be today. Any military person, man or woman, who is part of our armed forces, is considered to be in the general category of "troops".

You knew, of course, that you are a member of God's troops. However, you are in a much greater battle than any of our military personnel. You face a much larger army than any of our troops have ever faced. You have an enemy that is embodiment of evil. An arch-foe that has existed since before our creation, and an army at his disposal that is innumerable. The battle lines have been drawn, and there is no option as to whether you will enlist or not. The enemy has come to you, and you are God's warrior. You are a member of His troop, and you are called to fight the good fight of faith (I Timothy 6:12).

The Apostle Paul repeatedly reminds us, that we serve as soldiers for Christ. "Endure hardship with us as a good soldier of Christ Jesus. No one serving as a soldier gets involved in civilian affairs – he wants to please his commanding officer." (II Timothy 2:3-4) And, speaking of his fellow servant Epaphroditus, Paul says; "My brother, fellow worker and fellow soldier." (Philippians 2:25)

Dear friends, you are in God's military, you are a part of God's troops. The conflict is hot and heavy, the casualties are great. The enemy marches on ruthlessly, but you not only hold the high ground, you press the attack towards the enemy. You fight with all God's strength, and you have as leader, the Captain of God's Army (Joshua 5:14). The enemy is not lost people; the enemy is the one who holds lost people captive. But you will gain the victory through Christ; "With God we will gain the victory, and he will trample down our enemies." (Psalm 60:12)

I know the battle is long and hard. I know you have been weary and tired, but take heart, the King is coming soon for you. And, one day, we will be transported to heaven – not by a 747 or a DC-10, or any other type of aircraft – but by God Himself (perhaps using angels!). Then, we will see the sign; Welcome home troops!" You will receive a welcome you could never imagine, and you will enter a home that that will take your breath away. But, most importantly, God will be there to personally welcome you with outstretched arms. Those same arms that were outstretched for you on Calvary's tree. Welcome home troops!

# 83
# WHAT DO YOU GIVE THE PERSON WHO HAS EVERYTHING?

$B$ev is coming up on a birthday. I am facing my usual struggle of what to give her (by the way, the title of this devotional is not speaking about her!). Clothes? Forget that, she doesn't trust me picking them out for her. How about appliances? Yeah, right, that is pretty romantic! How about a trip somewhere? Well, let's see, we just back from Russia, Finland, Germany and Greece, and next month we go to the Philippines. Ok, forget that one too.

There certainly have been times down through the years when I surprised her with something she always wanted, but it seems to be getting harder. So, like a lot of husbands, I often times get her a gift certificate. Pretty romantic, huh? Then there is the meal, should we go out to dinner, or stay in and have a nice meal – cooked by family. Decisions, decisions! And if you think Bev is hard finding a gift for, you cannot imagine how difficult and challenging buying a gift for the pro ball players was. We worked with them for 14 years, and always struggled with what to get the person who has everything.

Speaking of the person who has everything, what do you get the Son of God for a gift? Talk about a monumental challenge! It is challenging enough for us, but what would His Father get Him? What would God the Father choose to give His Son, the King of Glory – who has everything? Well, He would only get Him something He really wanted, and God would have no challenge in getting Him the perfect gift.

We do not have to guess what that gift is, because Christ in scripture has revealed it to us. Jesus tells us in John 17. Here are His own words uttered in prayer; "For you granted him (Jesus) authority over all people that he might give eternal life to all those you have given him...I have revealed you to those whom you gave me out of the world. They were yours; you gave them to me...Father, I want those you have given me to be with me..." (John 17:2, 6, 24) Wow, pretty amazing! Did you get that? What does Jesus really want, and what does the Father really want to get Him? It is us! The One who has everything – wants us! God could think of no better gift, and the Son desires no other gift.

We talk much about the gift of eternal life given to us, and that is as it should be. We are blown away that God loved us so much that He gave us His Son. No greater gift could be received. But we rarely think about the gift we are to Christ. I know that may make some of us uncomfortable. I know, we think of our sins and our own unworthiness, and wonder why Christ would want us. But He does! Think of the gift you desired the most, and now multiply that an infinite number of times, and that is how much Jesus wants us. And He will get us; the Father will make sure of that.

So, start to think of the gift you are to Christ – purchased at an unbelievable price. Jesus wants you, and God made sure He had you. This day, this week, this life, think of how you are a gift to the Son of God. It will change how you think and conduct yourself. "I am God's gift to His Son". Don't hold anything back and make sure He has all of you. I am wanted, desired and purchased - what an amazing thought!

# 84
# SO, WHAT WOULD YOU PUT ON YOUR TOMBSTONE?

A strange question, right? Most of us do not sit around wondering about our tombstone, I mean, that means death! Besides, if you are like me, you are still holding out for the rapture!

Several years ago, I was in meetings in Indiana and a man approached me and gave me a book. The book was *Behold the Camels Cometh*. It was a very old book, and I assumed the man was giving it to me because he knew I collected old religious books – by the way, the book was on the encounter of Isaac with Rebekah (found in Genesis 24). But, as it turned out, it was not because I was a collector of old books. He said to me; "Look on the inside cover". I did, and I saw the name "Harold Jolliffe". Now, that name means nothing to you, but it was my grandfather's name. I was shocked! I asked this gentleman if he knew my grandfather, and he replied that he did.

Now, you have to understand that I did not know my grandfather, or at least, I do not remember him. He died when

I was a little boy. So, I was fascinated by having something my grandfather owned. This was before my mother died (1986), so I called her up and asked her about Grandpa Jolliffe. My mom was English, and her whole family was very reserved. They just didn't talk much about each other. So I knew very little. She didn't offer a lot of information, but she did say; "Well, I will tell you one thing about your grandfather, he had one word on his tombstone." "What's that?" I asked. "It is the word, forgiven'" she replied.

Harold H. Jolliffe 1897 – 1955

Forgiven

She went on to explain, that when the family heard what was to be on the grave marker, they wondered why he picked those words. Was it because he struggled with the concept of forgiveness, and it was always a question mark in his mind? No, the reason was that he could never get over the wonder of sins forgiven – his sins. It captured his mind and heart, and shaped him all his days.

Wow, I thought! I want to be like grandpa! I want to be a man who never forgets his roots – grounded in Calvary. The prophet Micah had it right; "Who is a God like you, who pardons sin and forgives the transgression of the remnant of His inheritance." (Micah 718) When was the last time we sat in wonder and awe, and contemplated God's forgiveness of our own sins? "I, even I, am He who blots out your transgressions, for my own sake, and remembers your sins no more." (Isaiah 43:25)

About three years ago, I was in meetings in Michigan, and in-between those meetings, I visited the cemetery where my grandfather was buried (I had not even known where he was buried). A friend went with me, and we found the spot where he was buried – but there was no grave marker! We doubled checked with the office at the cemetery, and they assured me he was buried in that location. So, we began to dig! After about 3 or 4 inches, we hit the grave marker. We began to scrape and clean, and eventually we uncovered the entire grave marker (it was a flat and low to the ground). The years and weather had covered it up. But, by the time we were done, it almost looked new. We both just stood there staring at it. I asked to be alone for a moment. A strong emotion filled my heart, and I was suddenly "choked up". These words came out of my mouth; "O God please let me be like my grandfather. Don't let my life become like this cemetery, and time and circumstances cover up my strong belief and gratitude for your mercy and grace".

We took a picture of the grave marker and I carry it in my Bible. As I type this devotional, I am looking at that picture. It is a vivid reminder to me. But, for each of us, we need only look to the cross as a reminder. Why not right now thank God for your forgiveness of sins, and why not right now ask God to "haunt" your life always with that glorious truth? And let's keep the gravesite clear.

Bruce McDonald

# 85
# WHAT MAKES THEM DO IT?

In World War II, the Army Air Forces lost 35,933 AAF planes. A staggering number, but when you add the 52,651 stateside AAF accidents that happened during that same time, the numbers are mind boggling. What would make a man want to pilot one of these planes?

Laura Hillenbrand, in her excellent book *Unbroken*, gives numbers unseen before of the casualties and accidents of B-24s during the Second World War. During one three month training period, she recounts that 3,041 of these planes crashed. That was non-combative! Add to that the wartime casualties, and you had a fifty percent chance of not returning when flying one of these missions.

Why would anyone pilot these planes? When I read those statistics, I thought of another branch of the Armed Services, our National Coast Guard. Their motto is, "Semper Paratus," which means "always prepared". But, within their ranks, they have another motto, one that the public hears nothing about. That motto or unwritten code is; "The book says you have to go out, it doesn't say anything about coming back." I think the Coast Guard and the early Army Air Force pilots understood the same principle. And, to be truthful, all who have or are serving in the military, understand this: "You fight; you serve, regardless of the outcome."

I think the early Christians were captivated by this same motto and spirit. In fact, not just the Christians of the New Testament, but the believers down through church history as well. For instance, there is a letter missionary Adoniram Judson wrote in 1809 to the parents of the girl he wanted to marry. Part of that letter reads:

*"I have now to ask, whether you can consent to part with your daughter next spring, to see her no more in this world; whether you can consent to her departure, and her subjection to the hardships and sufferings of missionary life; whether you can consent to her exposure to the dangers of the ocean, to the fatal influence of the southern climate of India; to every kind of want and distress; to degradation, insult, persecution, and perhaps a violent death. Can you consent to all this, for the sake of Him who left His heavenly home, and died for her and for you?"*

I know, that's a hard letter to read. Who would write such a thing? I think it was one who had the same spirit as those WWII pilots and the Coast Guard. It seems so foreign to us today. I heard the President of a Mission Agency say once that the greatest deterrent today to young people surrendering to missions, is that they want more "guarantees" of how they will be taken care of on the mission field. What promises they can receive of a "safe return". But it is not just the young men and women, parents are asking this of mission agencies for their adult children. A pretty sobering thought as it relates to "conditions of surrender".

So, what is it that makes people willing to go out in the face of uncertainties and, at times, dangers? Well, for the soldier, it probably is both a sense of doing what's right and necessary, but also realizing that there are no other options. This must be done, and they are willing to lay their lives on the line for it. For the believer, the call to unconditional surrender comes both from a sense of duty – a high calling, but also a glimpse of the One in whom we are serving. Isaiah saw the Lord and said "Here am I send me". (Isaiah 6:8). Moses "persevered because he saw him who is invisible." (Hebrews 11:27) Willing to "go out" certainly has a large element of seeing the cause, but it is more than that - it is seeing The One who has called us to such an adventure.

Make no mistake about it, there are casualties out there. Like the WWII pilots, we don't volunteer unaware. And like the Coast Guard, we understand the call is first to "go out", not to come back. But when we leave, oftentimes our areas of comfort, we find that God has not only sent us, but He is there waiting for us. The safest place is in the perfect plan of God. Safety may not mean "coming back", but even if we don't, we go on to be with Him.

Perhaps such a thought and challenge would seem appropriate being addressed to those who are contemplating surrendering to God in full time vocational service. I pray that would be the case. We need a whole new generation raised up to "heed the call". But it is also appropriate for all of us. We need a fresh challenge to "see the Lord". When we do, we are rocked out of our lethargy and comfortableness. Statistics and projections of uncertainties don't unsettle us. We have seen the Lord, and we want to join His cause. At home, at school, at work, or overseas, we hop into that cockpit or climb aboard that boat, and we "go out". We'll never be the same, and neither will our world. We never know what will happen when we go out, but, ultimately, we know that something wonderful awaits us; "And the ransomed of the Lord will return. They will enter Zion singing; everlasting joy will crown their heads. Gladness and joy will overtake them, and sorrow and sighing will flee away." (Isaiah 35:10)

# 86
# WHEN JESUS LEAVES

"When Jesus leaves" sounds rather frightening doesn't it? But there are times when believers struggle with a sense of God's abandonment. Saint John of the Cross (not to endorse him or his writings) coined a phrase, "Dark Night of the Soul", which many believers have felt they experienced when Jesus "seems to go away". The great Apologist C.S. Lewis, while watching his beloved wife Joy slowly die of cancer, wrote his powerful book, *A Grief Observed*. Many years before that he wrote *The Problem of Pain*. An excellent book, but his grief observed caused him to ask some powerful and penetrating questions that only one can feel in the dark night of the soul. Listen to these words from Lewis' pen; *"Go to Him (God) when your need is desperate, when all other help is vain, and what do you find? A door slammed in your face and a sound of bolting and double bolting on the inside. After that, silence. You may well turn away. The longer you wait, the more emphatic the silence will become. There are no lights in the windows. It might be an empty house. Was it ever inhabited?"*

As I have written at other times, many Bible Characters – stalwarts of the faith – struggled in the same way as Lewis (see

Jeremiah, David and Job, among others). But we don't need to look at great men and women of the past, or even from the pages of scripture, because, truthfully, we struggle with feelings of abandonment. I thought of the title for this chapter when I recently read the account of John the Baptist being beheaded.

Jesus' relationship with John the Baptist has always intrigued me, and, to be truthful, confused me. After all four gospels introduce John early – and Luke's account goes into great explanation of his miraculous birth (to aged parents), we really do not have much on John. He was highly anticipated as Jesus' forerunner; he baptizes Jesus, says much about Him, points others to Him as "The Lamb of God", but then, mysteriously disappears from Jesus' life. We really do not know if Jesus ever saw John again after the baptism. This is confusing! It would seem that they would travel in tandem, John setting the stage and then Jesus coming to the platform. After all the "press" on John's birth and ministry, he slips away, and except for two isolated references, we hear no more of him. John's ministry may have lasted less than a year! What was that all about? And besides Jesus not staying connected to the one who would be announcing Him, John was also a relative.

But here is the passage I want to bring to your attention. It is found in Matthew 4:12; "When he (Jesus) heard that John had been arrested, he left Judea and returned to Galilee." Did you follow that? Not only had Jesus not come to spend time with John, or even bring him along in ministry, but when John is arrested – Jesus leaves! No going to see him in prison (or confinement), no special miracle to release him. And here is the most amazing thing – no special words of comfort, either directly, or through another messenger. In fact, even as John sits in his cell, and begins to have doubts – so much so that he sends some of his own disciples to Jesus to get some words of comfort – Jesus does not say a word to his (John's disciples) about His love and concern for John. He doesn't even give hope for a promised future (read Matthew 11:1-19). And then John dies - perhaps shortly after he sent his disciples to Jesus - a horrible death. Where was Jesus? He had left!

Okay, now I really have your attention! Like the quote from C.S. Lewis I mentioned, Jesus seemed to be absent when John needed Him the most. Why does this happen? And does Jesus really leave us when we need Him most? If I didn't believe that Jesus is always with us, especially in our time of need, I would never – ever – seek to serve and love Him. Life would be too frightening. Jesus' withdrawal is only apparent, not real. Oh, the feelings of Him being gone are real, but that is what they are - feelings. The fact of the matter is "I will never fail you, I will never abandon you" were Jesus' words to us (Hebrews 13:5). He has also said, "I am with you always, even unto the ends of the earth." (Matthew 28:20)

C. S. Lewis later gained that assurance and so did the men and women of scripture. The same Jesus who said to Nathaniel "I saw you under the fig tree" (John 1:48) is the one, who, though He was absent in body, was beholding John in prison – and upholding him. Jesus has never abandoned anyone, and He never will. God has many reasons, known only to Him, why He seems to "leave" when things get difficult. But He will watch over you as "the apple of His eye" (Psalm 17:8). He will be there, even when you think Him gone, to give you grace for any present situations. The good thing, make that, the great thing, is that He will be there for you even if you do not have enough present faith to believe He is there. The one who gave His life for you will not leave you in your darkest hour. He is there and He cares.

Bruce McDonald

# 87
# MY NEEDS AREN'T MET

It's not that I haven't heard this many times, or that I haven't felt or said it myself at times. But having two friends make similar comments within a short time of each other really touched my heart. One friend said, with tears in her eyes, "I have been praying so long for my two sons, and they still have not changed. Why won't God answer my prayers? It seems like evil is stronger than God. I don't know if I can trust him anymore." And then another friend said these words; "I have prayed so much and so hard for God to heal me and take away my pain, but I guess, because He is sovereign, He has already determined what He wants to do, and my praying doesn't matter."

I'm sure you have heard similar words, or have thought or expressed those feelings yourself. The topic of unanswered prayer is vast and complicated. The strange thing is, that it is generally those who walk closest with God and love Him dearly, that struggle the most with this. As followers of God, we realize that we are not our own, and that we have been bought with a price (I Corinthians 6:19-20). We also realize that, like our Savior Jesus Christ, we should always desire

314

God's will to be done, and not ours – unless it aligns with His (Matthew 6:10). But having said that, we naturally assume (excuse the bluntness of this phrase) – "That God will do His part of the relationship and take care of us." We understand desires are kind of "iffy", so when we pray about certain desires, we have somewhat prepared ourselves that those may not be answered. Although, truth be told, God oftentimes does give us the desires of our hearts. But when we bring our needs to Him – real needs, we believe that He is going to meet those and answer our prayers. After all, He has gone on record and said; "And my God will meet all your needs according to his glorious riches in Christ Jesus." (Philippians 4:19)

Philippians 4:19 is a wonderful truth and promise, make no mistake about that. But there are times when it sure seems like needs are not met and Christ-honoring prayers are not answered. So what do we do with that? What are our thoughts of God at that time? The Psalmist said; "I was young and now I am old, yet I have never seen the righteous forsaken or their children begging bread." (Psalm 37:25) Really? Do you believe it is only the lost and unsaved that have gone without food and have been forced to beg? Have God's children never experienced hunger – severe hunger?

Some of you are getting uncomfortable at this point. So, let me assure you, I am not seeking to doubt God or His Word. But let me just continue with this thought for a moment. Think of Proverbs 10:22; "The blessings of the Lord makes one rich, and he adds no sorrow to it." Really? Riches for everyone, and with it no sorrow? How does the believer respond when needs (seemingly) are not met? What happens when we pray – and pray, about something good and important – and potentially Christ-honoring, but still get no answer, or worse yet, things become worse? Why does God, at times, seem to not keep His Word? Unanswered prayer for a broken marriage, a wayward child, a split church, a harmful government ruling, or a job that keeps us afloat? Notice that I am not even mentioning health issues, or things that may seem to be personal desires. However, I'm talking about life, necessities and things honoring to God.

Not easy questions, and certainly, not easy answers. Unanswered prayer hurts, and especially so, when it is a legitimate need or an obvious Christ-honoring request. The Bible does not shield us from those who experienced these same dilemmas. The same book – the Bible, that gives us so many promises, also reveals times when its heroes experienced the lack of those answers and provisions. People prayed, and Peter is released and James is beheaded. People prayed, and John the Baptist's head is removed at the whim of a petty woman. The list of characters is extensive. But the issue is you, not characters from long ago. What about you, or better yet, "why you?"

I believe that one of the things about faith is believing that God is not only good and wise, but that He is mysterious. Jesus said to His closest friends; "You don't realize now what I am doing, but later you will understand." (John 13:7) Simply put, there are times when God's actions – or lack of them, will make no sense – at least right now. Why does God not answer certain prayers and meet certain needs? I don't know. He still wants us to come to Him – regularly, persistently, and in faith. But He may choose not to answer.

In some ways, trusting God in the midst of failed promises (read this line again), is the greatest act of worship. It really is. Not only praising Him for answers, but praising Him when He seems to not have kept His word. In John chapter 6, Jesus says and does something that doesn't make sense to His followers at the time. Many start to leave Him. Jesus turns to His twelve apostles and says; "You do not want to leave too, do you?" (John 6:67).

I guess, in some ways, that is where many of us are who

have experienced disappointment with God in not answering certain prayers. Will we leave also? Oh to have the faith of the Old Testament Prophet Habakkuk; "Though the fig tree does not bud and there are no grapes on the vines, though the olive crop fails and the fields produce no food, though there are no sheep in the pen and cattle in the stalls, yet I will rejoice in the Lord, I will be joyful in God my Savior." (Habakkuk 3:17-18) Notice Habakkuk didn't have his needs met, but chose to trust and praise God in spite of this. An earlier Old Testament saint voiced this conviction even stronger; Job put it this way; "Though he slay me, yet will I hope in him." (Job 13:15)

Life is hard, and finding answers to unanswered prayer can be difficult. Perhaps we'll never know the answers why in this lifetime. Remember Jesus' words; "later you will understand". In the meantime, keep praying, but also keep on believing that He is not only good, wise, and all-powerful, but He also is mysterious. He knows what He is doing. Heaven will be one of those "now I see" moments. But, even now, God is here and He loves you. He will work His perfect plan out for you. Perhaps He is giving you this time to trust Him in the dark, so that your praise and worship can ripple through a watching universe. You just never know.

Bruce McDonald

# 88
# WHISPER TO ME THOSE THREE LITTLE WORDS!

I know what you are thinking, but it's not those words! The three words "I love you" are wonderful, but there are actually three other words that are more special. They are "you are forgiven". Stop and think about it… Could any words be so meaningful and life-changing? I thought of that this morning during my Bible reading. I was reading in Isaiah, and I came across Isaiah 6:7; "Behold, this has touched your lips; your guilt is taken away, and your sin atoned for." Wow, what awesome news! This account has to do with Isaiah seeing God, and realizing that he, Isaiah, was a man of unclean lips. He was in the presence of a holy God, but God made provision for Isaiah by having a seraphim touch his lips with a live coal off of God's alter. He was declared clean and forgiven. How much more so each of us who has been forgiven and cleansed by the blood of Christ!

I believe that we do not stop and think about this enough. We need to hear those three little words over and over again, "you are forgiven". What are the best words you have ever heard? Perhaps some of the following:

- Yes, I'll marry you
- You are pregnant
- It will be a girl
- It will be a boy
- The test proved negative
- You have a refund coming
- The problem was just a loose wire
- You have a buyer
- They accepted your bid
- Eat all you want

No matter what you are currently experiencing, the news that your sins are forgiven should forever put a song in your heart. Think on some of the following verses; "In him we have redemption through his blood, the forgiveness of sins." (Ephesians 1:7) "In him we have redemption, the forgiveness of sins." (Colossians 1:14) "He forgave us all our sins." (Colossians 2:13) "Your sins have been forgiven on account of his name." (I John 2:12) We could never earn forgiveness, we do not deserve forgiveness, and we could never show enough gratitude to keep forgiveness in place. Our sins have been atoned for, completely paid for, and the slate has been wiped clean. O what great news! Go forth this day with a song in your heart for sins forgiven. Perhaps you will appreciate this old puritan prayer found in the excellent book "The Valley of Vision":

*"Blessed Lord Jesus,*

*Before thy cross I kneel and see the heinousness of my sin, my iniquity that caused thee to be made a curse, the evil that excites the severity of divine wrath. Show me the enormity of my guilt by the crown of thorns, the pierced hands and feet, the bruised body, the dying cries. Thy blood is the blood of incarnate God, its worth infinite, its value beyond all thought. Infinite must be the evil and guilt that demands such a price. Sin is my*

Bruce McDonald

*malady, my monster, my foe, my viper, born in my birth, alive in my life, strong in my character, dominating my faculties, following me as a shadow, intermingling with my every thought, my chain that holds me captive in the empire of my soul. Sinner that I am, why should the sun give me light, the air supply breath, the earth bear my tread, its fruits nourish me, its creatures sub serve my ends?*

*Yet thy compassions yearn over me, thy heart hastens to my rescue, thy love endured my curse, thy mercy bore my deserved stripes. Let me walk humbly in the lowest depths of humiliation, bathed in thy blood, tender of conscience, triumphing gloriously as an heir of salvation."*

# 89
# IN A HOLDING PATTERN

It is called a "holding pattern", and people who fly do not like to hear that announcement. A holding pattern is what pilots and planes are instructed to do when, for some reason, they cannot land at the airport at the designated time. So, the control tower sends them off somewhere away from the flight lanes coming in, and they simply do large circles until cleared to land. "Holding Patterns" can be short – say, 20 minutes or so, or they can be long – such as over an hour. No one likes to have a plane go on a holding pattern. There can be many reasons for holding patterns; weather issues, backed-up traffic, problems on a runway, or even having the President's plane on the ground (Air force One). A holding pattern can cause all sorts of problems; people missing connecting flights, and family or friends left waiting in cars or at the airport to pick them up. Holding patterns are not fun!

I recently had an experience with a holding pattern on one of my flights. It ended up being the most harrowing flying experience I have had in all my years of air travel. I was flying from San Diego to Denver, and an announcement came on

321

saying there were thunderstorms in Denver, and we had been instructed to go into a holding pattern for 1 hour. One hour, yikes! So, that is what we did, and then we were instructed to wait another hour. All this time we were in turbulent clouds and being bounced around like I have never experienced. Suddenly, the pilot pointed the plane down and we dropped to a low elevation. We were bouncing back and forth, and then we hit a "wind-sheer" (the pilot told us afterward). So, we lurched forward, and for a moment, I, and all the other passengers, thought we would crash. The pilot suddenly pulled up, and we landed on the runway – oh, not the Denver runway, the Colorado Springs runway. We had been diverted! We sat on the tarmac at the Colorado Springs Airport for an hour and a half. We were not allowed to get off the plane (though by now, there were several panicking passengers). The pilot finally got the go-ahead to try Denver again, and this time we made it. It took us 6 hours on a flight that normally is 1 hour and 45 minutes. As you can imagine, several missed their connecting flights.

Now, right at this point, several of you are saying; "You see, that is why I don't fly!" But you know what? You don't have to fly to experience maddening – and frightening "holding patterns". Many of you have experienced these in your life, or you may be experiencing one right now. And perhaps you have been in a long holding pattern. A holding pattern is any time we are stopped in our pursuit of a desired destination or expected plan. Like myself, when I couldn't do anything about it (for some reason they didn't want me to take over the plane, and I had already tried to change the weather pattern), we feel totally helpless. And, truthfully, we sometimes feel totally frustrated.

The Bible calls holding patterns waiting on the Lord. Times we are called to wait are both unexpected and unplanned for. It seems like our heavenly pilot, or, better yet, our heavenly life controller, makes calls and plans without consulting us. And

He even seems indifferent to our schedules. Take heart friend, you are not alone in this experience.

In fact, it is the lot of all true followers of Christ. Think of all the saints in scripture who had to wait for God's promise – or promises. Noah, Abraham, Joseph, Moses, David, and just about anyone who is profiled in scripture. They all had to go on holding patterns. Perhaps that is why the command and counsel in scripture is, over and over again, to wait on the Lord. "Wait for the Lord; be strong and take heart and wait for the Lord." (Psalm 27:14) "Be still before the Lord and wait patiently before him." (Psalm 37:7) God's people are told to wait for His purpose to be fulfilled in their lives; to wait for the answers to their prayers; to wait for the Return of Christ (I Corinthians 1:7; I Thessalonians 1:10; Titus 2:13). God can be counted on to keep His word, even if it is not in our timing.

It may be difficult to imagine God in a "Control Tower", but realize He is always our "guide". "For this God is our God for ever and ever; he will be our guide even unto the end." (Psalm 48:14) And at the end of each hope and dream, He is there doing much more than we can imagine. "He stilled the storm to a whisper; the waves of the sea were hushed. They were glad when it grew calm, and he guided them to their desired destination." (Psalm 107:29-30) He is always our Shepherd "Who guides me in paths of righteousness for his sake." (Psalm 23:3)

May God encourage all of us with this wonderful promise; "The Lord longs to be gracious to you; he rises to show you compassion. For the Lord is a God of justice. Blessed are all who wait for him." (Isaiah 30:18) Oh, and by the way, you do remember, that all those saints who were made to wait on God (some didn't do well in the waiting part), they all eventually, and in a very unique way, saw God's promises fulfilled.

There is one other thing you might like to know; that

holding pattern of mine and the diverting to Colorado Springs? It really wasn't a wasted time. Though I never saw this coming, God opened the door for me to share with a young Jewish man who was sitting behind me. I would not have had that opportunity, unless the plane had sat on that runway for an hour and a half. We were all allowed to stand up and walk around. And it also just so happened that I was just pulling out a copy of *Israel My Glory*, the magazine put out by "The Friends of Israel". I was able to leave that with Him. Hmm…maybe God does know best! I don't know how long you have been in your holding pattern, but it will not last forever, there is a reason for it. Trust our Guide in the Control Tower.

# 90
# WHO DID THIS?

If you are a parent, or for that matter, if you had parents (which includes all of us!), you have heard the words, or have uttered them, "who did this?" Milk is spilled, a glass is broken, a husband's razor was used to shave legs, or games were left out on the table. Most of the time, the question is answered, but sometimes it is not. "It just happened" or "no one did it". Perhaps it is confessed years later; "you know that last piece of cake you were saving for yourself, well I ate it!" But now it is years later and it really doesn't matter.

We had a funny thing happen a few years ago. We were watching an old home video of the boys and I playing basketball (a small ball and hoop) in our living room, something which Bev often frowned on – "you'll break something", she would say. Well, as we watched the video, one of the boys (honest, it wasn't me) knocked over a lamp and broke it. The age old mystery was solved! He was "busted" years later. Pretty amazing evidence! It took a while, but we discovered the culprit.

Bruce McDonald

As I write this, it's the Easter season and an age old question must be asked; "Who did this?" The cross of Christ, the crucifixion, who did this to Christ? The most heinous crime in the history of our earth, who was the perpetrator? This is a very important question, and the answer has far reaching implications. Let us see if we can figure it out. Was it the Roman soldiers? They were the ones who roughed him up, literally tortured Him. They led Him to the cross and nailed Him there. Certainly they were guilty! How about Pilate? He vacillated and washed his hands after condemning Christ to be crucified. He most assuredly was guilty. If Pilate was guilty, then the Jewish leaders were even more guilty. Jesus indicated this; "The one who handed me over to you is guilty of a greater sin." (John 19:11) How about the Jews themselves? When given the chance to set Christ free, they demanded Barabbas instead. And even said the horrible words; "Let His blood be on us and our children". (Matthew 27:25) Yes, all these were guilty, but perhaps you are thinking, "What about Judas?" Certainly, him too, most assuredly so; "Judas, are you betraying the Son of Man with a kiss?" (Luke 22:48)

However, there are two more people who have to come forward to confess this crime. The first one is….you and I. That's right, we did it. It was our sins that drove Christ to the cross. I Corinthians 15:1 puts it succinctly; "Christ died for our sins." Christ was spotless and blameless, He never sinned, ever. But our sins had to be paid for, so He chose to pay for them. "For Christ died for sins once for all, the righteous for the unrighteous, to bring you to God." (I Peter 3:18) "The Lord has laid on Him the iniquity of us all." (Isaiah 53:6) "God made Him who had no sin to be sin for us, so that in Him we might become the righteousness of God." (II Corinthians 5:21 "Who did this?" We did! Our sins made it necessary to go to the cross. Our sins were the nails that held Him fast.

But, wait, there is one other as guilty as we are. In fact, there is one who was the most responsible. Are you ready for this? It was…God Himself! The Godhead chose the payment for sins, the only payment that would satisfy a holy God, to be that of the Son of God. It is true that there could be no other way, but, still, in eternity past, God chose this ultimate payment of love. "For God so loved the world He gave His only begotten Son." (John 3:16) The crucifixion, even the betrayal, did not come as a surprise to Christ. He constantly told His disciples this would happen (see Matthew 20:19; 26:2 and other passages). He came into this world for this very reason.

Oh dear friends, think of it! Christ was not a victim. Though the Jews, Romans, Pilate, Judas and the religious leaders were all guilty, He was not a victim. Though you and I put Him on the cross – our sins did this – yet He still had a choice. And that choice was exercised in eternity past. God chose this, and the Son volunteered. No wonder Christ could say; "Greater love has no man than this, than He lay down His life for His friends." (John 15:13) Yes we are His friends – now, but He laid down His life when we were His enemies! "For if, when we were enemies, we were reconciled to Him through the death of His Son" and "Christ died for the ungodly" (Romans 5:10, 6). Today, be in awe, and be forever grateful, that you know "Who did this"! The cross was planned out of a heart of love and mercy – for you.

Bruce McDonald

# 91
# SOMEONE IS WATCHING YOU

In 1546, a young man of 32 years of age stood before a religious tribunal made up of the Cardinal of Scotland and two Bishops. Also in attendance were several other Bishops and a vast audience of people from throughout Scotland. The young man's name was George Wishart, and he was being tried for preaching the gospel to the people of Scotland. George was a school teacher by trade, but God marvelously saved him – at the time, the only genuine believer in all of Scotland!

Young George began to grow quickly in Christ, and even snuck out of the country to sit at the feet of John Calvin. Though he had religious freedom while in Switzerland, his heart ached for his homeland Scotland, lost in religious darkness. At cost of his life, he went back to Scotland and began preaching. Soon he was arrested and thrown in a dungeon at Saint Andrews castle, where he waited to be called to trial in the Cathedral at Saint Andrews. In a mock trial, he was sentenced to be burned at the stake. And, just before sentencing, his accusers said; *"if we give him license to preach, he is so crafty, and in Holy Scriptures so exercised, that he will persuade the people to his opinion, and raise them against us."* Wishart was taken back to the dungeon, lowered down into it, to await execution the next day.

The following morning, Wishart was tied to the stake. The stake was surrounded by sticks, which would soon be burning to consume his body. Bags of gunpowder were tied to his clothes, so they would explode in flames as the fire moved higher up his body. Hundreds gathered around him and wept openly. He was greatly loved, more than any man in Scotland. The man who was to light the fire cried out; *"Sir, I pray you to forgive me".* Young Wishart looked down at the man and said; *"Lo, here is a token that I forgive thee; my heart, do your office."* At this, he leaned down and kissed the man on his cheek. Turning to the crowd he called out; *"Christian brothers and sisters, be not offended at the word of God...Love the word...I suffer gladly for the Redeemer's sake...Fear not those who can slay the body, for they cannot slay the soul...My soul shall sup with my savior this night."* And then, the sticks were lit, and the body of young George Wishart went up in flames...And the enemy won...or did he?

As the crowd watched in horror, and saw the mocking of the religious leaders, many cried out in anguish. But far back in the crowd stood another young man, a slender figure whose face was illuminated by the flames. Tears ran down his face as he stood there clenching and unclenching his fist, wishing he could do something – be someone. That moment sealed the fate of that young man, and that moment changed the entire history of Scotland. For you see, that young man, unnoticed by the Roman Catholic leaders, was none other than John Knox. The man who would become Scotland's greatest reformer, was unleashed that night. The flames of the fire that consumed George Wishart ignited John Knox. It was John Knox, whom Mary Queen of Scotland would later say; *"I fear John Knox down on his knees more than all of England's armies."*

Little did anyone know there was a young man named John

Knox watching, and dear friend, little do you and I know who is watching our life. Is there a young Timothy watching an Apostle Paul? A young Joshua watching the great emancipator Moses? We forget "watching eyes", and those eyes especially are focused on us when we go through our own deep waters. The trials you are bearing up under, the ones that so constrain you and stretch you to the limit, are not only producing something in you. They are not only giving you an opportunity to trust and worship God when it doesn't make sense, but they are also being used to light a fire in others. That little girl or young woman who is watching you, may be the next great woman of God. That little boy or young man, who is secretly observing you go through this trial, may be being prepared for a great work of God. And not just younger ones, those our age and older, will be emboldened for Christ and challenged to join in the conflict for Christ.

Paul wrote that we are to; "Set an example for the believers in speech, in life, in love, in faith, and in purity." (I Timothy 4:12) Is this trial purposeless? Is this an end in itself? Or is someone watching – perhaps lurking back in the shadows, one you are not even aware of? "Watching eyes"…may we all be reminded that our lives affect others much more than we could ever imagine.

# 92
# ARE THERE TATTOOS IN HEAVEN?

His name is Matiu, and I met him while hiking up a mountain in New Zealand. Matiu, which is Matthew in Maori, is a man who would catch your attention if you saw him. A relatively young man, who is tall and muscular. But the initial thing you notice about Matiu, is that his face and head are covered with tattoos. Now I worked with professional athletes for 14 years, so I am used to seeing bodies covered with tattoos. But Matiu's tattoos would far surpass any of the NBA ballplayers. His face and skull (clean shaven) are completely covered with decorative tattoos. Part of this would be because of his Maori heritage (Maoris are the original Polynesian residents of New Zealand and many of the surrounding islands), but another part would have to do with his past.

You might not be drawn to Matiu at first, because, well, because he is rather intimidating in his appearance. He even dresses the part of a gang member. But you would be wrong in thinking this man is not a wonderful follower of Christ. In fact, he heads up a ministry in New Zealand called "Peacekeepers". Matiu and his ministry seek to reach not only gang members, but also any others out there who may be hurting, or have felt the sting of rejection. Matiu shared with me, that he himself, has often felt that rejection from fellow believers. But God has raised him up, and he is being used of God in an integral way in the Body of Christ.

I am not sure what you think of tattoos. It used to be that we would only on occasion run into Christians with tattoos. There was a time when this was especially an issue in the church, not to mention, in the family. Now, in most circles, the unusual has become the familiar. I recall a time when I was working with NBA ball players, and a player called me up and told me he was thinking of getting a tattoo, but wanted to know if I thought Christians should get tattoos. Things have changed much since that time.

This devotional is not about addressing the issue of "should Christians get tattoos". But what I want you to consider, is this, "Will there be tattoos in heaven"? I mean, just what will carry over? What about the hole in someone's ear from where they wear an earring? Will that be there? Will birthmarks still be on the bodies? Fun questions, but what I really want you to understand is that there will definitely be tattoos in heaven – for sure! And guess who will have this notable tattoo? Christ! Listen to this wonderful passage in Isaiah 49:15-16; "Can a mother forget the baby at her breast and have no compassion on the child she has borne? Though she may forget, I will not forget you! See, I have engraved you on the palms of my hands; your walls are ever before me." Wow, did you catch that? God – Christ, has engraved you on the palms of His hands.

When you think of tattoos, there are a few questions that come to your mind. 1) What is tattooed there? 2) Where is the tattoo? and 3) How long will it last? Well, number one, as far as God's tattoo, your name is what is tattooed there. Tattoos usually have a name or title a person likes to be known as.

Some pretty bodacious names on entertainers and athletes. Or there will be symbols, something they want to identify with, or something they think is special. Think about it, God could have engraved one of His Names or Titles – "The Rock", "The Truth" or "All-Powerful". But He didn't. He could have engraved the sun, the moon or any other part of His creation. But He didn't. Your name is there!

Now, secondly, consider where His tattoo is. For some, tattoos are concealed, or on a part of the body that is less noticeable. For others, it is out in plain sight for others to see. But, sometimes, the one with the tattoo can't see it themselves. Where is God's? On His hand, where He can see it at any time, and also where He can hold it up for others to see.

And third, how long will it last – forever! Throughout all of eternity, your name is before Him. But what exactly is this tattoo of your name? It is this, "The nail prints on his hands from the cross." Because you see, it was not the nails that held Christ to the cross, it was you. Your sins and His love for you, kept Him on the cross until the price for sin was paid. The amazing truth is that the only reminder of sin in heaven is on the hands and feet of Jesus. Remember His post-resurrection appearance to the apostles? He said; "Put your finger here; see my hands." (John 20:27) In the book of Revelation, it is recorded that when John saw Jesus, he saw a "freshly slain lamb" (Revelation 5:6). Evidently, the marks on Christ throughout eternity will be freshly visible. Amazing thought, Christ has engraved us on His hands for all of eternity.

And, here's a story I've heard to further illustrate this point. During Word War II, young RAF pilots (Royal Air force Pilots) often suffered severe burns in the line of duty. These young pilots would fly the British "Spitfires" to ward off the large lumbering German "Luftwaffe Bombers". The bombing of London lasted for over 40 days and nights, and it was only these courageous pilots flying the small spitfires that saved

England. The problem was, these planes were built for speed and not protection, and the engine sat right in front of the pilot. Whenever the plane was hit, the engine would burst into flames, and often severely burn and disfigure the pilots. The doctors did what they could, but many of the pilots would still remain disfigured and scarred. The medical staff felt horrible that they couldn't do more for these young heroes. They wondered how they would adjust to society in this condition, and more importantly, how they would be treated. But a strange thing happened, the very disfigurement, and the very scars that had been a concern, became, instead, the badge of greatness and honor. The public – and oftentimes, the children, would point with admiration to these scarred (sometime horribly) pilots, and say, "Look mommy, there's one of the heroes". People saw in the scars the great price that was paid for their freedom.

Oh dear friends, one day we too shall see the scars of the One who paid the greatest price for our freedom. His scars – His tattoos – will look so beautiful. He will hold His arms wide apart and show us His scars, and say, "This, my child, was for you. I have engraved you on my palms for forever."

# 93
# AGAINST ALL ODDS

On October 6, 1973 – Yom Kippur, the holiest day on the Jewish calendar, Egypt and Syria opened a coordinated surprise attack against Israel. The combined armies of Egypt and Syria dwarfed the military size of Israel. In the Golan Heights, 180 Israeli tanks faced 1,400 Syrian tanks. Along the Suez Canal, 436 Israeli defenders were attacked by 80,000 Egyptians. The attacks happened simultaneously. In addition to Egypt and Syria, nine other nations aided in the attack. Iraq sent 18,000 soldiers and hundreds of tanks. Saudi Arabia sent 3,000 troops and Libya gave 1 billion dollars for the war effort. Tunisia sent 2,000 troops, Sudan sent another 3,500, and Morocco commissioned 2,500 men. Jordan helped the cause by bringing 100 tanks into the conflict. The Soviet Union did its normal nefarious deeds, by sending weapons and military experts to help with the cause. The result? Israel overwhelmingly defeated the combined forces of these Arab States. So much so, that the United Nations had to come to Egypt's rescue. Beating the odds is a God thing!

Almost 3,000 years before the Yom Kippur war, Israel

faced another humongous army. The odds were even more in favor of the enemy than during the Egypt/Syria conflict. The Philistines were set to attack a small army of Israeli soldiers led by King Saul. Let me read the passage for you: "The Philistines mustered a mighty army of three thousand chariots (some manuscripts read; 30,000), six thousand horsemen and as many warriors as the grains of sand along the seashore." (I Samuel 13:5) How many did Israel have? Here is what scripture records; "Saul was staying on the outskirts of Gibeah…with him were about 600 men." (I Samuel 14:2) What was Israel's response? "When the men of Israel saw the vast number of enemy troops, they lost their nerve entirely and tried to hide in caves, holes, rocks, tombs, and cisterns." (I Samuel 13:6) Things were hopeless, and to make things worse – Israel had no weapons to fight with! I Samuel 13:22 says; "None of the people of Israel had a sword or spear, except for Saul and Jonathan."

Wow, how would victory ever be possible? How does anyone face such overwhelming odds and win? The answer is, "there always needs to be a Jonathan!" You see, one thing the Philistines did not reckon on, was that Jonathan stood between them and victory. Jonathan had already won an important victory earlier (I Samuel 13:3), and this really made the Philistines angry. This is why they marshaled such a great army against Israel.

But, get this, remember how I read where the Israelites were terrified, and went into hiding? Well, they did - that is everyone except Jonathan. What did Jonathan do? Let's listen in; "Jonathan said to his young armor-bearer, 'Come, let's go over to the outpost of those uncircumcised fellows. Perhaps the Lord will act in our behalf. Nothing can hinder the Lord from saving, whether by many or few." (I Samuel 14:6) Don't miss that, Jonathan had tapped into something that no one else had, not even his father the king. Here it is, "Odds mean nothing to God! In fact, God loves overwhelming odds –

against His people! Abraham with 318 of his servants fighting against 4 kings and their armies (Genesis 14:14); Gideon with his 300 men against 135,000 Midianites (Judges 8:10); and now Jonathan and his armor-bearer against countless thousands. Jonathan started out by killing 20 men in hand-to-hand combat. Then, the 600 men chased and defeated the large Philistine army (God threw an earthquake in for good measure).

So what is the point? I wonder what odds you may be facing today. Does it seem that you are facing something so big – it seems countless? Perhaps it is an enemy that has struck terror into your life, or at the least, has caused you to run out of all options. Maybe it is a health issue, or a financial problem. Maybe it is a relationship difficulty, or maybe a lack of relationship. Perhaps a dead-end job or lack of job. It might be a ministry challenge or a failed dream. I realize it could be countless things, but the one unifying factor is this, you are at your wits end, and the odds are overwhelming and foreboding. Dare to be a Jonathan? Did you hear his words? "Nothing can hinder the Lord from saving, whether by many or few."

Odds mean nothing to God, except that it gives Him an opportunity to shine and do something no one else can do. But here is the kicker; "He is looking for Jonathans!" Perhaps this day or night as you read this, you are one statement of faith away from a great victory. 599 soldiers missed out on the chance to see God bring a great victory through them, but one man defied the odds. He believed God. Oh Lord, give us the spirit – and faith, of Jonathan. Beating the odds is a God thing!

Bruce McDonald

# 94
# WILL I EVER LEARN?

We've had a minor emergency as I write this - our water went out. As I've mentioned before, we live almost 9000 feet up in the Rockies. Our development is on a couple of shared wells, and every once in awhile, the water drains out or the pump malfunctions. It seems that it usually happens when one of us is in the shower! Any way, it went out this morning as we were seeking to get ready to go down to the Colorado Springs to celebrate our anniversary. I found myself panicking and being "touchy" to Bev's comments. I immediately felt frustrated with myself, and asked God to forgive me.

It seems there have been many things lately – actually, this entire year – that have tested my patience and challenged my joy and faith. This has been a year of multiple surgeries, lightning strikes, computers going down, family crisis, disappointment in a ministry vision, and the death of our much loved dog. These are just to name a few. Yet, even as I mention these things, I realize how blessed we have been, and how much things are worse for others.

There is a reason I am sharing this with you, it is because of something God showed me today. Actually, reminded me once again. For most of my life, I have prayed – very hard – that I would live to "The praise of God's Glory". That I would really grow as a believer, and be a blessing in people's lives. But, especially, that I would bring God much glory. Today I read this in my Bible; "You rejoice in this (Peter had been writing about the blessing of our guaranteed inheritance), though for a time you have had to be distressed by various trials, so that the genuineness of your faith – more valuable than gold, which perishes though refined by fire – may result in praise, glory, and honor at the revelation of Jesus Christ." (I Peter 1:6,7) There it is!

If I want to have Christ receive much glory in my life, I must welcome trials. They are the chief means to give God glory, and for Him to receive praise. AND, they are the best means for spiritual growth. I know this, but why do I fight it so much? God is answering my deepest prayers and desire – to live for His glory – by sending and allowing trials. This morning, the water going out, was an opportunity to respond properly, rest in God, and even rejoice. The major events that have happened in our lives this year are opportunities to bring God glory.

God reminded me of this today, and then, to gently further this truth and reminder in my life, he had me read Spurgeon's devotional. Here is part of what he wrote-I think you can get the point clearly. Spurgeon was liking Christians who only grow when things are pleasant to that of a certain type of bush:

*"Its greenness is absolutely dependent upon circumstances, a present abundance of water makes it flourish, and a drought destroys it at once. Is this my case?...Do I love the Lord only while temporal comforts are received from His hands?...Can I honestly assert that when bodily comforts have been few, and my surroundings have been rather adverse to grace than*

*at all helpful to it, I have still held fast my integrity?....A godly man often grows best when his worldly circumstances decay. He who follows Christ for His bag is a Judas; they who follow for loaves and fishes are children of the Devil; but they who attend Him out of love to Himself are His own beloved ones. Lord, let me find my life in Thee, and not in the mire of this world's favor or gain."*

Ouch, I needed that! And perhaps you can somewhat identify with me in my weakness, and oftentimes failure. May the Lord help each of us to rejoice in the midst of our distress, and see these as opportunities to live for His praise and glory – in the midst of a watching universe!

# 95
# YOU DON'T WANT TO SEE ME ANGRY!

There is a popular comic book character – The Hulk – who utters these lines. If you do not know who the Hulk is, well, ask your kids. Bruce Banner is a mild-mannered (aren't all super heroes?) scientist, who, when he loses his temper, turns into this powerful, raging hulk of a man. You don't want to see him angry!

I hesitate to use a comic book figure to illustrate something of our Lord Jesus Christ, but I want you to see reality in the light of a fictitious character. Jesus is loving and long-suffering, and, most of the time while He was on earth, He displayed His meekness. But there is coming a day when people will see His anger – His wrath unleashed.

One of the most wonderful accounts of Jesus' miracles is found in John chapter 11, and it concerns His raising Lazarus from the dead. I want to pick a passage out of that chapter to remind us of something about Jesus. The passage goes like this; "When Jesus saw her weeping, and the Jews who had come along with her also weeping, he was deeply moved in spirit and troubled." (John 11:33) In our English reading you

341

might not catch this, but the word translated "deeply troubled" is a word that means angry, indignant or outraged. He was not angry at the crowds, or Martha and Mary, but He was angry – outraged– at sin, and the result of sin - death. This was not how He designed it to be! His creation has fallen under sin, and is in the (temporal) dominion of a usurper – Satan. And Jesus is angry (dare I say ticked off?). Not lose control angry, but righteous indignation that will be satisfied. Jesus is outraged at what sin has caused (in this case the death of Lazarus), and He is going to do something about it.

I think there are a couple reminders here for us. First of all, God is not just a sovereign, complacent God. "Well, there is going to be sin, and one day I'll do something about it." Oh no, God is sovereign – you can take that to the bank – but He is not complacent. He is angry at sin. In fact, God is so angry at sin, that He poured His wrath out on His Son to pay the penalty for our sin. But those not under the blood of Christ will find out what that wrath looks like.

There is a picture in Revelation of a true event where God is pouring His wrath out on the earth during the Tribulation period, and this is the response of the people; "Then the kings of the earth, the princes, the generals, the rich, the mighty, and every slave and every free man hid in caves and among the rocks of the mountains. They called to the mountains and the rocks, "Fall on us and hide us from the face of him who sits on the throne and from the wrath of the Lamb." (Revelation 6:15-16) Later on in Revelation, the scene switches to the end of earthly time and it portrays all lost mankind before God Almighty. This is what it says; "Earth and sky fled from his presence, and there was no place for them." (Revelation 20:11) You don't want to see God angry!

Perhaps one more picture of Jesus' wrath; "God is just: He will pay back trouble to those who trouble you and give relief to you who are troubled, and to us as well. This will happen when the Lord Jesus is revealed from heaven in blazing fire with his powerful angels. He will punish those who do not know God and do not obey the gospel of our Lord Jesus Christ." (II Thessalonians 1:6-8)

Let us never think God is indifferent to sin, wickedness and death. He is angry at it. You and I get grieved – ticked – over wickedness and sin. Injustice frustrates us, and we get angry thinking that evil is running unchecked, and that there never will be accountability. There will be, and it is coming on fast.

There is one other word I want to point out in John 11:33 and it is the word "troubled". It is a word that means "emotional turmoil". Jesus was not only angry at sin and death, but He was moved emotionally at Martha and Mary's heartache. Jesus is angry at the sin and evil that assault you – and He will do something about it. But right now, He also identifies with your heartache and confusion – He cares. So. let's take comfort in the fact that Jesus will do something about sin, wickedness and injustice, and, wow, will He ever! But in the meantime He is grieved over your hurts and sorrows. He cares, and He is a sympathetic High Priest.

Today, if you think He has forgotten, or that He will never do anything, remember that He will, and it will be pretty terrifying when He does – a lot more than the Hulk! And right now He wants to help and comfort you. He is that close.

Bruce McDonald

# 96
# YOU HAVE ONE!

Por favor, onde fica o correio? I wonder how many of you could read that opening line? It is Portuguese, and it says, "Please, where is the post office?" I did not have a clue what it said. We are leaving tomorrow morning for Brazil, and Bev has been brushing up on her Portuguese. She grew up there, but has not been back since she was 16. She is doing well, and like several people have told her, "It is like riding a bike, once you are back there you will pick it up." But she has not taken much solace in that!

In the midst of getting ready for the trip and all the meetings, I have tried to both listen to a CD and read a pocket book on "Conversing in Portuguese". In addition, Bev has tried to coach me through some words – none of this has worked. This is embarrassing to say, and admit, but I am language challenged! I have been in many countries around the world, and have failed in all of them with the local language. To be honest with you, I struggled in school with learning a foreign language. Like I said, it is embarrassing since I am a missionary myself. I have often asked God why He didn't give me the gift of languages, or at least a better aptitude for picking up some of the words. Many of my ministry friends are adept at languages, and worse yet, three of my brother-in-laws. Ouch!

You know what? I really feel like a one or two-talent guy (I added the two in there). Sometimes it is discouraging, and very humbling. I would like to use this as an excuse to not serve Christ. But the fact of the matter is I have no leg to stand on, as far as an excuse. You see God HAS gifted you and me too. It doesn't matter how much, or what type of gift. They all come from the hand of a Sovereign God who knows what He is doing. If you have not spent some time in I Corinthians 12 lately, you should. In describing some of the gifts – in a representative way – Paul says, "All these are the work of one and the same Spirit, and give them to each one, just as He determines." Later on in the chapter, he writes, "God has arranged the parts in the body, every one of them, just as He wanted them to be." Just think, God in eternity past, selected you, and chose the gift or gifts that would best fit His program.

The bottom line is that you are special, and uniquely gifted. God knew what He was about when He made and gifted you. He determined several things. Where you would be born, and where you would live (Acts 17:26), how you would look and what family you would come from (Psalm 139:13). He even handcrafted every day of your life (Psalm 139:16). Yes, God has allowed you to have input, and in His sovereignty, He uses your choices (deep stuff, I know). But make no mistake about it, God is at work in your life to bring about His eternal plan. Ultimately, it is for His glory, but also for your good too.

So lift up your head, and do not be discouraged (are you listening Bruce?), because you have your place and fit. Oh yeah, we are to serve and be faithful in many areas, and we cannot use the excuse "That is not my gift". But there will be at least one area where you will shine, and be most effective. Ate' logo! (You'll have to look that one up).

345

# 97
# YOU'RE TOO NICE!

Those words, believe it or not, came from one of my sons. To be honest, he was not saying that as a son to his father. I am sure, that at times, he probably thought I was the meanest man on the face of the earth! But he said this in regard to my coaching.

I have coached (long time ago) basketball and baseball, both on the High School and the College level. However, my son observed back then, that I was not enough of a disciplinarian, or hard enough on the players. If they felt bad, I felt bad. At least, that was his take. I thought I was a modern day Vince Lombardi, or maybe Tony Dungy, Joe Torre, and Phil Jackson all rolled into one! It is hard to know when to be kind, forgiving, understanding and loving, and then when to be firm, unmoving, and disciplinary. Parents have struggles with this, and coaches and people in positions of leadership have always been challenged by this in their roles.

What about God? Talk about a challenge! How does He act

346

consistent with all His attributes? How does He act within His nature to not violate one aspect of His Being over another? If you have been a follower of Christ for very long, you know that the cross was a beautiful picture of how mercy and justice was met. You know that God's holiness and love were satisfied in the Person and work of Christ on the cross. Much has been written (and rightfully so) on the Character and Nature of God. Volumes could be written on each attribute of God (loving, merciful, holy, just, etc.), but that is not my purpose here.

I want to pick up on my original theme "You're too nice". Make no doubt about it, God is not a God who is up in heaven as a kind, grandfatherly figure. He does not just wink at sin, and He never says "boys will be boys"! God is a holy, majestic and glorious God. But we are definitely recipients of His grace and kindness. I found a wonderful verse in, of all places, the book of Judges, on the mercy and tenderness of God. In the midst of all the rebellion going on in that book, and in the midst of God's disciplining His children (and those who professed to be), He lets shine His tender-heartedness. Here it is; "And He became impatient over the misery of Israel". Other translations say; "And He became weary of Israel's misery" and "And He could bear Israel's misery no longer". Fascinating, because God was the one that brought that misery on in His discipline and punishment.

Even when He (God) disciplines, His heart goes out to the one who is under His discipline. This is important to know, because if you and I were under the hands of an angry and capricious God, who was all-powerful, we would be in deep trouble. I know that the cross, that is Christ satisfied payment, settled this for us, but this verse is long before the cross. And it is a good reminder that God has always had a tender and compassionate heart for His people - actually, for all of His creation. I think this passage in Psalm 103 really captures the heart of God. "He does not treat us as our sins deserve or

347

repay us according to our iniquities. For as high as the heavens are above the earth, so great is His love for those who fear Him; as far as the east is from the west, so far has He removed our transgressions from us. As a father has compassion on his children, so the Lord has compassion on those who fear Him; for He knows how we are formed, He remembers we are dust."

Perhaps at this time, you are feeling like you have blown it, that you should be under God's displeasure. Keep in mind two things; one, God exhausted His wrath on Christ at the cross on our behalf, and two, He longs to be gracious to you. Even when under His discipline, He cannot stand to see you in misery for very long. One of my favorite verses, and pictures of God, is Job 36:16; "He is wooing you from the jaws of distress to a spacious place free from restriction, to the comfort of your table laden with choice food." Is God too nice? Well, I do not want to minimize the awesome presence of a Holy God, but I do want to report to you what God has said, and gone on record saying. Wouldn't you agree, that often times we would have to say; "God, you are too nice to me".

# 98
# YOU'LL MAKE YOUR CONNECTION

We were in the midst of several flights around Brazil, when the woman at the check-in counter for Tam Airlines made that comment. We had just checked in at the ticket counter and found out that our plane was going to be delayed an hour and a half. We were flying out of Campo Grande through Sao Paulo and on to Rio De Janeiro. I was concerned that we would miss our connecting flight to Sao Paulo. I did not speak Portuguese, and she spoke very limited English. But she kept repeating, "You will make your connection".

Our flight finally left Campo Grande and arrived very late into Sao Paulo. We wondered if we could get off the plane and make the connecting flight before it left, which seemed very doubtful. As we were getting our stuff gathered together, the man in front of us asked where we were flying to. I told him Rio, and gave him our flight number. He calmly said, "That is this plane". I was stunned! The connecting flight was actually the same plane, and we didn't even need to get off. It would have been impossible to miss it! I thought back to the woman at the ticket counter. She obviously knew this and was trying to reassure me with this information. I just misunderstood her. All the worry or concern was for naught, we were on the right plane anyway.

As I sat back down in my seat, I thought to myself, I wonder how many times I have needlessly worried about God making the right connections for my life? So often, I allow unexpected or unanticipated events that have come into my life to cause me to worry and fret if God is still in control. I think I know the destination that God has me traveling, but something happens that seems to ruin all hope. "Lord can there be any good in this? This event or difficulty will surely cause me to miss the direction and timing you have for my life."

Can you identify? The very thing that we would think is the antithesis of what should happen for things to work out for good, becomes the very instrument that God uses. I imagine Joseph in the prison could not comprehend how any of this was part of God causing him to arrive at the right destination. Ditto for David hiding out in the caves of En Gedi, "How could this be part of my anointing to become the next king"? And what about Abraham being told to offer his son Isaac as a sacrifice, the same son that God said He would multiply his offspring through? The list of Bible characters that experienced concern over "missing connections" is great.

That day on the plane Psalm 48:14 came to my mind. "For this God is our God for ever and ever; he will be our guide even to the end." The check-in lady knew something I did not know, there was no way I could miss my destination, and I was already on the same plane that would take us to Rio. The reason I did not know that was that I really was having difficulty understanding her; in addition, the flight number was different on the flight to Sao Paulo than on the one to Rio. I had no idea they would change the flight number on the same plane. It is kind of like me trying to figure things out here when a Heavenly Mind has comprehension beyond my abilities. So my word of encouragement to all of us is keep in mind that we will make our connections, God will make sure of it. And when we look back it will all make sense, and we will see that our worrying and fretting was unnecessary.

I risk losing you here by closing with a lengthy quote from Alexander MacLaren that I wrote in the front of my Bible 30 years ago. But I think God can powerfully encourage you if you read it.

*"Everything that befalls us, every object with which we come into contact, all the variety of condition, all the variations of experience, has one distinct significant purpose. They are all meant to tell upon the character, to make us better in sundry ways, to bring us closer to God, and to fill us more full of Him. And that one effect may be produced by the most opposite incidents, just as in some great machine you may have two wheels turning in opposite ways, and yet contributing to one resulting motion; or just as the summer and winter, with all their antithesis, have a single result in the abundant harvest, one force attracts the planets to the sun, one force tends to drive it out into the fields of space; but the two, working together, make it circle in its orbit around its center. And so, by sorrow and by joy, by light and by dark, by giving and withholding, by granting and refusing, by all the varieties of our circumstances, and by everything that lies around us, God works to prepare us for Himself."*

You will make your connection. God is your travel agent and pilot, and you can trust Him in this.

# 99
# A GOOD SELFISHNESS

Selfishness, just hearing or reading the word brings disgusting thoughts to our minds. It seems we live in a day when there are constant reminders of the awfulness of that word. It's not that selfishness is new – it came with the fall of man, it's just that it seems to be trumpeted and displayed in a greater way than at any other time. And you may be tempted to say, "Well, that's just because we have access today to media and instant information." While there may be truth to that statement, the Bible does clearly say that, "But mark this: There will be terrible times in the last days. People will be lovers of themselves..." (II Timothy 3:1) If this book were a blog, right now several of you could write on incidences of "selfishness" you have observed, read about or, unfortunately, experienced. For me to illustrate an act of selfishness, the challenge would be, not in finding one, but selecting which one to use.

Though it would be tempting to reach into the world of Professional Sports, or the Hollywood Industry, or High Finance, or the Political World, to illustrate the "badness" of selfishness, the truth is, it is all around us, and all too often, in my own life. As a "frequent flier", I have often – seems like most times – been on flights that are "overbooked". When this happens the people at the gate will announce, "We are overbooked on this flight, and we're offering money for someone to give up their seat and take a later flight." Sometimes the offer increases with monetary gifts and even free tickets for a future flight. That scenario happened recently at Reagan National Airport in Washington D.C., and even though I wasn't on hand for that flight, I read about it.

The announcement was made that the flight was overbooked, but in this case, there was a specific request made in regards to the overbooked flight. The plane was carrying the body of a young Marine, Lance Corporal Justin Wilson. This young soldier was killed in a roadside bombing in Afghanistan. He was only 24 years old. The announcement came to the passengers that Justin's parents and family wished to travel with Justin's body back home for his funeral. In the words of one of the passengers, "We all just sat there just kind of looking at the family. The announcement went on for 30 minutes, with the offer going up to $500 and future tickets. But not enough people would give up their seats, even though they could catch the next flight out." Now, truthfully, I'm sure that many could not give up their seats, either for pressing connections or important deadlines. But I do find it hard to believe that everyone on the plane had that same problem. Selfishness? It does seem like that could have been a big part of not giving up their seats.

So selfishness is bad, but is it bad all the time? A safe answer would be "yes"; just by definition a selfish act is bad. But as believers, I want you to consider one selfish act that may be considered good, in fact, very good. Our motives for serving Christ should always be high and lofty, and the highest motive, is of course, our love for Christ (because He loves us). Our desire to live a holy and pleasing life before Him should be because He deserves it, and He has purchased our life at a great cost. However, there can be a "selfish" reason for our obedience and holy life style. Let me explain. In a nutshell, when you or I live a life pleasing to God, we "reap" something, we experience a great benefit, and it brings us something pleasing. Proverbs 11:28 puts it succinctly; "He who sows righteousness reaps a sure reward." That couldn't be clearer; "we" reap something-something good.

But sometimes we think that "good thing" is only something in the future, something we'll receive in heaven. But there is something specifically, we receive now, and selfishly, we should desire it. What is it? It's peace of mind and a godly confidence that God is pleased with us. These two things should not be taken lightly; they're something we all crave. Listen to what the Psalmist – and King, David says; "Happy are those who keep His decrees and seek Him with all their heart." (Psalm 119:2) There is a selfishness about keeping God's decrees (living in obedience), and that is, that it brings us "happiness".

Now here's something we don't often consider, or at least, don't often talk about – Christians can be more miserable than unbelievers. It is true, and most of us have experienced that. Unbelievers can sin, and for the most part, not feel bad. When we sin as believers, we feel bad, even miserable. The Holy Spirit, using our conscience, has a lot to do with that. When believers sin, we can't just "shake it off or ignore it." We feel bad and we lose our happiness and joy. King David shared his "journal" with us, stating his misery when he was struggling with sins and seeking to ignore them. "Restore unto me the joy of my salvation" he writes in Psalm 51:12. Earlier in that Psalm, he writes, "My sins are always before me." In a moment of hyperbole, he says "Let the bones you have crushed rejoice". God certainly did not "crush" his bones, but the misery of the weight of sin made it feel that way.

Christians are the happiest people on the face of the earth; they can also be the most miserable. No Christian puts his or her head on the pillow at night and says, "Ah that was a wonderful sin. Now I'll sleep like a baby!" Our sins are forgiven, and Christ will always hold us securely in His hands. But when we sin – and we all sin, it grieves His Spirit and He knows it is also harmful to us, so He allows, in His grace and kindness, for us to "feel" miserable, even alienated from Him. So, obviously, I don't want to feel miserable-selfishly, I want to be happy! So, seeking to live a holy life, one that's pleasing to Him, reaps benefits to me. And when I sin, if I confess that sin, He immediately restores that "feeling" of a wonderful relationship with Him. It makes me happy!

I know that several pastors and missionaries may read this book, and at the risk of losing some of the rest of you, let me share something that I have written in the front of my Bible. It speaks specifically to those of us in Ministry, but is certainly applicable to all of us. This quote haunts me, and I wish I could say it has been a total deterrent to me sinning – it hasn't! But it has helped, and I think it can help all of us. Here is the quote:

*"The better the man, the better the preacher. When he kneels by the bed of the dying or when he mounts the pulpit stairs, then every self-denial he has made, every Christian forbearance he has shown, every resistance to sin and temptation, will come back to him to strengthen his arm, and give conviction to his voice. Likewise, every evasion to duty, every indulgence to self, every compromise of evil, every unworthy thought, word or deed, will be there at the head of the pulpit stairs to meet the minister on Sunday morning, to take the light from his eyes, the power from his blow, the ring from his voice, and the joy from his heart."* (Clarence E. Macartney, 1879-1957)

Normally I would never encourage someone to act selfishly, but in this case, go ahead, seek to live that pleasing life to God, and you – yourself – will receive something, - happiness.

# 100
# YOUR LIFE MEANS MORE THAN YOU CAN IMAGINE

I came across an unusual verse speaking of the life of Christ. It is found in Daniel 9 and verse 26. Daniel 9, verses 20-27 speaks of the entire future of Israel. It is a vision given Daniel by God and explained by the archangel Gabriel. The vision gives the actual time when Jesus the Messiah would be "cut off" (killed). Space does not allow me to go into detail of the "seventy weeks of Daniel", but you might want to reread it if you have not done so in awhile. But, picking up the dialog between Daniel and Gabriel, Gabriel explains this part of the prophetic utterance to Daniel; "After this period of sixty-two sets of seven, the Anointed One (Jesus Christ) will be killed, appearing to have accomplished nothing." I was especially taken by the phrase "appearing to have accomplished nothing".

For those of us living almost two millenniums after Christ, this seems like an impossible thing to say. But what Gabriel said was certainly true in Jesus' day. Many – most, thought that His life was not that extraordinary, and they certainly believed

His "movement" would die with Him. His life of relative obscurity and His ignominious death all lent credence to a failed life. The prophet Isaiah records these words (written more than 700 years before Christ came to earth); "He had no beauty or majesty to attract us to him, nothing in his appearance that we should desire him." (Isaiah 53:2) It took the resurrection and the centuries of changed lives to correct that thinking.

You know by the title of this chapter that I want to press home an important point, and it is this; "Your life means more than you can imagine". Jesus' life seemed to have accomplished nothing, but the truth was, that it was the most accomplished life ever lived. The quote from Daniel 9 was about what people living at that time would feel about Jesus' life. But the greater struggle we all have, is not so much other people thinking our life doesn't count, but us thinking our life doesn't count ! A person does not have to be middle age for them to begin contemplating whether their life has meaning or not. It is a malady that all of us struggle with.

I came across an interesting site on the internet that was titled "10 People who became famous after death". A fascinating list, and one that included names such as Galileo, Mendel, Thoreau, Poe, Dickinson and van Gogh. These people not only did not become famous until after death, but during their lifetime they felt like they were not accomplishing much of any value.

I had an interesting experience on one of my overseas trips. After speaking all week at a conference for missionaries, I had a couple come up to talk to me about some personal struggles they were having. The couple had been on the field for many years and were contemplating resigning – and not just from missions, but from serving God in any capacity. I asked them why, and the husband in particular shared that he felt they had accomplished nothing and had been failures; even wondering if anything good had ever been accomplished in their ministry. This was a shocking statement, especially considering the fact that they had been used by God to start several churches, and God had opened up new doors to reach national students. I had met with several missionaries that week, and one of the questions I asked them was; "If you could be another missionary, who would you like to be?" As I talked with this couple, I asked them who they thought the missionaries chose. They replied that they didn't have any idea. They were stunned when I told them it was them!

In my library are many biographies, and several of those are of people who had no idea of what their life was accomplishing. People such as William Cowper, Oswald Chambers (his wife published *My utmost for His highest* after he died), Robert Murray McCheyne, David Brainerd, and a host of others. I share this with you, because your life does count.

There are no little people in God's program, and no spiritual task that is insignificant. Others may not see your value, and more significantly, you may not see it, but your life IS accomplishing something. Occupation does not define you, nor does exposure or breadth of influence. You may feel like Isaiah when he said to the Lord; "I have labored to no purpose; I have spent my strength in vain and for nothing." (Isaiah 49:4) But your life is accomplishing much; God has not allowed your life to be wasted. One day in glory you'll see the full measure of your accomplishment – now hidden from your eyes – and you will rejoice that your life was a specially designed instrument to accomplish all that the Master so chose.

# CONCLUSION

I hope these thoughts and words have indeed been strength for the journey. Life can be hard, and the Christian life a challenging adventure, but God is there with us every step of the way. This book has sought to lift up Christ in a special way before our eyes. For when we know Christ better, we will live more valiantly. But this book has also sought to remind us of the wonderful truths of what the Word of God reveals about our identity in Christ, and the hope of our calling and inheritance. If you have found this helpful and Christ-exalting, then I would encourage you to continue this "Speaking to the Heart" journey, by reading volume two.

God bless,
Bruce W. McDonald

Made in the USA
Monee, IL
21 October 2021